To my mother:

*One of the best things about our long good-bye
has been writing this for you.*

acknowledgments

If you want to see your life flash before you—at least in a way that it can be appreciated—I suggest that you write a book. It's been said that you can't do so before you turn forty. Until then, you're not wise enough, for you haven't failed enough. Your life has been too short. I didn't buy that, so I boldly began the project at thirty-eight. I turned forty-four by the time it was finished. Common wisdom, at least in my case, was right.

Writing this book was a harder task than I ever imagined it would be. I discovered that it wasn't the first 5,000 words that were tough, but the other 95,000. Enormous thanks to the team of Rick Kot, my gifted editor at Viking, and Stephen Fenichell, a real writer, both of whom taught this rookie how to actually *write*. Rick's uncanny ability to visualize and organize this entire project in his head, while ordering lunch, was something out of *Rain Man*. And for someone who didn't know much about the nuances of brand development before we began working together, Stephen, I am convinced, could today open his own brand consultancy.

I never would have met Rick or Stephen had it not been for David Black, my literary agent. David sought me out when I was at Nike and persuaded me in the ensuing years that I could do more than sell sneakers, and later at Starbucks, lattes. He made me believe that I could write a book, and that it might even be a good one. I think what he meant to say was, *with the right people* I could make it happen. Such has been the case. You can only imagine how I tested the team's patience when the marketing world took a turn one way or the other and I went following close on its trail. I wanted to write about everything. Fortunately for you, they pared it down to what was relevant.

Over my career I have been fortunate to work alongside some remarkable people. I have gained from their intelligence, their wit, their humor, their patience, and most of all, their creativity. It would be impossible to thank everyone who made me a better brand fool, but I must single out a few of the exceptionally bright lights that illuminated the path for me.

To Phil Knight, thank you for demonstrating how to unleash innovation and passion around core brand values—and for not telling me exactly what to do in the process. You inspired me, along with a few thousand other swooshers, to do great things and take chances. I am still amazed that you trusted all of Nike's advertising to a thirty-year-old.

To Howard Shultz, thank you for giving me the chance to help build a company that did not leave its employees behind—or anyone anywhere more than a short walk away from a great cup of coffee. Nike taught me the value of saying something interesting to millions of people at once, but Starbucks taught me the equally important value of building a great brand one cup and one person at a time.

To Dan Wieden and David Kennedy, thank you for never becoming just another advertising agency, for never selling out, and for always putting the work first. Thanks for making me appreciate the difference between the stuff that typically passes for advertising and the meaningful communication you always made your goal. Thanks for telling us at Nike when we were off base, in no uncertain terms, and for creatively acknowledging those rare occasions when we weren't.

But no company can be great, whoever is in charge, without a staff of good people. The tiny Wieden and Kennedy Nike account team grew to become an enormous talent pool that included Jim Riswold, Billy Davenport, Susan Hoffman, Dave Luhr, Kelley Stoutt, John Russell, Tim O'Kennedy, Michael Prieve, Deb Weekly, Jerry Cronin, Jelly Helm, Jamie Barrett, Buzz Sawyer, Tom Blessington, Janet Champ, Charlotte Moore, Cheri Rogers, Paul Manganello, Canice Neary, Chris Mendola, Tom Noble, Bob Moore, Scott French, Chris Riley, Mark Barden, John Jay, and the late Steve Sandoz. They went far beyond what was expected in the pursuit of great work and they made us all proud—even when they were thrown out of beer halls in Munich.

As a company, Nike defined the term "dream team" back in 1987. Harry Carsh, David Kottkamp, Ron Nelson, Dick Donahue, Tom Clarke, Mark Parker, Lisa McKillips, Tinker Hatfield, Steve Nichols, Jerome Conlon, Stephen Gomez, Liz Dolan, Ron Hill, Peter Ruppe, Skip Lei, Mike Wilskey, Bob Wood, Tom Hartge, Claire Hamill, Chris Van Dyke, Bink Smith, Deb Johnson, Chris Aveni, and Ron Dumas were all capable of shooting from long range with their eyes closed. I am enormously proud of the leaders who made Nike advertising a genre unto itself. Bill Zeitz, Nancy Monsarrat, Rob DeFlorio, Mark Thomashow, Liz Christiansen, Mike Beckerman, Ann Marie Lei, Saga Hamilton, Kassia Sing, Gina Mazza, Sandy Manning, and Stuart Redsun were the nucleus of the greatest team I have ever had the honor to lead. Thanks to Bill Barrett, formerly of SFM Media, for his sage media counsel around the world, and heartfelt thanks to my assistant, Dawn Smith, who kept me organized, sane, and laughing during the most stressful period of my life.

Starbucks was no less steeped in talent. People like Howard Behar, Dave Olsen, Mary Williams, Arthur Rubenfeld, Yves Misrahi, George Murphy, Deidra Wager, Christine Day, Myra Gose, Harry Roberts, Jennifer Tisdel, Wanda Herndon, Georgette Essad, Gabe Goldberg, Nancy Kent, and Cristina Prather made Starbucks Brewtopia. My assistant, Linda Van Beek, could walk right through a wall in pursuit of something for me (and that was without coffee). Somewhere in heaven she is optimizing God's daily schedule and screening his calls like no other. She could keep Jesus on hold, if necessary.

Special thanks go to Mary Jackson who worked tirelessly as my assistant at Brandstream. In addition to her other duties, she critiqued every chapter draft and questioned anything that did not make sense to her. She made the book much more readable for those who do not consider themselves a marketing genius.

As a marketer, I am amazed by what I continue to learn from my kids. They have kept me young at heart and aware of a world much larger and more precious than I could ever have known on my own. Nothing prepared me for the day I saw my then eight-year-old son discuss world politics with a stunned Henry Kissinger, complimenting the geopolitical legend on how he "proved that the pen is mightier than a hundred armies" during the Paris peace talks. At ten, he had surpassed my own understanding of contemporary culture, much less the conflict in Bosnia. Now that he is twelve, I don't dare go shopping for music, soft drinks, or clothes without him. My five-year-old daughter has taught me the things only a girl can teach her dad—tenderness, compassion, the fleeting gift of innocence, and the steely desire to flatten anything that threatens her. I am already dreading future boyfriends. But it will all make me a better marketer.

And then there's my wife, Sam. For twenty-two years she has been my greatest fan, my best critic, my soul mate, and my best friend. I have never met anyone more in step with the world than she—though exactly how much I may never really appreciate. While I can hardly remember what I had for dinner on any given night, she can recall the music in the restaurant, the aroma from the kitchen, the quality of the napkins, the stoneware, everyone who came to the table, the lighting, the people seated within thirty feet of us (and what each of them wore), and what we *both* had for dinner. She follows all music, the arts, politics, Wall Street, and, most recently, the Seattle Mariners. As I was completing the first rough draft of the book, I told my agent that should something happen to me, should my plane never make its gate, she could finish it. She gave up a promising career at Nordstrom's corporate headquarters (she was in fact making more money than I was at the time) to raise our family and to make me a better husband, father, marketer, and writer.

In writing this book I have learned that authors can be inspired in many ways. They sometimes turn to scotch, double lattes, or whatever works to keep the ideas flowing. I personally invoked the "Hemingway Amendment" on a few late evenings when only a Macallan single malt could unlock the mental mystery before me. I have become known for my double-short non-fat latte at more than a few Starbucks in Seattle, San Francisco, New York, and London. They may not know my name but they know my drink. Those experiences confirmed something I suspected when I first joined Starbucks: Writers have been inexorably linked to coffeehouses since the sixteenth century. Visit any crowded coffeehouse and you can easily spot the stymied writers. They sit and stare a lot, looking for words.

And finally, I must thank you for trusting me enough to read this small opus. I hope that it is worth your time, and that I pass the audition.

SB

contents

———

introduction

————————

Confessions of a Brand Fool

If you're like most readers of business books, you've probably familiarized yourself with such hot-button topics as corporate reengineering, process improvement, customer centricity, and one-to-one marketing. At some point you may have been inspired by the Internet geniuses who boldly proclaimed the death of traditional business models and of mass marketing as we know it. In the good new old days, "New Economy" concepts like permission marketing and customer relationship management (CRM) tools were expected to render everything else obsolete—as irrelevant as hay was to the Model T.

Today, the buzz is about a business practice that is not really new. It is a practice that for me has always existed somewhere above and beyond all other business strategies. It is an organizing principle so broad yet so defining that it can shape and direct just about everything a company does, and, most important, *how* it does it. I'm referring, of course, to brand building, a process that, when it works well, should leave no facet of a company untouched. And no business practice unexamined.

Brand Building, Broadly Viewed

Brand building is much more than the responsibility of the marketing department or even of the CEO, although both functions must participate actively in championing and protecting the brand from within for the effort to succeed. Building and supporting a great brand is everyone's job, from the CEO on down.

But brands have been around for centuries. Why all the buzz and bother at the moment, as we begin a new century?

I submit that brand building's big cultural moment has arrived right around now for three basic reasons.

One: We are awash as never before with products, services, companies, and brands, all aiming to set themselves apart from the pack, to be distinct, and most of all to be loved and desired. In the meantime, the grand solution to the problem of undifferentiated products and services has been broadly judged to involve something "more" than spending truckloads of cash on marketing the way it once was, or even as it might have been. The consensus is that for better or for worse, all the money in the world can't buy you love or trust. You have to earn trust and love by how you behave over time. Some of the world's most beloved brands, Starbucks among them, spend next to nothing on traditional marketing activities. Yet Starbucks employees *know how to behave.* Their training, their benefits, their sense of solidarity—and therefore their attitude and presentation—are consistently a cut above those of employees in the rest of the restaurant-and-fast-food industry. Which is a prime example of how, if you understand your brand—its values, its mission, its reason for being—and integrate it consistently into everything you do, your entire organization will know how to behave in virtually any and all situations. Behavior and quality, over time, build trust. Advertising, if it is any good, should help to confirm what already *is,* not what should be.

Two: The most valuable assets of a company are no longer physical. Factories, trucks, warehouses, materials, employees, and even palatial corporate headquarters buildings are no longer credible badges of corporate success. These once-vaunted tangibles now hang around the neck of many companies as liabilities on the balance sheet, or as poorly performing assets. Today, no one wants to own a factory, not if they can possibly help it. Companies like Handspring, maker of the Visor personal digital assistant, which in 2001 projected $400 million in revenues with 400 employees, began business in much the same way Nike did: with no intention of ever building its own products. Instead, Handspring invests its capital where it obtains the best return, particularly over the long haul: on innovative product design, engineering, marketing, and brand positioning. Everything else is outsourced to specialists who manufacture and distribute more efficiently than Handspring ever could do because it is *all* that they do.

Nevertheless, there is one asset, an intangible one, that stands head and shoulders above all the others and that cannot be easily outsourced: the brand. If Handspring wants to thrive, not just survive, in the current economic climate, it will have to do something more than efficiently source its product. It will have to become a great brand. Which is, believe you me, a more complicated process than sourcing a piece of electronics.

Three: There is and will continue to be increasing pressure on corporations, especially the large ones, to behave more responsibly as citizens—a trait that I've labeled elsewhere "using your superhuman powers for good." Companies will need to become more human and walk more lightly on the land. In the New Brand World, there will be fewer hiding places for companies that disrespect this fundamental social dynamic. Thanks to the advent of the Information Age and unabashed media scrutiny, nearly every industry and the players within them are more transparent than ever. Unethical CEOs and CFOs will have much more difficulty filling their pockets with stakeholder equity and twisting balance sheets. Everyone is pretty much buck-naked out there. And spending money on expensive clothing—such as elaborate television commercials, brochures, and magazine ads—won't hide the ugliness if it exists. Brand karma is real.

Where I Am Coming From

So who am I? And what do I know about brands?

The simple answer is that I have been fortunate to find myself in key marketing and strategic positions inside two of the last century's fastest-growing brands, Nike and Starbucks, during their most pivotal periods. For more than a decade I worked alongside brilliant and passionate people focused on reinventing two forgotten product commodities, sneakers and coffee. I did whatever I could to shape these products into more valuable, more relevant, more exciting, and more rewarding experiences. For seven years, from 1987 to 1994, I headed up Nike's worldwide advertising efforts, perhaps one of the world's greatest jobs one could ever wish for. Even though it was a much smaller company in 1987, with roughly $800 million in sales versus $10 billion ten years later, it was a rocket ride of sorts. We shot from number 3 to number 1 worldwide in a few short years. Along the way we also reinvented much of how marketing was supposed to work. It should be noted that we also had a few beers.

In 1995 I traded in my sneakers for coffee and spent three highly caffeinated years in Brewtopia (local lingo for Seattle) as Starbucks' chief marketing officer. My ambition there was pretty straightforward: to help build another great global brand, this time for a retail chain without the support of mass marketing. No small challenge, that. But the effort worked, for reasons that you will learn in this book. It should also be noted that we drank a lot of coffee. Without it we could never have achieved our 40-plus percent annual compound growth rate.

At both companies, I often found myself more perplexed than amused by the high-flown theories, guidelines, case studies, and even "immutable laws of branding" espoused by lifetime academics and career management consultants. They were usually more wrong than right, but the point here is not to criticize. It can be hard enough to know a company—especially one as private as Nike—from the inside, let alone from the outside. There's a lot more to Starbucks than a double-tall nonfat latte served up promptly in a clean, well-lit, comfortable environment. Brands are complex characters—as you will learn.

Which is why I can't provide a slick elevator pitch for explaining how great brands take off. Building a brand is the most challenging, complicated, and painstaking process that a company can embark on. It's more intuitive than analytical, and most of the time it can't be seen. But it can always be felt.

My personal fascination with brands began long before Nike broke the "Just Do It" campaign and decades before Starbucks began to weave itself into the five-hundred-year-old coffeehouse tradition. It began, in fact, with my growing up the son of a car salesman.

My father was not your average car salesman; he didn't just "sell" cars. He preached brand gospel from the showroom pulpit, as many as seven days a week, twelve hours a day, for nearly fifty years. Some of my earliest memories are of Dad trying to convert souls lost to the religions of Chrysler, Ford, and Honda to the Oldsmobile and Cadillac faith. He must have been pretty good at it, for he not only supported a family of eight but was one of a very few people in his profession to benefit from repeat customers. He was one of General Motors' greatest brand disciples ever, a task that became harder for him as Oldsmobile and Cadillac began to lose their way in the late 1980s and '90s.

Ironically, as I was writing this book, Oldsmobile, the oldest car brand in America, announced that it would cease production. This was no surprise to my father or me. In the eighties he knew the company was headed down the wrong road when it launched its notorious "This Is Not Your Father's Oldsmobile" campaign—a botched attempt to lure younger consumers to the brand franchise without alienating its older core customers. I didn't buy it. Oldsmobile *was* and *would always be* my father's Oldsmobile. It would take more than advertising to change that.

I studied advertising at the University of Oregon School of Journalism with hopes of becoming the next David Ogilvy. Upon graduation in 1980, I took a job in product management for a small food products company, a great place for any brand fool to start. After learning those ropes I went to work for the largest advertising agency in Seattle at the time, an Ogilvy & Mather affiliate by the name of Cole & Weber. While there, I was blessed with some of the world's best and worst clients, and learned equally from both.

In 1987 I was recruited to help turn around the struggling number 3 athletic footwear brand, Nike, as director of corporate advertising. My first efforts focused on what became the "Just Do It" campaign. In the years that followed, we expanded the brand with innovative products and equally innovative communication programs, from television commercials to women's print advertising to retail concepts like Nike Town. But after seven years and a few million air miles, I felt I'd accomplished much of what I had set out to do and left the company to spend a year with my young and growing family. I didn't set foot on a plane for six months. I taught my then five-year-old son how to ride a bike, how to swim, how to fish, and how to deal with flirtatious kindergarten girls.

While on break, I read business books, something few of us had the time—or the interest—to do at Nike. I quickly realized just how far ahead of its time Nike was in its brand-building practices. We had, it seemed, about a ten-year leap on the rest of the world. After weeks of ranting to my wife about how far astray most companies had gone, she suggested that I put my money where my mouth was and write my own book. Frankly, by that point I think she probably just wanted to get me out of the house.

Before I could think of reasons not to become an author she had rented a remote summer cabin high in the Oregon Cascades on the banks of the Metolius River—in the dead of winter. With my Apple PowerBook, coffee, scotch, mountain bike, and fly-fishing gear, I headed for my snow-covered enclave in the woods. My wife left me there without a car and would visit only on weekends. Let's just say that my novice writing experience contained a few moments straight out of *The Shining*.

A few weeks later, I sent some sample chapters to a handful of CEOs to see whether my Nike-centric views would have relevance for industries like oil, computers, entertainment, or even a commodity as boring as coffee. The day after he received his package, Starbucks' CEO, Howard Schultz, summoned me from my cabin to his headquarters in Seattle where we shared an incredible cup of Sumatra. Before I left his office he asked me to

consider joining him as his chief marketing officer. At first I politely refused the offer. Undaunted, Howard kept pursuing, and I finally relented
a few weeks later. My family and I packed our bags and headed north to
Brewtopia, the vibrant town we had left eight years before to follow the
swoosh.

At Starbucks, I shelved the book project for what became a wild three-
year coffee break. During that time, we tripled the number of stores, introduced products into the grocery channel, formed alliances and joint
ventures with companies like United Airlines and Pepsi, and opened our
first overseas cafés. Having done my share of stamping out bad coffee, I
left Starbucks in 1998 to finish my book and launch a brand consulting
practice. I sought out a broad range of clients, from Silicon Valley start-ups
to the world's most powerful brand, Coke, and to see if the branding principles that worked for Nike and Starbucks could work elsewhere.

Fortunately for me—and for them—they did.

So here it is, a half decade later, give or take a year or two. The world
and the brands in it have come a long way since I first began thinking long
and hard about brands in that cabin in the woods in the dead of winter. I
certainly hope that the pages and ideas that follow will bear fruit for you,
as they have for me, and that they provide inspiration for your own business
and reveal new ways to make your own brand more desired, more relevant,
and more enduring. The concepts in this book apply, I am now confident,
to big and small companies, products and services, and business-to-business
and business-to-consumer industries. They have always felt like common
sense to me. In time, I hope they will to you too.

As was the case with my work at both Nike and Starbucks, nothing
I've written here has been pretested or filtered down to the lowest possible common denominator like most marketing concepts. Every word and
thought in this book has been informed by the mind, inspired by the gut,
and written from the heart. These are the experiences and views of one
person fortunate enough to have worked with gifted and visionary people
who were part of companies that cared deeply about their brands. At
times, I suspect that *you* may suspect that I am either a genius or an exceptionally lucky idiot. Personally, I've always found the fine line dividing
the two a razor-thin one.

Seize the Day—Today

Given the near collapse of public trust in large institutions—from major
corporations like Enron and Worldcom to organizations like the Catholic

church—there has never been a more important time to establish and strengthen brand trust. In the New Brand World, there will be no shortage of competitors and no limit on the expectations that customers will place on corporations that have already become more powerful than some governments. The noise, static, and confusion have, particularly in the preceding decade, become amplified to an uneasy roar. But I sincerely believe that the challenge of being seen, heard, and remembered—not to mention desired and respected—amid the evolving chaos of change will not just test but will bring out the best in every one of us.

So let's get to it.

all aboard
the brandwagon

Principle #1
Relying on brand awareness has become marketing fool's gold.

You've probably noticed in the past couple of years that once-arcane phrases like "brand dilution," "brand synergy," "brand equity," and "brand recognition" have begun tripping lightly off just about every tongue in the business punditocracy. Such glib terms and phrases are typically uttered not only with a straight face but also with a solemn pursing of the lips and no detectable trace of irony.

"In the landmark 1967 film *The Graduate*," the *New York Times* business reporter Joel Sharkey recently wrote, "there is the famous scene at the cocktail party where a helpful older man whispers this single word of business advice into the ear of a callow, befuddled young Dustin Hoffman: 'Plastics.' Remake the movie today, and you'd have to change the line to 'branding.'"

These days, the term "branding" is being uttered in the same pious, reverential tones formerly reserved for buzz words like "synergy," "leverage," and "strategic planning." The brand idea is no longer confined just to packaged consumer products. Today the word "brand" has become part of the vernacular within every department of any progressive company. It is on everyone's radar screen, though not everyone really knows what it means. Personally, and speaking as something of a brand fool, all this loose talk makes me nervous. For it was only a few years ago that everyone had given brands up for dead.

Brand Awareness Versus
Brand Strength

Step back to the spring of 1993, when Marlboro, one of the world's most recognizable brands (if not *the* most recognizable) stunned the marketing world when it announced that it would have to aggressively cut its cigarette prices to stay competitive. The move was prompted by an onslaught of lower-cost, less-known competitors. Some of these were essentially generic, without any real brand sensibilities or public recognition in the market, other than that they were cheap. Others were barely brands in their own right. Wall Street analysts hammered Marlboro's parent company Philip Morris's stock, and several business magazines heralded the death of branding the very next week. According to them, it was price, not brand image, that would matter in the future. Building a strong brand was a concept that had run its course.

My friend Watts Wacker, a professional futurist, had it right when he stated at an Association of National Advertisers conference that year, "I believe the nineties officially began with Marlboro's inability to sustain its price. When the number one brand realized that its value proposition (what the brand was really 'worth' in the minds of the customer) was out of sync, that underlines the difference between a pig and a hog."

Asked by one conference participant to define that difference, Wacker gamely replied, "You feed a pig, but you slaughter a hog. Brands can be piggy, but they can't be hogs."

To me, the Marlboro Man had not fallen off his horse because the limitations of branding had finally revealed themselves. What sent him plummeting to earth, spurs pointing skyward, were two things: the product had lost any real differentiation in the marketplace from the equally blurred identities of a growing number of competitors, and its marketing strategy had become entirely predictable. By simply resting on past laurels, which was acceptable in the Old Brand World, the Marlboro brand eventually rejoined the larger pack, if you will, of all the other brands of cigarettes. It began to look like one more player in a very large, mostly unremarkable commodity market. The only distinction between Marlboro and its competition was Marlboro's heavier marketing and higher price, something that must have perplexed more than a few smokers.

To Marlboro's credit, it had established strong emotional connections with millions of core users, thanks to decades of rich imagery of the open West: vibrant vistas of cowboys, cattle, campfires, and coffee. Transcending a product-only relationship and connecting the brand to powerful and often timeless emotion—"emotional branding"—will continue to be important in the New Brand World, but it can never replace meaningful product innovation. Emotional branding merely augments and extends a powerful product or service platform by recognizing that some of the most important product benefits are emotional rather than physical. What is new is the need for greater innovation in both product development and marketing communications. In the future, standing still will be lethal to any brand.

Not unlike Marlboro, Nike also wove its brand into timeless emotions by becoming the category protagonist for competitive sports and fitness. But unlike Marlboro, Nike never stopped reinventing its products and its marketing. It is safe to say that Nike Advertising took a thousand different creative tacks on the same core brand positioning during my eight-year watch, from 1987 to 1994. While Nike Advertising was constantly refreshing the marketing and brand positioning, Nike Design became one of the world's premier product design and development organizations. Speed of change was also important to Nike. Just when Marlboro was beginning to falter, Nike was introducing so many new products and marketing campaigns that it had reduced its average product life cycle from one year to three or four months.

Relevance and Resonance

But change for the sake of change can also be marketing fool's gold. The best reason for change is to expand brand *relevance* and brand *resonance,* two measures of brand strength that are much more valuable than mere brand *awareness* can ever be. Perhaps this is the greatest single change in the concept of "brand" in recent years. Where we once looked at brands on a surface level, we now view them in more intimate and multidimensional terms. We plumb their depths, looking for reassurance that they are good, responsible, sensitive, knowing, and hip. Never in the history of business has there been such scrutiny of brand performance.

So how do brands become more relevant and resonate more deeply with customers? One of the most rewarding strategies for achieving this goal has been *mass customization,* the process of creating a broader array of "niche" products that emanate from one central brand position like spokes on a wheel. Executed properly, mass customization enables large brands to build and retain relationships with smaller subsets of a mass market while growing the entire brand franchise.

Consider Harley-Davidson. Yet another brand with a timeless emo-

4 ⬚ SCOTT BEDBURY

tional position—the open road, personal freedom, and rebellion—Harley-Davidson also understands the value of providing customers myriad ways to customize its core product or embrace its brand. For FY 2000, Harley posted $2.2 billion in revenues from its motorcycles. *It also posted $600 million in revenue on parts, accessories, and general merchandise.* The latter delivered more than just high profit margins to the company. It also enabled consumers to customize their own Harley-Davidson brand experience.

Another brand historically hell-bent on change has been Intel, with its "self-cannibalization" of Pentium technology in the nineties. Intel was well aware that with every new, faster chip, it was essentially killing its young, but it recognized this violent act as a form of what Intel chairman Andy Grove called "creative destruction." (This term was originally coined by the early-twentieth-century Austrian economist Joseph Schumpeter and was later popularized by both Grove and General Electric's CEO, Jack Welch.)

Marlboro's plight gave the big, traditional, Old Brand World brands much to ponder, especially the *Über*-brands like U.S. Tobacco, Unilever, Procter & Gamble, General Foods, and Nestlé. For them, "Marlboro Friday," as they called the day the price cuts came down, threatened the foundation of trillions of dollars' worth of merchandise and services derived from their brands—brands that had by then apparently grown too similar, too complacent, and too reliant on outdated and conservative marketing practices. The notion that a brand could survive for years, even decades, without significant change to its product or marketing had to be abandoned. Branding had become a game of fast-break basketball. The fastest and most innovative team would win. Branding, it also became clear, was no longer a straightforward concept.

Fortunately for Nike, it never looked to the postindustrial brand juggernauts for best brand-development practices. In fact, we steered clear of anything that felt like Old Brand World logic. Nike committed a form of "creative destruction" comparable to Intel's by creating literally thousands of products and hundreds of print ads, billboards, and television commercials every year. It aggressively began to mass-customize with new "collections" of products that amounted to sub-brands within categories like basketball and tennis. Each sub-brand and collection beneath the Nike brand umbrella was geared to a particular customer segment or distribution channel. The overall effect of Nike's brand segmentation was to burnish the brand in the mind of the consumer in more creative, more relevant and dynamic ways. Like Intel, the Nike brand became as much about change as about continuity. Both brands kept consumers happy and on their toes, and grew into global powerhouse brands by constantly refreshing and reinventing themselves—remaining forever the same, yet forever new.

The Value of Brand for the Commodity

Nike and Intel had succeeded brilliantly in precisely the area where Marlboro had so dismally failed: the fertile mind of the consumer. Marlboro had been forced to cut prices to match Brand X inferiors and no-name interlopers because cigarettes were increasingly perceived by consumers as commodity products—goods that are essentially "fungible," or mutually interchangeable and undifferentiated, like wheat, pork bellies, or sugar.

This dreary perception of what marketing people call, with justifiable dread, "product parity" erased the value created by literally billions of dollars expended on marketing, promotion, and advertising over the years. Marlboro had spent billions building up the global image of the Marlboro Man as the epitome of rugged American individualism and free-wheeling masculinity, yet this great American icon was being increasingly regarded as representing "just another cigarette." At the same time, Nike and Intel accomplished precisely the reverse. *They* took what for decades had been considered commodity products, athletic shoes and computer chips, and transformed them into something not merely different, but better.

Almost every brand in existence today can be reduced to the status of a commodity if it fails to effectively evolve both its products and its marketing communications. You can't do just one or the other. The most innovative product line will grow stale in the minds of potential customers if the marketing has become static, undifferentiated, or—even worse—irritating for lack of change. Even the best marketing campaign will be run into the ground when it becomes so repetitive that it wears out its welcome. Stay with a marketing campaign too long and it will send your brand into reverse as consumers lunge for the remote control, change radio stations, or flip past your print ads the nanosecond they recognize that it's just you, *again*. On the Web it's no different. Consumers will curse your Web banner, too, at some point. Even "permission marketing," a method of marketing where customers "opt in" to be contacted by companies (usually on the Web) for new products and services or to participate in promotions, will wear out its welcome for many unless it is respectful and kept vibrant. Unsolicited e-mails and "notifications" are only marginally more acceptable than unsolicited telemarketing to your home phone during dinner.

The issue of branding has become topical in nearly every business, and in recent years it has become even more critical to industries where competition is particularly fierce *and* where technology has become a disruptive force. We have witnessed the effects of information technology on stock trading, travel, and even shopping (not necessarily on buying, though that will evolve). But this pales by comparison to the technological changes in the telephone, cable, and wireless industries. An exponential expansion of capacity (thanks to fiber-optic, cable, and wireless technologies) has dropped prices as well as barriers for entry to potential competitors. At the turn of the century, it became a price-driven war for survival. Profits have crumbled and many question what the future holds for some of the biggest and once-strong brands in the world. In the March 19, 2001, issue of *Forbes* magazine, the publisher, Rich Karlgaard, put his thumb on the plight of a number of large companies with enormous brand awareness but downward-spiraling profits in a column that illuminated many of the shortcomings of traditional brand thinking.

"The 20th-century idea of a brand is inadequate protection these days—a castle wall in the age of cannons," Karlgaard writes. "Needed is fresh thinking on a brand's new responsibilities." Why, he wonders, are the brands that enjoy the greatest awareness facing such a hard time in the marketplace? The answer is simple: awareness is just about all that some of them have to show for themselves anymore.

This complacency is not limited to the tired old brands that have been sitting on their "old economy" butts. Also at the turn of the century, quite a few newer brands sought to create brand awareness and ended up with *only* that. The failed Internet brand Pets.com built huge brand awareness with its admittedly cloying sock-puppet mascot, and eToys also created enormous name recognition for itself en route to bankruptcy court. Massive levels of brand awareness will not correct a flawed business model. Excessive marketing spending will only accelerate the demise of any poorly conceived company.

These companies are mere blips on the screen when compared to a massive, established juggernaut like AT&T, but even AT&T has been having its own brand troubles lately. By the turn of the century the phone industry had become a textbook case of what happens when a product or service becomes invisible at best, frustrating at worst, and so omnipresent that it generates excitement in no one. And the overabundance of capacity created a marketing war that none of us could possibly have missed.

At one point AT&T was spending more than a billion dollars per year on marketing, mainly to mitigate the negative effects on its bottom line from disloyal-customer "churn," an outgrowth of the widely available and heavily discounted offerings by competitors. Just as computer chips and sneakers once were no-frills items, phone service has become a commodity. Rather than reinvent the commodity, however, most phone companies opted to do what they had done ever since deregulation first hit in the mid-eighties. They plowed more and more money into traditional marketing schemes, nearly all of them complicated and sometimes deceptive promotions and dial-around services with myriad 800 numbers that connect callers to discounted long-distance providers.

I strongly suspect that most of these companies assumed that outlandish promotional budgets would help strengthen their brands, but in reality such excessive expenditures may have had a reverse effect. Nearly all of that high-cost telecom advertising delivered one brand-fatal message: *the only factor that matters when it comes to phone service is price.* Not service, not new technology, not friendly customer support, customer relations, or the quality of the people behind the brand. Any market in which the only critical factor is price is by definition a commodity market. Take wheat, pork bellies, gold, and silver—in every one of these markets, the only factor is price per pound on a given day. A rare exception to this rule is Morton Salt, which built a viable brand out of a commodity and made it synonymous with quality and value. What's the principal difference today between Sprint, MCI, and AT&T, or a whole host of smaller, rival phone services? Price, of course. Perceptions of product parity are the death of the brand in any business. It takes great creativity for any brand, once immersed, to pull itself out of the murky soup of product parity. The future for this industry may rest with companies like Tellme Networks, a voice-recognition communications company located in Mountain View, California, that may render the buttons on the phone unnecessary. "Dial Tone 2.0," as we liked to refer to it while I was helping Tellme map out its own brand architecture in 2000, will marry the information power of the Web with the simplicity and omnipresence of the phone. Interestingly, AT&T was one of the early investors in Tellme.

Branding a Commodity: The Right Way

Part of the appeal for me in joining Starbucks in 1995 was the prospect of helping create another powerful global brand from within a commodity business, as we had accomplished at Nike with sneakers. But this time around, we would not be able to rely on major advertising or any of the beneficial awareness that marketing might bring. Starbucks was investing more than $100 million each year in opening new locations and also had one of the best—and most expensive—employee benefits programs ever offered anywhere. As a result, it had very little left over for mass marketing.

When I left Nike, I left behind a $200 million marketing communications war chest, up significantly from the $17 million budget I had started with seven years earlier. Interestingly, the percentage of sales that Nike committed to marketing remained the same over that period. As top-line revenues grew, so did our marketing. Starbucks CEO Howard Schultz had been able to scrape together a $5 million marketing budget for my first year there. We invested the money in redesigning the stores and every aspect of product packaging, in new product development, and in grassroots marketing, particularly in new markets. During the time I was there the budget never increased much, and Starbucks never bought network broadcast or national print advertising, though we made several stabs at seeing what it would look like, creatively, if we ever needed it. Starbucks was blessed by the fact that the rest of the coffee world was still fast asleep at the switch, pumping out undifferentiated products for the grocery channel, manufactured to the lowest possible price. For decades, industry innovation had been leveraged to get costs down rather than quality up. And in the fifty-year race to see who could make the cheapest three-pound can of coffee and stack it high and deep on the end of the grocery aisle, the coffee brands spent billions of dollars on marketing that was at best unremarkable.

As it turned out, the industry giants essentially sat on their hands while Starbucks reinvented a nine-hundred-year-old product they had dominated for generations. Was Starbucks any more convenient than a home-made cup of coffee? Not really. Most customers have to drive or walk to their nearest Starbucks, and wait another six or seven minutes to get their morning drink. Was it cheaper? Hardly. On a per cup basis, a double-tall nonfat latte costs ten times more than a cup of sour, scalded Joe made from a six-month-old can of barely roasted, one-grind-fits-all low-elevation robusta bean shavings. Rather than compromise on product quality in order to have money to spend on expensive media campaigns, Starbucks served up a steady stream of hand-crafted, customized products in a welcoming, well-lit, clean, and comforting environment. The Starbucks experience proved relevant from Times Square in New York to King's Road in London to the Ginza in Tokyo. It also works well in five thousand other locations around the world today.

But Starbucks didn't limit the process of brand development to coffee alone. In 1995 it began to sell its own music compilations on CDs, as well as its own books, pastries, and other merchandise. Starbucks didn't really make the coffee kings nervous until it successfully entered their own turf, the grocery store, with bottled Frappuccino, Starbucks coffee ice creams, and whole-bean coffees, all in the span of a single year. They thought we were out to get them, but we were just following our Golden Rule: brewing unto others as we would have them brew unto us. We believed that no one should have to drink bad coffee at work, eat coffee ice cream that had no real coffee in it, or brew poor-quality coffee at home, even if the Starbucks choices cost a little more.

Branding a Commodity: The Wrong Way

The confusion between brand *awareness* and brand *strength* reached its zenith six years after the Marlboro Man fell off his high horse, as the technology sector—especially Web-based e-commerce companies, software companies, and e-business consulting companies—took center stage in the battle for brand differentiation. For a time, the new brand battles were fought between Intel and AMD, Compaq, IBM, and Apple; between Amazon.com and Yahoo!; between eBay and eToys.

Nothing was more important for many of the freshly minted dot coms, in those halcyon days, than immediately establishing themselves as *the* brand in their space. To do so, they figured, would require loads of advertising. In the span of a few short years, billions of marketing dollars evaporated at the hands of young, restless, well-funded, and inexperienced entrepreneurs in the pursuit of "brand building." Despite the revolutionary nature of the business, most followed the misguided example of their Old Economy predecessors and equated brand *awareness* with brand *strength*.

In the wake of the dot-com bust, many companies overreacted and fled to the opposite extreme, reflexively deeming all forms of mass media a complete waste of time. They turned their attention instead to Web-based marketing, usually in the form of issuing blizzards of unsolicited e-mails and banner ads wherever they could get them. I encountered the fallout of this approach firsthand at a board meeting for one of Silicon Valley's most promising start-ups. One board member who had funded a number of by then failing companies remarked, "I can't think of too many of my portfolio companies that are happy that they spent a ton of money on advertising lately."

Another board member added, "Television doesn't work. Never has and never will." This "insight" amazed me. Apparently the speaker's experience had been formed at Microsoft, a company that could not buy good advertising no matter how hard it tried. And it spent a lot of money trying. Microsoft had even hired Nike's agency, Wieden & Kennedy, in 1994 for the launch of Windows 95 and to help it "with its brand work." Save for the "Start Me Up" commercial, the relationship was a complete disaster and was not long-lived. But I don't believe for a moment that the problem was the fault of the agency, for Microsoft is a notoriously difficult client and Wieden is a notoriously gifted agency. Shortly after this board meeting I spoke with one former Microsoft marketing executive turned venture capitalist who also thought that television was a waste for any company, click or mortar. I asked him how he felt about the creative process with Wieden & Kennedy.

"Wieden & Kennedy never got the heart of Microsoft," he complained.

"That's funny," I replied. "I never knew Microsoft *had* a heart."

To their credit, the Portland, Oregon–based creative powerhouse Wieden & Kennedy—which has kept a relationship with Nike since the agency opened its door in 1981—had sought in vain to find something deeper within Microsoft that would resonate with the world, not unlike what they had accomplished for Nike. They tried to define something in the brand that was more meaningful to people than mere software, but they came up empty-handed. Even the best advertising cannot create something that is not there. If a company lacks soul or heart, if it doesn't understand the concept of "brand," or if it is disconnected from the world around it, there is little chance that its marketing will resonate deeply with anyone. It's a lot like putting lipstick on a pig.

Shortly after the 2000 Super Bowl, I was asked by a writer from *USA Today* to comment on the televised ad presence and creative performance of the dot coms. The writer informed me, half kidding, that he was starting to think that all the creative disasters he had been treated to that past Sunday could be blamed on Nike.

"You made it all look so *easy*," the reporter observed. "They think that all they have to do to create a great brand is to hire a hot ad agency, tell them they want 'Nike advertising,' and 'spend lots of money.'"

"They overlooked three things," I replied. "We had a compelling product that everyone understood. We had a business model that actually worked. And we had common sense when reviewing creative ideas."

I can't think of much better advice for any brand in any industry. Start with a great product or service that people desire and that you can sell profitably. The best brands never start out with the intent of building a great brand. They focus on building a great—and profitable—product or service and an organization that can sustain it. Once that has been accomplished, you can slam your foot on the marketing accelerator and let the whole world know about it. But get ready to meet the demand created by that marketing or you will destroy your brand before it ever gets off the ground. And also know that your advertising must create a proposition that your product or service delivers on, time and time again.

Defining "Brand"

So now we know that in the New Brand World, brand awareness and recognition, even when judiciously used, do not necessarily a viable or powerful brand make, though they are key aspects of the process. What then is the complete equation? What are all the forces that shape a brand? Is there one completely accurate definition?

For starters, let's examine what a brand is not. It is not, to cite just one example, best defined by an entry in a recent edition of the *Random House English Dictionary*.

> 1. A word, name, symbol etc. esp. one legally registered as a trademark, used by a manufacturer or merchant to identify its products distinctively from others of the same type and usually prominently displayed on its goods, in advertising etc. 2. A product, line of products or service bearing a widely known brand name. 3. informal. A person notable or famous, esp. in a particular field: The reception was replete with brand names from politics and the arts [1925].

This outmoded definition relies far too heavily on tangible quantities like products, services, and trademarks. Yes, brands are in part physical. They are often represented by products, places, and people. But we're now turning away from a half century best described by Diane Coyle in her excellent work *The Weightless World* as "the tyranny of the tangible." Since the advent of the Industrial Revolution, all that mattered in business were tangible assets: physical entities that either appeared on the corporate balance sheet as "hard assets" or, in the realm of abstraction, such easily quantifiable concepts as price-to-earnings ratios or quarterly earnings. The materials and power sources that drove the Industrial Revolution—steel, oil, electricity, lumber, heavy equipment, concrete, and automobiles—formed the tangible bedrock of the value equation. But in today's knowledge-based, experience-driven society, intangible and often weightless notions, intellectual properties, ideas, products, and services are driving more wealth creation than are materials.

Nowhere is this more evident than in the realm of brand development. It can safely be said that Coca-Cola's total market value is more an emotional quantity than a physical one. Hard assets like bottling plants, trucks, raw materials, and buildings are not as important to Coke—or Wall Street, for that matter—as the consumer goodwill that exists around the world toward the brand. Put another way, the loyalty that Coke has created is worth many billions, possibly hundreds of billions, of future dollars. Attempting to quantify this part of the balance sheet can drive even the best CFO nuts, but the value is there. In 2001 I was retained by Coke to help drive an important new brand-development process that would help reveal the dynamics that drive Coke's brand strength and help establish a tracking system that would monitor how the company's most important beverage brands were performing in key markets around the world.

Defining the Softer Side of "Brand"

The more enlightened definition of branding that I'm going to propose here originated many centuries in the past. Well ahead of his time, Plato believed that behind and above and beneath everything concrete we experience in our daily lives is the *idea* of that thing, which gives the thing lasting, even everlasting, meaning. In a comparable way, every brand has a fundamental essence. This essence is not physical or defined exclusively or entirely by products or services.

Today, a brand is, if it is any *thing,* the result of a synaptic process in the brain. The great nineteenth-century Russian behavioral psychologist Ivan Petrovich Pavlov would understand this conception of branding. The pleasurable sensation that his dogs felt when he rang his famous bell—and their eager anticipation of the imminent arrival of food, which they demonstrated by salivating—is perhaps the best analogy I can think of to the psychological process that branding elicits in us when it works successfully. The concept of the brand—the Platonic idea, if you will—creates a response in its audience without the audience's seeing the product or directly experiencing the service. Think Godiva chocolates for a moment: the very name, perhaps even the logo, conjures up an image of sinful indulgence. Yes, it represents chocolate or ice cream, but it is the feeling and the anticipation of that feeling that the brand conveys most compellingly.

But for our purposes, even the Pavlovian model comes up a little short. I believe that the twentieth-century humanist psychologist Abraham Maslow offers us a model that may be more relevant for the more nuanced consumers of today.

Maslow's Hierarchy of Human Needs

The founder of what later became known as the "human potential" movement, the Brooklyn-born Abraham Maslow (1908–1970) completed his training in psychology when the field was dominated by the school known as behaviorism, led by B. F. Skinner. Behaviorists believed that the "human animal" was not fundamentally different from any other animal, and as such was primarily motivated by the basic physical and physiological needs for food, sex, warmth, shelter. Any "higher" emotions, goals, or ambitions were merely abstracted from these basic drives, and were thus not worthy of serious study.

But Maslow was not convinced that that was all there was to human psychology. By nature an independent spirit and thinker, he was no more impressed by the Freudian school (then gaining ground in America) than by the behaviorists. To illustrate his own theory of what motivates people, Maslow created a pyramid-shaped *hierarchy* of human needs. The primary, physiological needs for food and shelter are at the bottom, and progressively more complex needs—for safety, belonging, love, and esteem—are ranked progressively higher. At the top are our "highest" needs, for self-actualization and spiritual fulfillment.

Old Brand World thinking concentrated on what marketers call "top-of-mind" awareness, which, ironically enough, is precisely the opposite of what Maslow put at the top of his mental model. In traditional marketing lingo, "top of the mind" refers to unaided awareness of a brand, a product, or a product feature. This surface-level measure does not impart enough insight in today's fiercely competitive and commoditized marketplace. And it does not begin to approach the notion of measuring brand loyalty. I am personally aware of a great number of brands I have no intention of ever buying because they are irrelevant to me, or they don't resonate deeply enough for me to trust them.

Today's brand positioning and behavior must reflect an understanding of the deeper psychological issues that Maslow placed at the apex of his pyramid. Brands that respect the "higher" consumer needs and develop products, services, and marketing communications that intelligently leverage them will rise above the commodity fray, for they will become more meaningful. These emotional needs include more powerful, more subtle, more complex motivations like yearning to belong, needing to feel connected, hoping to transcend, desiring to experience joy and fulfillment. We will discuss these emotive drivers, particularly as they relate to Maslow's theories, in greater detail in chapter 4. But for now, keep this "higher ground" concept in mind as we attempt to redefine the notion of a brand. Henry Ford did more than create the concept of mass production. The real power of the automobile in its early years was probably more emotional than it was physical. It must have been much more than getting from one place to another. Imagine the emotional rewards that came with owning an automobile for the first time or just riding in one. If that's difficult, remember back to your first bike. Mine was a Huffy. Some of our greatest brand memories are primarily emotional.

Brand Alchemy

If in today's competitive environment a brand can be bound by the laws of psychology at all, the process by which it evolves into a marketer's most powerful tool is most akin to alchemy. This is the ancient and quasi-mystical practice of transmuting base elements like iron into precious elements like gold.

> *Branding is about taking something common and improving upon it in ways that make it more valuable and meaningful.*

A coffee bean is just a coffee bean until someone like Howard Schultz and Starbucks comes along, and creates from it a branded product—a hand-crafted espresso drink served in an environment such as a coffee-house.

The sneaker was just a sneaker, in every way pedestrian, until Phil Knight and Nike came along and connected the aspirational and inspirational rewards of sports and fitness with world-class innovative product performance like that of the Nike Air shoe. Nike could have spent millions preaching the value of encapsulated gas trapped within a thin, pliable membrane in the midsole of a shoe, encased by a molded foot frame and attached to a dynamic fit system. Instead, it not only simply *showed* the product but also communicated on a deeper, more inspirational level what the product *meant* within the wider world of sports and fitness. It transcended the product. It moved people.

The alchemical process described above—the transmutation of "base" materials into gold—occurs in the deepest recesses of the human brain as a *memory*. This memory may be sharp, or it may be out of focus; it is of everything that the consumer in question has seen, heard, or felt about that particular brand. The products themselves are just one contributing factor among many in this mental construct. Therefore:

> *A brand is the sum of the good, the bad, the ugly, and the off-strategy. It is defined by your best product as well as your worst product. It is defined by award-winning advertising as well as by the god-awful ads that somehow slipped through the cracks, got approved, and, not surprisingly, sank into oblivion. It is defined by the accomplishments of your best employee—the shining star in the company who can do no wrong—as well as by the mishaps of the worst hire that you ever made. It is also defined by your receptionist and the music your customers are subjected to when placed on hold. For every grand and finely worded public statement by the CEO, the brand is also defined by derisory consumer comments overheard in the hallway or in a chat room on the Internet. Brands are sponges for content, for images, for fleeting feelings. They become psychological concepts held in the minds of the public, where they may stay forever. As such you can't entirely control a brand. At best you only guide and influence it.*

The most successful brands consistently evoke positive feelings over time. With each new product, service, or marketing campaign the brand is refreshed and recharged. Great brands do this around a core theme or idea and draw each new product or service into its narrative as another engaging, relevant, new chapter in a story that, like a great piece of mythology, can never be completely told. But they do all this with the customer, not the company, as the story's main protagonist. To do this requires that the company change the way it looks at the marketing universe.

Brand Astrology: The Copernican View

One essential difference between the New and the Old Brand Worlds is that in today's brand equation, the consumer to whom you are telling your story—the listener, the viewer, the customer—has more control than ever before. Whether the name of your game is pure bricks-and-mortar (physical-world retailing, wholesaling, manufacturing, or services) or "clicks-and-mortar" (employing elements from the virtual and physical worlds), or you meet the public entirely on-line, the fact remains that the world has unalterably changed because of the Internet. What the Web and the Net have accomplished—and this is a potentially earth-shattering feat—is to put consumers in the driver's seat of the economy. Ignore them at your own risk. This is as major a perceptual transformation in the universe of marketing as Copernicus's realization that the earth revolved around the sun, not the other way around. Likewise, the New Economy revolves around the consumer. In the future, business will ultimately rise and set with the customer, not your best retail distributor or reseller.

The long-term implications of this astronomical shift are both profound and perplexing. According to the University of Michigan business school professors C. K. Prahalad and Venkatram Ramaswamy, the swing of the power pendulum to the consumer makes a product *"no more than an artifact around which customers have experiences."* This notion is potentially so far-reaching that I believe it bears repeating:

A product is no more than an artifact around which customers have experiences.

Over time, products and services will come and go, but the brand that provides them will remain a constant. And brands will be defined by the sum total of those experiences, rather than the products or services themselves. It is precisely because we live in this new Copernican universe of marketing that we must now pay more attention to the consumer experience. We must recognize that a great product by itself is just one more chit, one more token, one more piece of currency in the relationship between consumer and brand.

We must also recognize that not all exchanges between brand and customer are good. In fact, some are disastrous, and these exchanges test the strength of the relationship. But brands that have built a strong emotional bond with customers are far more likely to recover from a misstep or an unwarranted tragedy than those that are perceived as merely products, no matter how good those products may be.

When the McNeil pharmaceutical company, the manufacturer of Tylenol, was hit by a mad poisoner, it was a tragedy for the consumers who were victims of the crime. It was also a particularly undermining attack on the integrity of the brand. What ultimately allowed Tylenol to recover was its immediate recall, an aggressive couponing program (as much as $2 toward purchase of a new package), and, perhaps most important, a deep reservoir of brand trust. Tylenol had never given rise to questions concerning the integrity of the brand. The way in which it behaved in the days following the tragedy ultimately built even more trust in the brand.

When AOL's brand became, for a time, synonymous with "busy signal," it was bad news for both the customers and the brand. What allowed it to recover from that debacle was the enduring strength of its brand position, and the consistency and coherence of its brand promise. That, and the rapid installation of a good many more phone lines. Never closely associated with cutting-edge technology, AOL instead built a credible brand by being the most "user-friendly" Internet service provider. It was one of the first businesses to successfully market basic e-mail services for the masses. It was first to market easy-to-use instant messaging. AOL's brand strength and its stock price accelerated to the point that it was able to acquire Time Warner at the peak of the dot-com boom. And while that acquisition may look out of balance in the wake of the subsequent market sell-off there is no denying that AOL established one of the most trusted media brands in the world.

For an illustrative counterexample, consider the *Exxon Valdez* oil spill in Prince William Sound, Alaska, in 1989. At the time it occurred, Exxon's brand image with the consumer was not exactly a deep pool of good feeling. When in the face of ecological crisis the company seemed to be bent on evading its moral and ethical responsibilities to the environment, the public came down on it hard.

Nine years later, when the Justice Department and twenty states' attorneys general accused Microsoft of unfair competitive practices, Microsoft customers' brand loyalty and the company's market position were not such as to make the public rise up in outcry in defense of a beloved brand. Microsoft built an incredibly rich and powerful company but an incredibly shallow brand. A paradox like this suggests business practices that may not have been entirely in the best interest of the consuming public, not to mention the brand itself. Bill Gates and Steve Ballmer hastily concocted television commercials in which they begged for forgiveness and sympathy from the American public in the days preceding the Justice Department's announcement that it was charging Microsoft with antitrust law violations, which ultimately went badly for them. The commercials represented a comically feeble, and long overdue, attempt to change public opinion.

"Product purists" would beg to differ with this interpretation. Product purists insist that products speak for themselves. They would claim that all the above is just "branding BS," and that what allowed Tylenol and AOL and other strong brands to stay strong even in the face of adversity was the fact that they are *great products*. In other words, if the public doesn't have an unshakable faith in your product, it's because your product sucks.

Don't believe them. Microsoft and Exxon both put out great products, certainly as good software and gasoline as anyone else. But when external events turned against them, the public just as quickly turned on them too. That just didn't happen with AOL or Tylenol. And that's the difference, pure and simple, between having a strong brand and having a weak brand.

Even the greatest brands, of course, go through their rough spots, and experience some prolonged periods of severe stress. What enabled Nike to triumph over innumerable adversities—including being practically boycotted for supposedly underpaying its suppliers' Asian contract workers—was the underlying strength of its brand. What permitted Starbucks to overcome the accusation that it was becoming "too much like Taco Bell" has been a consistent record in doing good things for its customers and its employees. These include full medical benefits for part-time employees and stock ownership available to all employees no matter how many hours they worked—benefits and rewards that most fast-food brands had never dreamed of offering. The end result: employees like their company and in turn create a better *brand experience* for their customers.

Products and services will continue to come and go. But the residual experiences of customers who consume them will ultimately define the brand. Even the world's greatest brand spokesman, even Michael Jordan, will one day fade away. At Nike we knew Michael Jordan was ultimately just another contribution to the totality of elements that constitute the Nike brand—albeit a critical one. Years before Michael first retired from the NBA to pursue baseball, we were already at work envisioning our business without Air Jordan. Even the world's greatest athlete was for us a means, even if an immensely powerful one, to a greater end.

Brand Metaphysics

Ask yourself the question "Who am I?" Your initial answer is probably something quick and obvious, like your name. That was my response the first time I was asked the deceptively simple question "Who are you?" as part of an executive training session led by Deepak Chopra. The exercise was straightforward: after answering the question, no matter what your answer was, you were asked it again. And again. With each answer I had to dig a little deeper as I tried to explain who on earth I was. It quickly became apparent to me that I was not just a name, not just a father, not just a husband, not just a son. And I was certainly not merely my job title, a response offered by some of the others participating in the exercise.

If you have read any of Deepak Chopra's books, you know that it is a fundamentally flawed and limited view of our lives—not to mention the universe—to define ourselves by our physical presence, since that is temporal and fleeting. I'm not talking about reincarnation here, or at least not yet. The human body pretty much regenerates itself every year, some organs faster than others. Hair continues to grow no matter how we cut it (for most of us, anyway), and the skin you sport today was not there six months ago. Nor will it be with you six months from now. Even your internal organs slowly die and rebuild.

So if we aren't entirely defined by our physical attributes or the name we give ourselves, how *are* we defined? Some believe we are defined by a spirit or by the spirituality that guides the decisions we make in life. I think that approach is part of the answer, but I have a somewhat more concrete suggestion than that.

We are defined by the experiences and actions of our lifetime. So are brands.

We are defined by years of fun and boredom, of excitement and terror, of pleasure and pain, of love and loathing. Some portion of the weathering and scars is visible. Some of it lies much deeper. We are defined by the friends we have kept as well as those we elected not to. We are a product of the things we controlled as well as stuff that landed on our laps courtesy of fate, chance, bad luck, or destiny.

As I related Chopra's riddle to my wife that evening I was struck by the similarities between defining a person and defining a brand. Understanding what constitutes a brand is an equally daunting exercise. In the end, as we have seen, brands are not physical things that can be held in your hand, placed on your feet, or measured accurately on a scale. Such characteristics belong to products. Likewise, brands don't insure your house, connect your phone call, change your oil, advise you about your business, or bring you your e-mail. Those are services.

Brands are living concepts that we hold in our minds for years. What goes into them is both logical and irrational. Some of the most lasting brand images are purely emotional—memories of exceptionally bad service, of a product that failed to deliver on its promise, or of one that exceeded our expectations and blew us away with its screaming performance. In our minds we store all the moments in time when a brand stopped us in our tracks and made us think deeply or inspired us. This is where we remember the brands that marked an important passage in our lives. Gerber baby food is an excellent example. As a brand, Gerber consistently ranks among the most powerful on earth. It delivers trust where we most appreciate it.

We also remember the brands that have nearly killed us. For me that's a certain brand of tequila that will remain nameless, and a Third World airline that for similar reasons will also remain nameless. Thanks to these negative associations, I now steer clear of all tequila-derived cocktails and commercial pilots from Third World countries who are quite comfortable with the idea of reincarnation. People and brands also share a concept that the pilots of such airlines understand completely: karma. *Webster's* dictionary defines karma as "the force generated by a person's actions held in Hinduism and Buddhism to perpetuate reincarnation and to determine the nature of the person's next existence."

I believe that brands have karma. If brand awareness was once the standard measure for brand strength, and brand resonance and relevance are the new yardsticks, I suspect that brand karma will be the ultimate definition of brand strength one day. But as you can see by that transition, we have gone from something easily measurable (how many people are *aware* of your brand) to something far more difficult to measure (how do people really *feel* about your brand). Brand karma reflects everything a company does as well as everything it elects not to do. Ignoring a public relations debacle is very bad for brand karma. Thanks to the media and the Information Age, a brand's karma will be more exposed and studied than ever before.

The world has no shortage of companies, of products, and of means by which to get them. In the New Brand World, successful brands will set themselves apart not just by how well their products and services perform, but by how they create and deliver them to the consuming public and how they communicate and interact with the world around them. Top-of-mind awareness and other surface-level viewpoints of a brand reveal little about a brand's real strength or weakness. To fully understand a brand you have to look much deeper. You have to strip everything away and get to its core and understand how it is viewed *and felt* by people inside the company and the world outside.

So How Do You Build a Brand?

In the coming pages, we'll take a look at several principles that I have been fortunate enough put to work in once-small companies that over time became powerful global brands and industry leaders. Some of the key learnings are:

1. How to define and protect your own-brand DNA.

2. How to create intelligent brandwidth and grow your company.

3. How to establish lasting emotional ties with your customers that transcend your product or service.

4. How to become a protagonist for something timeless and valuable.

5. How to make size an asset, not a liability.

6. How to use your God-given, unique superhuman powers for good.

7. How to make your brand values pervasive in your organization.

8. How to be a good brand parent.

These principles have always felt like common sense to me. I've been fortunate to see them honored or ignored at small companies when I was in the advertising agency business, I saw them put into practice with stellar results at Nike and Starbucks, and more recently I witnessed how they could help technology companies quickly rise above all the rest and how one of the oldest and most trusted brands, Coca-Cola, could reinvent itself. But it was just a few years ago that most traditional business thinkers scratched their heads when they studied Nike or Starbucks and deemed them reckless or unsustainable over the long term. We certainly gave these business types much to think about. We didn't play by their rules. At Nike we probably didn't win many Wall Street friends in the early years because we didn't pay as much attention to them as other companies did. Instead, we spent most of our time looking at consumers and the world they, not the analysts, lived in. Interestingly, what has proved to be reckless and unsustainable are many Old Brand World marketing and brand-development practices. That paradigm shift is the crux of this book.

So now that we have defined what a brand is, let's get on with the task of learning how some of the best brands have been built. There is no better place to begin than with the foundations and core values that great brands are built upon.

cracking your brand's genetic code

─────────────

Brand Principle #2
You have to know it before you can grow it.

"Know thyself."—ARISTOTLE

NOVEMBER 30, 1987   On my first day at Nike, I found myself sitting in the private conference room of the company's CEO and founder, Phil Knight, in the old Murray 1 Building in Beaverton, Oregon. This was three years before Nike built its impressive corporate campus—an enormous hundred-acre shrine to sports and fitness—and its headquarters back then was spread across six nondescript leased office complexes in Portland and Beaverton.

In those days, Nike was running a distant third in the sneaker world, behind the German juggernaut Adidas and its chief domestic rival, Reebok. Nothing in the appearance of Nike's corporate offices suggested it would one day become a global powerhouse, much less an international protagonist for sports and fitness in the highest sense. Apart from the occasional poster of an athlete or a shoe framed on a wall, any of the headquarters buildings could easily have been mistaken for an insurance office, from the inside as well as out. Phil Knight's office windows looked out at a strip mall, anchored by a Kmart.

In my first few hours as Nike's director of corporate advertising, I'd done a little snooping around, hoping to find among the papers and records left behind by my predecessors some clues to my future existence. Rob Strasser, Peter Moore, and Cindy Hale, the threesome that had kept a tight rein on Nike design and marketing matters for more than a decade, had left in their wake an advertising plan that consisted of little more than three pages of budget numbers, grouped under two seasonal product launches. Such informality was typical of Nike in those days. Insofar as I had been able to ascertain, the marketing department's traditions, like those of the Bedouin, were entirely oral.

In the absence of any formal or written direction, I decided to seek out Phil Knight for some verbal guidance. Unfortunately for me, Knight was not one to tell any of his staff—especially a key employee, and a new hire to boot—exactly what to do. He spent a good deal of time recruiting talented people who, he hoped against hope, would intuitively grasp the core values of Nike, and then he very deliberately got the hell out of their way. As some of those new hires would learn to their distress, Phil Knight would only reemerge—and loom large in your presence—if you really screwed up.

"What would be the single most important thing I can do for you right now?" I asked, after taking a seat in the sparsely furnished conference room adjoining his office. Hardly anyone ever entered his *actual* office. That was his inner sanctum. Knight pondered my request for a moment and, with a strange combination of a grimace and a shrug, effectively parried my opening thrust.

"Just do great things," he replied, rubbing one hand across his grizzled jaw.

"But what if I end up making mistakes?" I wondered out loud, feeling not much more enlightened by this broad exhortation than I had by the so-called marketing plan.

"Oh, don't worry about that," Knight replied cheerfully.

By this point, I felt the unnerving joy of being granted incredible latitude—combined with a fear of not knowing where I might find the potholes that I knew would be in the road going forward. Then Knight turned deadly serious as he leaned forward and fixed me with a disconcertingly direct gaze.

"Just don't make the same mistake twice," he said.

On the short drive back to my own quarters in Nimbus A—a fitting name for a building that housed design, the product lab, and advertising—I began to suspect strongly that everything that Knight did or said in the presence of key employees was carefully considered. This didn't mean, of course, that he necessarily thought long, hard, or abstractly about his remarks. In fact, that was precisely the point: he deliberately did *not* think long, hard, or abstractly about them. It was simply that everything he said was judiciously weighed from an intuitive point of view. His opinions were genuine, not the sort of pronouncements that fill the air around so many CEOs who assume the position of being the ultimate authority on everything. If Knight preferred to give me general direction rather than a specific job description, I was going to have to live with it. Or find a new place of employment.

When I returned to my office I took the first step in following the program I'd been given and began ruminating on the gamut of mistakes that I believed Nike had made in the past few years, some of them probably committed at least twice. Nike's greatest recent error, in my humble opinion, had been to first ignore and then deny the growing strength of a new competitor: Reebok.

By the late eighties, even those in Beaverton who were inclined to stick their heads in the sand and ignore the more unpleasant realities of life were finding it harder and harder to dismiss the depth and breadth of the threat posed by a soft leather shoe called the Freestyle. Reebok's Freestyle was hardly what hard-core "Nike guys"—there were very few women in any position of power in Beaverton in those days—would have respectfully referred to as "high-performance sports gear." That the Freestyle lacked the firm torsion control and deep, durable cushioning of Nike Air scarcely mattered, however, to the millions of men and women who had enthusiastically purchased it in the early eighties. Some proudly wore theirs on the street, while still others wore theirs to the gym, to practice a strange new fitness pursuit called "aerobics." Some actually ran 5K and 10K races in them. It was all totally absurd from Nike's point of view, which was that there was no point in wearing athletic shoes that weren't "court-worthy," meaning a pair of finely tuned precision instruments exquisitely designed for imparting a critical competitive edge on whatever playing field you were on.

The real lesson to be learned from the threat posed by the Freestyle was not so much that it had trumped Nike on the style front. Or even that its stunning success in cornering the aerobics market—and with it the exploding fitness market—had helped knock Nike off its proud perch as the number 1 athletic shoe company in the country. The point, rather, was that Nike's outlook had become insular, arrogant, and complacent. For too long, management had flatly insisted that aerobics was nothing more than a passing fad. This high-handed attitude would, I feared, be their undoing.

As Ronald Reagan once said in a different context, "Mistakes were made." But did I possess the experience and skills to help fix them? On my first day at Nike, it would have been safe to say that I had just joined a company caught at a strategic crossroads. Andrew Grove, the former Intel CEO, would have recognized instantly what we were facing: a classic "strategic inflection point."

Brand Darwinism

A "strategic inflection point," for those who have not read Andy Grove's modern classic, *Only the Paranoid Survive,* is a critical juncture in the evolution of any organization. It is a time, to quote Tom Paine, that can "try men's souls." A time when a company finds itself faced with a great self-defining challenge, which it can meet only by answering in some detail these four critical questions:

1. What are our goals?
2. Where—and what—do we hope to be in the future?
3. What do we do if and when we get there?
4. How will we measure success?

Some companies, when confronted with a real live strategic inflection point, freeze in their tracks like a deer caught in the headlights. As a result of this paralysis, these institutions become excessively fearful of change. Most of the time, the strategic direction in which a company must head is far from obvious, even to those at the top. Nevertheless, companies faced with these vexing dilemmas are still obliged to grow or die, to change or to expire, to redefine themselves or join the dismal ranks of the also-rans and the once great.

Nike's unique strategic inflection point was clear. It had to grow beyond its narrow core of aspiring competitive athletes and make itself more relevant to a broader consuming public. Like all brands, it had to move forward or die. Yet even to entertain such a solution to Nike's mounting problems had become, for many of the old guard at Nike, a form of heresy. How could Nike, they asked, dare to consider betraying its identity as a pure athletic brand by targeting more casual athletes, who seldom if ever played a "real" sport?

The crux of the problem as I—a newcomer without preconceptions—saw it rested in the narrow way that "Brand Nike" had been defined up to that time. The brand's essence—its genetic material, if you will—was testosterone-heavy; it was geared principally toward young male athletes and projected a "wimps need not apply" ethos. But if this was all Nike would always be at its core, if this was to be its image and its legacy, the awesome organism that Knight and his old college track coach Bill Bowerman had founded would never achieve its full potential as a brand.

A few weeks earlier, when I was first interviewing with Knight for my job, the dilemma of Nike's brand limitations was obviously of great concern to him. Nike had recently lost a quarter of its revenues in a very short period of time and given up the number 1 position in North America to Reebok. Trailing twelve-month revenues were around $800 million. Knight had recently laid off nearly 20 percent of the employees, the first layoffs in the history of the company. On the heels of all this he asked me just how big I thought Nike could be someday.

"Easily, two, maybe three billion dollars," I said confidently.

Knight rubbed his chin and then asked me something I never would have anticipated: "What if I told you I only wanted to be the world's best-run one-billion-dollar sports-and-fitness company? Would you still want the job?"

"I'd be happy to help you do that," I replied. "But I'd regard it as a missed opportunity. This brand is capable of much more." Perhaps better than any other CEO in the world, Knight knew that every brand had its limitations, but that those limitations are usually self-imposed. Brands can get bigger without destroying what they once were. They just need bridges to connect the past to the future. Knight was looking for bridge builders who would respect what he had worked so hard to build.

The challenging situation that I was fortunate enough to find myself in at that time would repeat itself again and again in my subsequent experience with helping other companies build brands. In today's no-holds-barred drive to create powerful brands and brand images, some companies have spent vast sums of money on ambitious marketing programs without taking the most important first step: understanding exactly what it is that they are seeking to build upon—their brand's foundation. This substructure, as pointed out in the last chapter, is not built from tangible materials like steel and rebar, but fashioned by circumstances from intangible, dynamic forces that are often nearly impossible to define, let alone quantify.

This misperception of the primary focus of brand building is hardly a new phenomenon. The world has seldom suffered from a shortage of once cash-rich but now poorly managed companies lacking the faintest idea of what the brand development process is all about. But in the late 1990s, thanks to hundreds of desperate dot coms and their often blissfully ignorant investors, this affliction blossomed into a full-blown epidemic. Led by intelligent and lavishly funded but often inexperienced management teams, a new breed of company turned to aggressive consumer marketing in the hope of creating strong, high-profile brands in the blink of an eye.

To these often quite capable souls, building a brand involved little more than throwing limitless advertising budgets at the problem, and hoping that the public would bite—big, long, and hard. The lessons learned from this experience—the ads run during the 1999 and 2000 Super Bowls were cases in point—were both painful and expensive for many now-embittered participants. They discovered that even the most dazzling and even high-impact commercials did not necessarily a relevant or admired brand make. The most important of the lessons that can be drawn from such fiascoes is the following:

Every brand has at its core a substance that gives it strength. You have to understand it before you can grow it.

Some call this substance the brand's "essence"; others prefer the term "core brand values." As I once described this admittedly vague concept to the management team at Tellme Networks, a Silicon Valley start-up, a brash young engineer immediately "got" what I was trying to put across. "I know just what you're driving at," he offered brightly. "You're talking about brand *mojo*." Mojo works, too.

Personally, I prefer to think of this ethereal substance as a brand's *genetic structure*. Consider this: no two brands are exactly alike. Company founders are a little like parents: each of them contributes something unique of their values, disciplines, and visions that, if all goes well, will in combination create, nurture, and strengthen an entity that will outlive them.

All too often, when the corporate leadership changes, the genes mutate along with it—unless the brand is well understood across the company. In these traditional states, brands that are poorly defined often become deformed versions of the strong, vital substances the world once loved and respected. Only in very rare cases does leadership churn succeed in strengthening brands. More typically, a brand subjected to the inconsistent twists and turns of management pressure just degenerates into a confused, unremarkable mess. Specialty retailer Nordstrom experienced this shortly after the Nordstrom family stepped out of several key leadership positions in 2000. The key to Nordstrom's recovery? The family stepped back in.

But even the sorriest cases of brand dilution and convolution possess somewhere deep inside their stressed-out DNA a blueprint of the unique set of values that originally defined them. If carefully restored, these values still can continue to define the brand in the present as well as the future. Likewise, every brand contains a characteristic set of weaknesses, some of which can't be fixed with even the largest marketing budget. One of the most important lessons that I have learned over the years is that there is only so much any one brand can do. Nike once thought it could market denim jeans as an accessory to its footwear. It even signed up star athletes Wayne Gretzky and Kirk Gibson to promote them. A few months later, sanity prevailed. Smart brand stewards recognize the intrinsic limitations of their brands, as well as the wealth of opportunities that lie within their grasp.

Brand on the Run

One shining spot on an otherwise gloomy horizon for Nike in 1987 was its product innovation. Nike had introduced two revolutionary cushioning designs to the footwear market, thereby pioneering the then-novel concept of "high-tech footwear." Nike's first proprietary cushioning system had been the "waffle shoe" that the company's cofounder, the legendary University of Oregon track coach Bill Bowerman, developed one morning in 1970 while standing in his kitchen staring at his wife's waffle iron. The idea occurred to him that if he poured latex into the waffle iron, using it as a mold, the resulting material would resemble a baffled ceiling and would provide a dynamic air cushion for the foot. When Nike brought its "waffle sole" to market in 1977, it quickly became the sensation of the running world. Two years later, Nike introduced an even more revolutionary cushioning system for the midsole, based on a polyurethane bag in which was trapped a "super gas" made up of unusually large molecules. This system was branded "Nike Air" and became the core of the company's product success.

Eight years later, however, Nike Air was becoming "just another technology" in a raging battle between Reebok, Nike, Adidas, and other new entrants to see who had the best shoe laboratory. And then Nike changed the playing field. Nike's lead footwear designer, Tinker Hatfield, discovered a way to remove sections of the midsole on either side of the shoe to reveal the impermeable polyurethane bag of large molecular gas. Somehow, the fact that its upper came only in a blazingly garish Day-Glo reddish orange made the air bag beneath seem even more conspicuous, not to mention "very Nike."

"Vis-Air" might well have become a sensation all by itself, since the design was certainly "radical" in the most appealing sense of the term. But there was little doubt that the commercial success of Vis-Air owed a great deal to the equally compelling advertising campaign that the company had mounted to support it. Since it's unlikely that you will recall the details of this groundbreaking campaign nearly fifteen years after the fact, it's worth reviewing a few of the highlights of "Revolution." It was named in honor of the Beatles song penned by John Lennon and Paul McCartney, which provided the score. The TV commercial, which started running in March 1987, featured a complex juxtaposition of gritty black-and-white 8mm film images that ranged richly all over the cultural map, including:

- A group of exceptionally fit distance runners rounding the corner on a cinder track (actually, a hastily recruited battalion of Nike product line managers with Tom Hartge, the Nike Running PLM, leading the way).

- The emerging basketball star Michael Jordan wearing (incongruously) a white tennis shirt.

- John McEnroe on the brink of another nuclear meltdown.

- A thousand triathletes entering the water en masse.

- Inner-city playground hoopsters hitting the blacktop.

- Aerobics enthusiasts (some of the first television imagery of women in a Nike commercial) rocking a gym during the lunch hour.

- Most memorably, at least to me, in the midst of this moving montage, a young toddler (actually, a cousin of the agency account supervisor) running with his arms raised out in front of him, legs turning as fast as they could to keep pace with his upper body. His torso was tipping forward as only a toddler's can, when discovering what it's like to run full out for the first time.

These images were not merely evocative and beautiful, but meaningful, particularly in juxtaposition to each other. The message behind this med-

ley of images marked a new outlook for Nike: the Nike brand now spoke
to old as well as young, to women as well as men, to world-famous
champions and obscure street athletes, using different images but the same
voice. Nike, proclaimed "Revolution" without directly stating so, was an
inclusive, not an exclusive, brand.

One unexpected development, which even more unexpectedly served
to reinforce that core message, was the litigation that Nike's use of the
song prompted on the part of the surviving Beatles. The rights to "Revolution" had been acquired by Nike from SBK, negotiating on behalf of
Michael Jackson, who had purchased the rights to the entire Beatles catalog from EMI several years earlier. But that didn't stop Nike from being
unwittingly drawn into a tangled web of legal skirmishing among and between the surviving Beatles, Apple records, EMI, and SBK. What from a
marketing and PR perspective could have turned into a total fiasco for
Nike instead turned into an unanticipated media bonanza. As far as the
public was concerned the nuances of the case didn't much matter. "Beatles
Sue Nike" made for an eye-catching headline, even if the truth was a bit
more complex. The surprise for Nike was the way in which nearly every
network news show in the country, and many overseas, ran the spot in full
to illustrate their stories on the controversy—giving us a priceless amount
of free advertising time. Countless magazines featured a news story on
the lawsuit, and newspapers reported it on their front pages. After being
the beneficiary of this windfall of unpaid publicity for a few weeks, Knight
found that being sued by the Beatles didn't feel bad at all, especially since
he knew Nike had not acted improperly. If anything, the company's brush
with the Beatles only seemed to reinforce its hard-won image as part jock,
part rebel.

What interested me far more than the consequences of the lawsuit
were the particulars of the creative process that had led to "Revolution"
in the first place. In the course of an informal investigation into the gen-
esis of the campaign, which I embarked upon within days of arriving at
Nike, I learned that many of the most compelling images, including the
most striking one of the toddling toddler, had never been storyboarded.
So much of what made the campaign memorable had been the result of
a create-as-we-go, we'll-figure-it-all-out-later attitude on the part of the
creative team. I was further surprised to learn that Nike had not specified
in a brief that they were looking for anything even remotely resembling
"Revolution" from their ad agency, Portland-based Wieden & Kennedy.
In fact, not wanting anything too razzle-dazzle to detract from their goal
of showcasing its new "Vis-Air" technology, the client had originally indi-

cated that it was looking for a far more straightforward product-oriented campaign. As a bemused Wieden & Kennedy staffer later advised me, "They were hoping for an extended shot of a shoe, on a rotating lazy Susan, with a light shining through the air bag."

The genius of the agency had been to take that particular brief and run with it—straight to the nearest circular file. The agency's principals, Dan Wieden and David Kennedy, decided on their own that they wanted to create a campaign that would break the mold, not just to conduct an abstract aesthetic exercise but to say something enduring and meaningful about the Nike brand. In keeping with this approach, they were even willing to entertain a concept for the musical score that certainly came from left field. The idea of scoring the images to the Beatles' "Revolution" had been the inspiration of a woman named Janet Champ, who at the time was a receptionist at the agency. Champ quickly became a senior writer in W & K's creative department, and helped to conceive Nike's award-winning women's print advertising campaign a few years later.

Despite the strength of "Revolution" and "Vis-Air" in 1987, some of Nike's core problems remained as acute as ever. I became convinced that if anything, these minor victories in what might turn out to be a larger war could create a sense of false confidence that would obscure deeper problems. The company desperately needed to capitalize on the success of that year's product and advertising to help build something that was more than a sum of the parts: that ethereal thing called the Nike brand. I believed that Nike needed to lift the entire brand and redefine it in a way that was far more inclusive, without compromising Nike's authentic athletic spirit.

"Hayward Field"

The eagerly anticipated encore to the "Revolution" campaign had been in the works for fully two months before my arrival. The kick-off commercial was slated to be unveiled before a worldwide sales meeting in Palm Springs, California, in December 1987—just two weeks after my first day on the job. I spent several days of those first impressionable weeks holed up in a dark, airless editing room in Los Angeles with Dan Wieden, David Kennedy, and the rest of the W & K creative team on the Nike account—all four of them (in those days, there were just twenty-three people in the entire agency). The spot we were working on was called "Hayward Field," in honor of the University of Oregon track in Eugene, Oregon (Eugene is known as Track City, USA), where Nike's co-founders, Phil Knight, a runner, and Bill Bowerman, the coach, had first met.

The visuals that made up "Hayward Field" were gorgeous and haunting. The ad was artfully composed of solemn shots of an empty, lonely, rain-slicked track, with an equally somber audio commentary featuring an evocative collection of voices from Nike's glory days. The voices included those of Bill Bowerman and the late lamented Steve Prefontaine, the young Oregon running hero who, just twenty-five, had died in a heartbreaking car wreck in Eugene, becoming in the aftermath the bereaved running world's, and Nike's, tragic James Dean. The commercial's concluding voice-over was a deep, God-like pronouncement from heaven. The tone was elegiac, almost dirgelike.

"It all began here," the voice intoned. "The Fitness Revolution that changed America."

Impressive? Yes. But these many years later, I ask you one key question: What was wrong with this picture?

What was wrong with it was not immediately apparent to us sweating inside that editing room. Even I, the new recruit, had a hard time being critical of the spot, since it was so authentic and so deeply relevant to Nike. On the other hand—and this realization was not all that long in coming—"Hayward Field" was probably the best example of corporate navel-gazing ever produced. It was, in other words, intensely meaningful to Nike, but irrelevant to practically everyone else. No one outside of Eugene, Oregon, and a small, tightly knit club of running geeks gave a damn about the origin of jogging in the United States. The ad was inward and backward-looking at precisely the time that Nike needed to be forward and outward-looking. In strategy, it bore no resemblance whatsoever to "Revolution." If anything, it sent precisely the opposite message.

"Hayward Field" was a mess and a mistake, but with two weeks to go until the sales meeting, it was all we had. During the week I spent with Wieden and Kennedy in the editing room in Los Angeles, we shut our eyes to the conceptual problems and chose to pray that something miraculous would occur in the editing process. Which it occasionally, albeit rarely, does.

In my capacity as the new director of corporate advertising, I was saddled with the dubious honor of presenting the spot on opening night in Palm Springs as the next big advertising idea to follow "Revolution." After the spot ran, the thousand-plus sales reps did not exactly stand up and cheer in the aisles. Instead, the emotional response could be characterized as somewhere between tepid and respectful, between a long suppressed yawn and a moment of reverent, mournful silence.

Thirty minutes after the ad resoundingly failed to bring down the house,

Phil Knight, Tom Clarke—then Nike's head of product management, soon to be head of marketing, and eventually president—and I stood facing each other backstage, in a huddle, in a state of mild shock. All of us were silently wondering whether there was any way of salvaging something of value from this fiasco. Then, as was his right, Phil Knight spoke first.

"I think we can do better," Knight diplomatically began. Which meant, in plain English, that the commercial was dead. While we all quickly agreed that we had to strike out in a new direction—and fast—the unspoken question was, did we have the time? The sales reps would be leaving Palm Springs in a few days, armed with product samples for the biggest sales period of the year, the back-to-school season. Because we had set the bar so high with "Revolution," the absence of a follow-up campaign was particularly conspicuous and would, we feared, reveal our weakness to the trade.

T.C.—our nickname for Tom Clarke—was, understandably, angry at the agency. But personally, I couldn't blame them. On the basis of my limited experience with Dan Wieden, David Kennedy, and the rest of the agency, I viewed the root of the problem as lying elsewhere, closer to home. I faulted not the ad agency but the direction—or rather the chronic lack of it—they had been given by Nike. The turnover in Nike's marketing leadership in the preceding months had created a blind spot in the creative process. No one had been driving the bus when "Hayward Field" went into production.

"How should we proceed?" I asked my two superiors, feeling the pressure build among the three of us—and creeping up the back of my neck.

"That, Mr. Bedbury," Phil Knight dryly replied, "is what we hired *you* to figure out." And then he and T.C. turned and walked away. My honeymoon at Nike had lasted exactly thirteen days.

Defining the Nike Brand's Core Identity

Analyzing your brand's essence when things are going well, when the brand is flying along under its own power, when sales are strong, can present a significant challenge. But the same task is a far greater challenge when none of the above is going your way. Added to the nearly unbearable pressure I felt was the fact that Nike was not just in a race against time, but in a race against itself: we had to come to grips with a number of critical issues regarding the brand's core identity before it could evolve any further.

Basic questions like "What is Nike?" or, rather, "What is the essence

.of the Nike brand?" had become matters of fierce internal tension and debate as the company began to pick itself up off the floor after getting whacked by Reebok. Remember, none of the company's goals, missions, or marketing plans had been written down—doing so would have generated a great deal of derision from the old Nike hands, who regarded such notions as typical corporate poppycock.

Nevertheless, if the fiasco in Palm Springs taught me anything, it was that a lack of clarity on brand positioning was beginning to compromise Nike's ability to grow its brand intelligently. The sports-versus-fitness debate had created two warring camps within the company, whose members could see only the "either" instead of the "and" in the brand equation. Nike was a company defined by individual "silos"—groups within the overall structure devoted to advancing the interests of particular products or categories. As the director of corporate advertising, I was one of only a handful of employees charged with tying all these factions, products, and categories together in some coherent way. It was my job to surf across the silos looking for ways to connect them to some higher organizing principle, to weave a brand fabric that leveraged what each silo possessed toward a larger end.

To some at Nike, the solution to this conundrum was obvious: Nike should remain a tightly focused business, with highly specialized and separate product groups, and produce the world's finest athletic shoes for competitive athletes. Period. End of story.

Yet in this sort of rigid thinking lay, I believed, the crux of Nike's problems. To a key constituency within the company, Nike's story was to all intents and purposes over: growth would be predicated only on a rise in the number of serious athletes who chose to purchase Nike products. But I detected at least two problems with this as a growth strategy.

1. Nike was a publicly traded company, which needed to grow in order to build value for its shareholders, and it had already penetrated much of its core market.

2. Consumers were changing. Aging baby boomers were becoming more fitness- rather than sports-driven. A new generation of youth was as interested in skateboards and mountain bikes as they were in playing traditional sports. And as women participated in greater numbers of sports activities, they had become big spenders in the booming fitness category. In 1986, most women viewed Nike's product line the way they viewed jockstraps: as irrelevant.

To a rival faction of equally committed swooshers, this narrow way of defining the Nike brand by what it *had been,* presumably in its glory days, was a concept worth updating—and fast. To them—and I enthusiastically counted myself a spokesperson for this faction—Nike packed the potential to become the greatest "sports and fitness" company in the world. For us, the Nike "swoosh" should and could signify excellence and authenticity, whether emblazoned on a sweatshirt or a hat or a bag, or even a shoe that was designed specifically for something as unglamorous as fitness walking.

From my own biased point of view, the solution to bridging this great divide could already be seen inside "Revolution" like threads within a piece of fabric. Since first taking in the commercial in March 1987 as a mere "civilian" in my Seattle home six months before joining Nike, I had come to regard it as my talisman. Taken in its entirety, it provided Nike, even six months after its first airing, with an important strategic insight for growth, as well as a blueprint for immediate action. The message to me was simple:

> *Whether you were young or old, a professional athlete or a rank amateur, a daily runner or a weekend warrior, a tennis player or a walker, or even if you were just a kid, there was a place in the Nike universe for you.*

Once we established a consensus at the company around that core message, we would be if not exactly home free, at least more than halfway toward solving our problems. But as a realist, I was also keenly aware that even if we could successfully bridge the divide between the "exclusionists" and the "inclusionists," another divide still remained to be bridged. And that, unless resolved amicably, might present an even higher barrier to a redefinition of Nike's core values.

The chasm that concerned me nearly as much as the sports-versus-fitness debate was one that afflicts most companies. I refer to the almost spiritual division between those inclined to define a brand as a collection of *products* and those inclined to define a brand as a communicator of *core values*. I found myself pondering the difference between the ideas of Pavlov and Maslow. As mentioned earlier, Pavlovian psychology, and behavioral psychology in general, is primarily concerned with the issues involved in meeting the most basic human needs—food, clothing, shelter. Maslow's hierarchy of human needs, on the other hand, is concerned with a broader spectrum of needs: survival and physical needs at the base, with more emotional needs toward the top.

To me, "Revolution," unlike "Hayward Field," accomplished the hard-to-attain goal of appealing to both sides of this schism. It captured a more diverse set of emotions than anything Nike had ever done before. But it also helped to move an exciting new product out of the stores at an incredible pace. Unfortunately, the management team at Nike, in collaboration with Dan Wieden and David Kennedy, had shot straight past "Revolution" and moved on—without fully recognizing the brilliance of what they had accomplished. The real achievement of "Revolution" was to provide Nike and its agency with permission to play on a much larger field. They just hadn't quite realized that yet.

Widening the Access Point at Nike

The morning after we killed "Hayward Field," I met with Phil Knight to inform him that I had already met with the agency to advise them that I would be presenting them with a new creative brief just as soon as I was able to write it. I further informed Phil—although I couched this demand as a request—that we needed to double the agency's retainer fee immediately.

This was a bit brash, considering that at this very moment many within Nike were openly expressing a desire to fire the ad agency for poor service—a direct result of its being understaffed and underpaid—and now for the debacle of "Hayward Field." I was asking the boss to place even more confidence in them, and I was not inclined to go into a long explanation of why. To his credit, after some predictable grumbling—Knight had started out life as a CPA and for all his vision had never quite shaken the cost-cutting impulses of an accountant—he agreed to the fee increase. I suspected that in so doing he was testing his confidence in me as much as in Wieden & Kennedy. He was giving me adequate rope to hang myself with. I phoned Wieden with the news before leaving Palm Springs that evening to hop a red-eye out of L.A. to Philadelphia, to shoot a new commercial for Nike starring Charles Barkley. My plan was to write the brief on the plane.

At a few minutes before midnight, somewhere over the Rockies, I began to jot down my roiling thoughts. In the hours since we had killed the "Hayward Field" campaign, one thing stood out in my mind: we had been far too narrow in our approach and had become elitist. We were looking inward and we were looking backward. We needed to look broadly forward. We needed to plant one foot in the past and plant one firmly into a future that had as much to do with fitness as it did with sports, a future that would include women right alongside men, and a future where age was definitely a frame of mind.

"WIDEN THE ACCESS POINT," I wrote in capital letters across the top of the paper. I then sat back to think through precisely what it was I was trying to say. For four years I had been on the agency side of the fence, and I generally hated it when a client provided a creative brief. They were typically far too confining, and devoid of emotion or inspiration. But in a crisis like this, we needed a hard strategy, something to put down on a page and at least study for a moment. I also knew it would be tossed aside once the meeting was over. Nike had gone long enough without such a concrete direction. Two hours later, I felt I had the brief nailed.

> Nike is about to become a significant network television advertiser. We will spend nearly three times what we spent on "Revolution" in the fall of 1988. [Despite the high visibility of "Revolution," Nike had spent less than $5 million on TV that year.] This is a turning point for a company that not long ago spoke to its customers at track meets from the tailgate of a station wagon. This just cannot be a narrow look back at where we have been.
>
> We should be proud of our heritage, but we must also recognize that the appeal of "Hayward Field" is narrow and potentially alienating to those who are not great athletes. We need to grow this brand beyond its purist core. . . . We have to stop talking just to ourselves. *It's time to widen the access point.* We need to capture a more complete spectrum of the rewards for sports and fitness. We achieved this with "Revolution." Now we need to take the next step.

"Just Blank It"

The reconceived advertising proposal that Wieden & Kennedy presented to us two weeks later, based on that brief, was initially delivered by Dan Wieden himself. Tom Clarke and I were his audience on the Nike side of the table. Wieden spoke eloquently to the fact that consumers already knew as much as they wanted to know about fitness. And that most if not all of them were ridden by guilt about their failure to live up to their potential. Pleading the case of the ordinary as opposed to extraordinary athlete, Wieden said: So let's not rub their noses in it—at least not all the way.

"So we have this idea," deadpanned Jim Riswold, W & K's thirty-year-old rising-star copywriter, as he flipped open a piece of foam-core board to reveal the proposed new Nike slogan. There were only three words to it: "Just Fuck It." Needless to say, the room fell uncomfortably silent save for a few giggles from an agency staffer who had seen the line before.

"Now, of course," Riswold continued, still deadpan, without missing a beat, "since we can't say that, we'll just have to go with this." He then let the first piece of foam board fall forward to the table, revealing a second board, with a single change in the wording: "Just Do It."

Once again the room fell silent. It wasn't as if, taken at face value, "Just Do It" provided a compelling statement that had us jumping up and cheering spontaneously. But then Dan Wieden adroitly picked up the ball like an excited twelve-year-old with a new video game—it was like watching a tag-team match. "Okay, all by itself," he began, "'Just Do It' doesn't mean much, right? But watch how this works with what these guys have come up with." The creative team proceeded to present more than a dozen versions of the "Just Do It" theme, ranging from basketball to running to cross-training to walking to a spot aimed at kids. We began to see, as we moved through these iterations, that the dynamic spectrum of the work was compelling. While each spot was intriguing as a stand-alone, it was in combination and juxtaposition that the entire campaign transmitted a higher, more noble purpose. If one had to put the matter succinctly, it was that "Just Do It" was not about sneakers. It was about values. It was not about products; it was about a brand ethos.

Rather than giving Nike all the credit for the emotional rewards that sports and fitness can provide—which was the message of "Hayward Field"—the new advertising let the athletes speak for themselves. Just as compelling, some of those athletes were professionals while others were aging weekend warriors. One spot was even taken from the view of a dog on a leash, out for a very long walk on a hot day. It wasn't until a few months later, in the same editing studio where "Hayward Field" had floundered, that the magic of "Just Do It" became most apparent. Each commercial invoked a slightly different emotional response within an amazingly broad, uplifting platform that moved the brand boundaries outward on every corner. But it did not forsake its heart and soul in the process. If anything, it strengthened it by including the way jogging strengthens the human heart.

The first "Just Do It" spot aired on August 7, 1988, and featured a triathlete by the name of Joanne Ernst—an attractive, obviously highly fit woman. It would prove to be the most controversial spot in the mix—a great way to begin a new campaign.

VIDEO	AUDIO
Joanne on a weight bench.	"So, you want to get in shape and you can't decide between . . ."
Quick shot of Joanne running.	"running . . ."
Quick shot of Joanne lifting weights.	"weights . . ."
Quick shot of Joanne doing aerobics.	"volleyball . . ."
Quick shot of Joanne riding a bike.	"cycling . . ."
Quick shot of Joanne back on the bench.	"So don't . . . Just do it."
Montage of activity shots.	"Weights, cycling."
Tight shot of Joanne's face.	"Just do it!"
More montage footage.	"Just do it!"
Joanne's face in tight close-up.	"Just do it!"
The Nike "swoosh," with the "Just Do It" title under.	Silence
Joanne's face, in close-up.	"And it wouldn't hurt to stop eating like a pig, either."

Another spot, which also broke that same evening, was of a famous San Francisco–based eighty-year-old runner named Walt Stack, who was the oldest person—by about fifty years—ever to appear in a Nike ad. In the commercial Stack runs slowly (but without pausing for breath), shirtless, gray chest hairs to the wind, across the Golden Gate Bridge, waving at passing motorists who recognize the Bay Area legend.

"I run seventeen miles every day," Stack says as a title card appears with his name and age. "People ask me how I keep my teeth from chattering in the wintertime. . . . I leave 'em in my locker."

Within a couple of months of the first airing, three brutally simple words, "Just do it," were on everyone's lips. The campaign had become a part of the contemporary cultural vernacular—what every advertiser hopes for yet rarely achieves. A decade would elapse before Nike would ease off on the campaign, and even that would be only a brief derailment. A year later the company reconnected to the seemingly indispensable positioning line.

The deep secret to the longevity of "Just Do It" lay in the fact that its message possessed as much relevance for twenty-year-old triathletes as for fifty-year-old mall walkers. Tone and manner may change, but the message remained the same. The unique brand positioning of "JDI" simultaneously helped us widen and unify a brand that could easily have become fragmented under the stress of rapidly expanding product, category, and demographic lines. Not to mention the forces of global expansion and the brand stewardship problems created by the constant infusion of new people into the growing company.

It was intriguing that the more we pushed the dynamic range of the "JDI" commercials, the stronger the brand positioning became. "JDI" was not uniquely male or female, not just sports- or fitness-oriented, neither purist nor recreational. It embraced all categories. Most important to me, it codified an ethos that had always existed within the Nike brand, that was part of its genetic structure long before Dan Wieden identified it. We just couldn't see it until our backs were up against the wall and had to dig deeply into what made the brand tick.

The overwhelming success of that campaign further led me to a more general conclusion, one that I have helped to apply to other brands that have lost their way in the maze in the fifteen-odd years since the first "JDI" spot ran.

> *Cracking your brand's genetic code is not strictly about product, about the past, or even about things—it is about tapping in to an essence and an ethos that defines who you are to the folks who matter: your core customers, your potential customers, and your employees.*

The Problem with Most Brand Research

In most companies large and small, management attempts to determine the strengths and weaknesses of its products, services, and sometimes its brand image by commissioning some form of market research. The impulse behind this decision is more often than not a positive one: to reach outside the company as a means of gathering useful information about how the world and the public view it. But the problem with most traditional market-research approaches, which are typically based on such tried-and-true methodologies as phone polling, sending researchers with clipboards to question random consumers in shopping malls, and focus-group-testing products—is that they often lead brands down an uninspiring garden path.

The greatest problem with relying on traditional methodologies used by most outside market-research firms, I've found, is that they provide management with reams of statistical data, which may tempt those lacking in confidence to go against their common sense and gut intuition. That, to put it mildly, was not the Nike way. In fact, prior to my first interview with Phil Knight, I had been specifically advised to avoid mentioning the words "marketing" or "research" in speaking to him. Apparently he regarded both words as symbolic of what was wrong with most business.

Nevertheless, I was still taken aback to find as the "JDI" campaign got under way that no market research existed regarding either Nike or its products—none at all. Nike did, however, extensively test its product performance in its Beaverton lab and with the world's premier athletes.

Nike's Brand Strength Monitor

Instead of a market-research department, we had a person. His name was Jerome Conlon, and he occupied the office next to mine at Nimbus A. When I first stumbled into him in the hallway, he somewhat sheepishly introduced himself as the "product management information officer." When I asked him what that meant, he explained, "In any other company, what I do would be called consumer research. But we're very cautious about research around here. It's not part of our language or our culture. We don't want to ignore or diffuse our own instincts."

Even for a new hire like me, the logic of this approach was irrefutable. For sixteen years, Nike had successfully steered clear of traditional consumer research and had performed well, so long as it stuck to its core product areas and was content to be a sub-billion-dollar company. No one knew hard-core athletes better than Nike; they ran the company. But we once again faced a dilemma that threatened some of the time-honored traditions of this relatively young organization. Despite the realization that the terrain of the market was shifting in ways that were not always easy to track, not everyone in Beaverton was prepared to conclude that Nike needed to broaden its knowledge base. To me, it was clear that we would have to get to know—intimately—a different group of consumers if Nike was ever going to reclaim its number 1 position in North America from Reebok, much less overtake Adidas as the premier athletic footwear and apparel company in the world. We would have to understand that fitness and sports, though related, were distinct concepts with quite different drivers behind them. Nike, despite its embedded wisdom, did not own a single piece of paper that suggested that it knew the first thing about how to broaden its base of customers to include aerobics enthusiasts or women who liked to walk during their lunch break. There were several women in the marketing group who intuitively knew the way forward, but it would be another year before their voices would be heard.

Conlon had had no formal research or marketing experience prior to joining Nike, but that made him even more up for the challenge that I presented to him. We would have to conduct some sort of market research, and generate some hard data, but we would have to conceive the project in a "Nike way." In the years that followed, Conlon proved an invaluable guide as the company faced a series of critical marketing paradigm shifts that initially appeared to threaten its core. Looking back, there is no way Nike could have accomplished what it did in the late 1980s and early '90s if it had followed the brand-management and market-research textbook of a packaged-goods company like Procter & Gamble or Pepsi. On the other hand, I don't believe that it could have accomplished what it did without some sort of structured and useful knowledge of the market world that Nike people had come to refer to as "beyond the berm," the berm being a high wall of earth along the perimeter of the new corporate headquarters around which Nike employees often jogged.

Hence, our invention: the BSM (Brand Strength Monitor). One critical way in which our Brand Strength Monitor deliberately departed from the mold of traditional market-research methods was that Conlon and I were more interested in developing a methodology that kept us in touch with perceptions of the Nike "brand." We weren't interested in trying to predict how a particular product might be received at the shopping mall, or how a new advertising campaign might be received in the living rooms of America or at the newsstand. We didn't need, nor did we want, to "pretest" our creative concepts any more than we wanted to "pretest" Nike products. We instinctively recoiled at the notion of running a new print, radio, or TV advertisement by an ostensibly randomly selected group of consumers to find out how they might respond to it. To us, that approach lacked self-confidence and replaced gut instinct and creative intuition with conservative, risk-averse, lowest-common-denominator thinking.

On the other hand, we craved more information about how certain key consumer groups viewed a number of burning *issues*—as opposed to specific advertising *ideas*—that might greatly impact our business. To take just one obvious example, cracking the code with the women's market could not possibly be based on the intuitive insights of our senior management team, given that every member of it shaved his face each morning before breakfast.

So Conlon and I set out to concoct a brand-centric feedback loop that might help us determine how deeply the Nike brand resonated with specific groups of consumers. I had no interest in brand *awareness*. I wanted to know how Nike made people *feel*. It would have to be a broad study, encompassing several thousand interviews, conducted among several consumer groups across multiple markets. To take just one example, we already knew where we stood with most women: in the men's locker room. That was easy enough. What we had to learn in greater depth was exactly where we stood with our core consumer base, teen males, and track those perceptions over time.

Another need was to detect any sign of impending loss of esteem for our brand among our core consumer groups as we reached out to others beyond their narrow range. We had to feel confident about our tentative efforts to reach out to women and older nonathletes without turning off our core customers. We wanted to expand outward from our core without betraying it. The Brand Strength Monitor (BSM) methodology consisted of in-depth interviews conducted in several U.S. cities, to be repeated three times a year during our key selling seasons: back-to-school, holiday, and spring. The four groups we surveyed were:

Teen males (13–18)

Teen females (13–18)

Young men (25–34)

Young women (25–34)

Later, we would add annual interviews with boys nine to ten and eleven to twelve. We knew—and this knowledge was confirmed by our first set of interviews—that we *were* teen males. Nike's core consumer was in the throes of puberty, studying for a driving exam, taping covers of *Sports Illustrated* to his bedroom walls, and buying a lot of Clearasil. That came as no surprise. The big surprise here was the sheer level of unrequited demand for the product. More than 70 percent of teen males surveyed named Nike as the brand they most desired. This was a sure sign of current brand strength, yet also one of potential brand weakness. Was it possible that the brand could have become *too* hot among this core segment? Like metal that is superheated, exceptionally hot brands can crack and crumble quickly in the wake of a few key bad decisions.

I came away from perusing these surveys with an uneasy feeling that we were becoming overly reliant on our core customers for too large a portion of our business. This conclusion only tended to reinforce my growing conviction that if we failed to broaden our range, we ran a risk of losing a substantial slice of our market share if at any time the fickle teen fashion market were to turn suddenly against us.

Perhaps more than anything else, the BSM provided us with an index of *brand resonance*. It was like a Richter scale. When we moved consumers, we could see it in the numbers. Brand desirability, brand values, and brand characteristics were fed back to us in considerable detail, along with those of our competitors. The BSM was viewed as a novelty by some at Nike, but for Conlon and me, it became a veritable radar, a tool that warned when the brand was headed for trouble. In 1993, when we began to detect a slight softening among teen males, we were able to discover that the brand was losing edge and increasingly being viewed as "hype" and lacking substance. When the problem appeared to intensify in the next wave of interviews four months later, Conlon immediately fielded focus groups with alpha teen males that confirmed our suspicions. Again, there was no pretesting of creative concepts, just discussions about what the consumers felt about different brands and why.

As a direct result of these findings, we dialed up the edge meter by signing basketball stars Dennis Rodman and Charles Barkley; Barkley was given the equivalent of an open microphone. "Role Model" was our working title for a commercial inspired by a passage in Barkley's book *Outrageous!*, in which he complains that parents, teachers, and doctors, rather than athletes, should serve as kids' role models. It was produced two months after this latest and somewhat alarming research finding came in.

"Just because I dunk a basketball doesn't mean I should raise your kid," Barkley candidly announced to America in a commercial that created a record volume of calls and letters to Beaverton that were equally split in tone. Conlon left Nike in January 1996, and not long after that Nike abandoned some of the consumer insight instruments that he had developed, and essentially strayed into darkness. In the ensuing two years, its offshore labor controversy grew acute, and the brand made a serious gaffe with the oversupply of heavily branded (swoosh-only) products pushed into every conceivable distribution channel. Nike also misread the growing disconnect between the "average" consumer and the demigods of professional sports, many of whom were beginning to be perceived as spoiled, indulgent, and arrogant—not to mention occasionally immoral and immature. In July 1996, Nike incensed millions with an advertising campaign that broke during the Atlanta Olympic Games and featured images of an athlete vomiting on a track against a backdrop of headlines such as "You Don't Win a Silver, You Lose a Gold." But it's hard to criticize Nike. I respect a company willing to make mistakes. It's just hard to watch them make the same ones twice.

The underlying point of the BSM was not so much the specific methodology it employed as the emphasis it placed on a highly specific form of "consumer insight." Recall the new definition of "brand" offered in the first chapter:

> A brand is the sum of the good, the bad, the ugly, and the off-strategy. It is defined by your best product as well as your worst product. It is defined by award-winning advertising as well as by the god-awful ads that somehow slipped through the cracks, got approved, and, not surprisingly, sank into oblivion. It is defined by the accomplishments of your best employee—the shining star in the company who can do no wrong—as well as by the mishaps of the worst hire that you ever made. It is also defined by your receptionist and the music your customers are subjected to when placed on hold. For every grand and finely worded public statement by the CEO, the brand is also defined by derisory consumer comments overheard in the hallway or in a chat room on the Internet. Brands are sponges for content, for images, for fleeting feelings. They become psychological concepts held in the minds of the public, where they may stay forever. As such you can't entirely control a brand. At best you only guide and influence it.

The BSM represented our best effort at determining our brand's standing among a variety of consumer groups at a given point in time. If your company is small you probably don't need to go to the expense of the formal "brand audit" that the BSM provided. If you're not doing so already, talk with your employees and customers about what your brand means to them. What comes to mind when they think of your brand? What's good? What needs work? You may find that your brand doesn't conjure up much in the way of images, which is not necessarily a good thing. *Unless your brand stands for something, it stands for nothing.* Uncover what resides at the heart of your company. Where is the passion? What makes your company different, better, and more special than the next one? Once you have identified the values that are most essential to your desired brand definition, measure how well you're communicating and delivering on those values. This is your benchmark. Then do whatever you can to grow it, to promote it, and to make it a part of everything you do so that no one can miss it.

Cracking the Starbucks Bean Gene

One of my first executive hires after joining Starbucks as chief marketing officer was to lure Jerome Conlon away from Nike.

Much like Nike just a few years before, Starbucks was sitting on a large commodity that had been devoid of meaningful innovation for quite some time. Starbucks had the opportunity to reinvent a nine-hundred-year-old product category, coffee, but there was little in the way of research or insights to work with. We had no brand definition other than a corporate mission statement. Gut instinct and intuition had served Starbucks well to that point, but it would need something more to grow the brand faster and more broadly than ever before in order to maintain its first-mover advantage. It was Nike, Part 2. Howard Schultz also wanted more than financial success. He wanted to develop Starbucks into a world-class brand of which all employees could be proud. To do that would require some brand intelligence.

"I want you to conduct a Big Dig," I told Conlon, within days of his joining the company.

"A what?"

"A Big Dig. I want you to dig deeply into everything that has been written, felt, said, or thought about coffee."

It was an assignment that someone with as wide-ranging an intellect as Conlon's was bound to enjoy. Jerome conceived the Big Dig in three distinct phases. Phase 1 was an in-depth examination of every piece of readily available research about the entire product universe of coffee, from low-grade-left-on-a-burner-too-long restaurant swill to freeze-dried instant powder in China; from cold canned coffee available from vending machines in Kyoto to cowboy coffee in Wyoming. One of the first facts that we uncovered was that Starbucks represented roughly 1 percent of the total volume of green coffee beans imported to the United States. We also estimated that more than 3 billion cups of coffee were brewed around the world every day. Out of this, I figured that at least 2.7 billion of those cups sucked. In short, we faced a target-rich environment.

Phase 1 provided us with a feel for the language that people used to describe their coffee experiences. But given the emerging nature of the specialty (high-end) category, the language presented some problems. For example, the phrase "gourmet coffee" conveyed as many different meanings to people as there were categories of coffee. For some, "gourmet" meant an expensive can of grocery store coffee. For others, it meant hazelnut Irish crème vanilla instant coffee, which could double as a bad room deodorizer if you left the lid off. For still others, it meant—very specifically—a double-tall-not-too-hot-nonfat-caramel-latte-with-no-foam. At the very least, it was clear that we would have to watch our words. All future probing would be influenced by how we phrased the questions we asked.

So phase 2 involved conducting a series of focus groups with a range of coffee drinkers including but not limited to the core espresso drinker. It was here that we probed the conflicted lexicon of the coffee category to ensure that we would be able to establish a clearer dialogue with coffee drinkers on all levels. We asked our subjects to define their ideal coffee experience. And we tried to break down our data to both physical "need states"—"I need my caffeine fix right now or I'll throw myself in front of the next moving train"—as well as "day parts" and "lifestyle segments." In plain language, a "day part" indicates the time of day in which one consumes a particular product. In the coffee business, it is an inescapable fact of life that the vast majority of coffee is consumed between seven and ten in the morning. Of course, there are the late-night espresso sippers and the students and lawyers swigging to stay awake—and those fortunate few whom caffeine fails to stimulate at all. We further broke the "day parts" down into the before-work morning jolt drunk at home, the cup for the drive, the stop along the way, the midmorning break, the lunch cup, the afternoon cup, the after-dinner cup, and so on. As for "lifestyle segments," we identified coffee drinkers who surfed, coffee drinkers who drove, coffee drinkers who liked art, who liked music, who liked movies, and those who liked coffee ice cream.

In phase 3 we zeroed in on the Starbucks brand. By then we had established a usable context from which to drill into this subject more deeply. We knew the category, we knew the vernacular, we knew the physical need states, and we knew the emotional drivers. Now we needed to map the place where the Starbucks brand intersected with the world around it. Not just where we thought it should be, or should go, but where it now, in reality, stood. As a way of obtaining this information, we extensively interviewed heavy consumers of espresso drinks, both in and out of the Starbucks franchise. We listened closely to their stated perceptions of our brand in comparison to every other competitor. We spent time with the light espresso drinkers, the newcomers to the category, to see where the differences lay.

The news for Starbucks was, on balance, highly favorable. Among those who regarded themselves as "serious" coffee drinkers. Starbucks was perceived as an emerging high-quality brand, held in high esteem by the self-described coffee connoisseurs. But a few red flags also warned us of where danger lay, confirming that we would need to keep firm control of the brand. The biggest and brightest red flag was the very concept on which Starbucks' high growth rate was predicated: a *chain* of *coffeehouses*, which was regarded as an oxymoron by many. Here, we now knew for sure, lay the gravest danger to the brand, as well as, potentially, its greatest strength.

Let me explain. Perhaps the most important insight gleaned during our Big Dig was that to most people "coffee" was far more than simply a product to be consumed. A key part of the "coffee experience" for many consumers was the atmosphere and the conditions under which they savored this emotionally charged beverage. For nearly five hundred years the "coffeehouse" had evolved as a tradition in many cultures that served to deepen and even mystify the complex culture of coffee. And so, after conducting hundreds of interviews and poring over the immense breadth of coffee literature, from the psychoanalysts of fin-de-siècle Vienna—many of whom practically lived in coffeehouses—to Jack Kerouac's *On the Road,* we arrived at an inescapable conclusion:

> *The Starbucks brand's core identity was less about engineering a great cup of coffee than about providing a great coffee experience. Of course, it was about providing the highest-quality coffee beans, ground correctly, brewed with the purest water, at the right temperature, and for very specific periods of time. But just as "Brand Nike" was not simply about torsion control or midsole cushioning systems but about the pleasures delivered by sports and fitness, so the Starbucks brand was about what Abraham Maslow might have called the coffee "gestalt"—the atmospherics.*

Armed with these insights, it was far easier for us to focus on product opportunities that were more closely linked to the optimal coffee experience. For example, when proposals came forward from former McDonald's managers to drop the eight-ounce "short" cups and add to the menu a thirty-two-ounce monstrosity, the ensuing debate now had a useful context. When someone proposed replacing the standard white paper cups with polystyrene ones, the kind you find at burger joints and convenience stores, we pushed back. Starbucks was not just about driving unit costs down, but about elevating the experience around drinking a cup of coffee. The very vessel from which it was drunk mattered a great deal. Even the rolled paper lip and the bright white plastic lid with the little hole in it mattered a great deal. These were not to be messed with.

Perhaps even more critically, cracking Starbucks' brand code provided us with a rationale for forgoing opportunities, appealing as they might have been, that were not closely linked to our evolving conception of the brand. The idea of branding a high-end coffee liqueur seemed intriguing. We felt we could make some serious inroads against Kahlúa, should we choose to do so. But we elected to put the spirits channel on hold, because it seemed like too extreme a brand stretch. Not that it was a particularly bad idea; some of the test products we created were outstanding. The concept merely struck us as premature for a brand that was still undefined in most of America.

Near the end of our research project, Starbucks' CEO, Howard Schultz, stopped by my office to pass along a comment made to him by a barista, the person behind the espresso machine, that morning.

"One of our store partners made an amazing discovery this week," Schultz began. "He said that we are not, as he once thought, in the coffee business serving people. He said we are in the people business serving coffee." Howard beamed with pride. At every level of the company, Starbucks employees understood the complexity—and ultimate power—of the brand positioning.

Starbucks was well on its way to transcending the cup, to going far beyond the physical domain of the product. But it could not have gotten there if the Starbucks hourly employees had not known the value of delivering something more rewarding than just a cup of coffee.

Brand Mantras

My *Webster's* dictionary defines "mantra" as a Hindu term, derived from the Vedic texts, describing a hymn or portion of those texts "intoned as an incantation or prayer." The best known mantra is probably "om," a sound that Hindu practitioners believe can expand internally to encompass the universe. My friend Kevin Keller of the Amos Tuck School of Business at Dartmouth has defined brand mantras as "capturing the irrefutable essence or spirit of brand positioning. Their purpose is to ensure that all employees within the organization as well as external marketing partners understand what the brand most fundamentally is to represent to consumers, so that they can adjust their actions accordingly."

Brand mantras are not slogans, but touchstones that help shape what kinds of products and services companies create, how they conduct their business, and even how decisions are made as to what kind of people they hire. For many companies, brand mantras have provided a useful mechanism for succinctly expressing a brand's "genetic code" using a form of shorthand. Though they have since become commonplace at many forward-thinking companies, I believe that we originally coined the term "brand mantra" at Nike, to characterize a three-word encapsulation of the brand's core values. This came at a time in the company's evolution when we finally realized that it made sense to express those values in the simplest possible terms, instead of blithely assuming that employees either "got" the brand or didn't. The savvier we became about the internal dynamics of brand building, the more we came to consider crafting a "brand mantra" a critical step in cracking a brand's genetic code. We never stooped to printing the three key words on wallet-sized cards, much less to tattooing them on our skins, as some of us did the swoosh. But these values were indelibly etched into the mind of every employee deep enough so that it rarely needed to be explicitly invoked, even at times of brand crisis.

The Nike Mantra

In a mysterious process that no one ever seemed to grasp exactly—which was not a problem, since grasping things with anal precision was never a core value at Nike—our mantra had become "Authentic Athletic Performance." The fact that these three words ultimately inspired a thousand employees was an amazing phenomenon, because not only was the sacred text never written down, it was rarely even explicitly articulated or overtly referred to. And this too reflected a core internal value, because at Nike, the brand was supposed to be *felt*, not scripted. Everything had to be absorbed at a visceral level, not talked about, conceptualized, or abstracted. And *never* framed on a wall.

Nike's brand mantra put a particular emphasis on maintaining *authenticity,* by which we also meant integrity and purity, front and center. All images of and associations with our products had to be real, not contrived. Some mistakes are painfully obvious at a glance. I once pulled a golf catalog out of distribution when I discovered that the models wearing the Nike gear had obviously never held a driver in their hands, much less a putter. Golfers hold their clubs a certain way; nongolfers hold them like fireplace tongs or baseball bats. Nike Design had recruited a handful of exquisite-looking male models for the catalog, rather than real golfers. Even though it was a small thing, it was a very big thing in the way we presented our image to our sales reps and our customers. It became a learning experience for everyone in the advertising and design group. It was also a $35,000 error we would never make again.

All products and activities associated with Nike likewise had to be *athletic,* not leisurely. Thus, our brand mantra helped us to reject a proposal by one team attempting to develop "athleisure" products like "sports-inspired" dress shoes. Even footwear for boating was rife with problems. We moved forward with the aqua sock but dumped the topsider loafer concept. There were heated arguments about whether a walking shoe was actually an athletic product. For years Nike was adamant about excluding this category. Ultimately, the company resolved the controversy by expanding its interpretation of what it meant to be "athletic" and in so doing acknowledged the sweat and commitment of millions of consumers for whom walking is the daily fitness regime.

Finally, every Nike product had to exude world-class *performance* and meet the demands of the world's finest athletes, even though such athletes represented a microscopic piece of Nike's total business. We could not afford to let ourselves be swayed by the billion-dollar opportunity that existed by building cheap $29 sneakers for large discount department stores. Everything had to *perform.*

"Authentic Athletic Performance" was a simple idea, but like so many simple ideas, its execution and implementation could be complex, not to mention challenging, daunting—and even painful, when it came down to forgoing revenue-generating activities because they violated these accepted core values.

The Disney Mantra

For Disney, the brand mantra "Fun Family Entertainment" provided a broad yet highly directional mantra from which to map out growth opportunities, as well as to avoid opportunities that threatened long-term damage to its brand. "A brand," Disney CEO Michael Eisner has written, "is a living entity, and it is enriched or undermined cumulatively over time, the product of a thousand small gestures." Elsewhere in his memoir, *Work in Progress,* Eisner maintains, "Walt [Disney]'s genius had been to make Disney synonymous with the best in family entertainment—whether it was a theme park or a television show, an animated movie or even a Mickey Mouse watch. . . . The name 'Disney' promised a certain kind of experience: wholesome family fun appropriate for kids of any age, a high level of reliability and safety in its products and services, and a predictable set of values."

But by the time Michael Eisner joined Disney, nearly two decades after its founder's death, the brand struck Eisner, as well as many in America, as "awkward, old-fashioned, even a bit directionless." The challenge that Eisner and his new management team faced was to unearth "the underlying qualities that made the company special." As Eisner saw it, his job was not to "create something new but to bring back the magic, to dress Disney up in more stylish clothes and expand its reach, to remind people why they loved the company in the first place." Creating a cable channel or a network radio station centered around twenty-four-hour programming aimed toward children and communicating wholesome family values made perfect sense for Disney, in brand terms. But allowing its movies to be shown on an R-rated channel in Europe—a potentially lucrative growth opportunity deliberately rejected by the company—clearly did not. Forsaking a quick bottom-line hit was, for Michael Eisner, a form of "value investing" aimed at the future. Even in Disney's toughest financial hours, and it saw some in the late nineties, the mantra "Fun Family Entertainment" kept the Disney brand as pure as it could be, while the company looked to its other branded properties to grow the overall corporate bottom line.

The Starbucks Mantra

Thanks in large part to the Big Dig, we were able to distill the Starbucks brand experience into three words: "Rewarding Everyday Moments," which, in the spirit of the mantras crafted for Disney and Nike, would serve as our brand touchstone. We took note that the term "entertainment" for Disney could encompass a wide range of media, including theme parks, movies, radio, and television networks. We further noted that "Authentic Athletic Performance" provided Nike with a reach well beyond shoes and apparel, while not forsaking cohesion. In seeking to craft a simple statement that would be as broad yet defining for Starbucks, we made sure that the Starbucks mantra didn't even mention coffee. Because whether it be selling tea, Frappuccino, books, or newspapers, or just providing a comfortable, well-lit place to relax, providing "Rewarding Everyday Moments" encompasses all of these experiences within the Starbucks brand structure.

Cracking a Vintage Brand Code

One of the hardest tasks a company faces, as Michael Eisner and his team discovered, is to crack the code of an older, entrenched brand that has been subjected to decades of gene splicing by various executives.

Chrysler

Such was the case with Chrysler in the mid-eighties. It was during that low point for Chrysler, not long after Lee Iacocca engineered the company's infamous government bailout, that former Chrysler vice-chairman Bob "Guts" Lutz vowed to produce a new line of cars worthy of the proud Chrysler name.

More than anything else, Lutz yearned to create noticeable cars that would "stand out in today's supersaturated auto market," as he later put it in *Guts: The Seven Laws of Business That Made Chrysler the World's Hottest Car Company*. He urged his design team to immerse themselves in the once-great Chrysler brand's storied history. The problem with the American auto industry during this dismal period, Lutz later recalled, was that "nowhere in America was there a 14-year-old boy with tears in his eyes saying, 'Please Dad, let's buy a Lumina.'"

The eighties in general will be remembered by consumers and manufacturers alike as a peak of mass marketing amid a dearth of creative concepts. An absence of soul prevailed not only in the realm of marketing but also in manufacturing, where once the spirit of innovation had proudly flourished in America. In no place was this lack of soul more evident than in the depressed United States auto industry, which was reeling from the impact of classy new European imports, designed with a sense of flair and style, soul and character. From a design standpoint, the eighties were an unmitigated disaster for the U.S. automobile industry. Legendary cars like the Corvette and Thunderbird became fat and cheap. Car components like engines, transmissions, and even the chassis on which they all rested were commoditized and swapped out across different divisions.

In this environment, individuality became a much-noted fatality in the race to win market share—a race that Chrysler won on several mission-critical fronts. But the lack of soul was evident in the relatively cheap, undifferentiated steam of K-cars and minivans that streamed out of the automaker's factories. Lee Iacocca did whatever was needed to stay alive, and no one knew this better than Bob Lutz. But the observation wasn't his alone. Automotive critics began to deride Chrysler for being content with building affordable boxes on wheels for suburban families.

Lutz wasn't sure exactly which way to head, but he felt intuitively that he needed to reconnect the designers with Chrysler's original brand underpinnings, which had lain dormant for too long. By delving into the brand's past, Lutz and his team determined that Chrysler had always been—and would always be, if they had anything to do with it—"an engineering company" at its core. This was the original vision for the brand conceived by the company's founder, Walter P. Chrysler.

The award-winning results of Lutz's maiden efforts were the industry's first computer-aided "cab-forward" designs, a design reconfiguration that increased the interior space of the car while maintaining the same overall size and weight. To say the least, this was a giant step up from the dreary if practical K-car. Lutz's mandate had been to build cars that "ooze passion"; Lutz recalls, "The kind of products we started building at Chrysler were the kinds of cars we wanted to drive."

In addition to injecting creativity into Chrysler projects, this direction also justified an acquisition of the Jeep brand from American Motors. In contemplating Jeep, Lutz saw a brand with a tremendous set of enduring core values. While tucked within American Motors, Jeep had somehow succeeded in steering clear of the nerdy aura of AMC's Gremlin, Pacer, and Ambassador. By minimizing changes to the basic Jeep product, AMC had retained the vehicle's vintage connection to its military roots. No other brand invoked patriotism quite the way Jeep did. The genetic code for the Jeep brand was clear. It was rugged, timeless, and American. But the codes for Chrysler and Dodge were still not so crisply defined, so Lutz kept pushing.

Then, along came the Viper.

No single product—certainly no recent *American* product—has struck a more visceral chord in American drivers than the sizzling-hot Dodge Viper. The inspiration for the Viper, which hyped-up auto enthusiasts have dubbed "a masterpiece of yester-tech," was the Shelby Cobra, a legendary performance car developed by an automotive genius by the name of Carroll Shelby, who just happened to have a consulting agreement with Chrysler. The Viper—the "Cobra" echo was deliberate—came packed with what Lutz freely concedes were blatantly "Cobra-inspired visual cues." The stealth project was advanced under the radar of Chrysler's notoriously risk-averse bean counters by a skunk-works team Lutz dubbed "the snake pit," dedicated to the "right-brained"—i.e., creative—values that Lutz extolled. Lutz had a deep-seated aversion to market research as conventionally conducted, and throughout his career became increasingly convinced that his own gut intuition was his best navigation tool.

When Chrysler first displayed a prototype Viper as a "concept car" at the 1989 Detroit Auto Show, it caused such a sensation that the company overruled its own cautious middle managers and decided to build it for the 1993 model year. "Hard-core car people like the Viper because it looks, feels and sounds like a race car that has gone through a time warp," the *Wall Street Journal* recently observed. In fact, when a *WSJ* reporter recently took one for a spin, "passers-by yelled, whistled and gestured [while] a United Parcel Service driver offered his delivery truck in trade."

Following its original unveiling at the '89 automobile show, a crowd of Japanese engineers and auto executives gathered around Lutz and his team. They eyed the brave new beast with ill-disguised awe, not to mention a dose of envy. "You must have spent millions in market research to come up with that design," one of them remarked to Lutz, who feistily replied, "We didn't do any research at all—we just did it!" I do believe that he was, consciously or not, quoting Nike.

Getting to the Apple Core

When Steve Jobs returned to Apple with the task of restoring Apple to its former perch as the most innovative company in the computer industry, Apple mounted an effort strikingly similar to Chrysler's—to refresh the brand while restoring its core identity. The goal became to connect the present and future of a troubled brand to the vanished glories of the storied past, although in this case that past was not quite so distant as it had been for Chrysler.

In a desperate bid to recover an edge sadly dulled by poor development and product strategy combined with reckless management decisions, Jobs and his cohorts dared to imagine what the Macintosh would be like if reborn for a new generation. They delivered a stunning piece of eye candy: the iMac was a groove machine aching with attitude, which instantly bespoke what Apple had once been as a brand: cool, creative simplicity with an irreverent tone that openly challenged the complacent dullness of the status quo.

After more than a decade, Apple at long last regained its swing and its reputation for "daring to be different," as its ads proclaimed. It restored its wilting market share, and in 1998 announced to the world that it was not prepared to lie down and roll over in the face of the Wintel juggernaut. The new line of candy-colored iMacs in no way slavishly imitated the classic original except in the sense that they paid homage to the old Mac's simplicity of style and ease of function. In their time, the original Macs had been suave designs that were more intimate than the boring beige behemoths turned out by IBM and its cloning competitors. The new iMacs, like the old, poked intelligent fun at what has long been a staid, uptight category dominated by bulk providers for large corporations.

Even the advertising campaign that supported the new Macs was "future retro," consciously harking back to the seminal Apple work for the 1984 Super Bowl by the agency Chiat/Day. In that now-famous spot, the Macintosh was juxtaposed against the IBM PC as the machine of a new generation of rugged individualists determined not to be swamped by Big Blue and its hordes of faceless, soulless minions. Fifteen years later, Jobs, Apple's dollar-a-year CEO, revived his own reputation and that of his brand by bravely reinfusing the brand with its essence. Rehiring Chiat/Day gave Jobs a chance to strategize again with its chairman and chief creative officer, Lee Clow, who knew the Apple brand's genetic code better than anyone else.

As stated earlier, it is one thing to crack your code. It is quite another to bring it to life with products and communication that stop people in their tracks. Apple and Chiat/Day achieved this with their daring "Think Different" campaign, which brought together images of people who dared to "think different" as various as Albert Einstein, Arthur Miller, and the Dalai Lama.

Beetle Gene Therapy

That very same year of 1998, a similar scenario of revival and renewal was played out in a master marketing stroke by Volkswagen, with equally brand-positive results. VW had been stumbling through roughly the same type of hiatus as Apple with its prolonged slump, with a touch of Chrysler's doldrums: the post-Beetle VW's had come to be perceived as boring, not-very-stylish "economy cars." By the late nineties, the VW brand not only lacked sizzle, it lacked the whimsy of earlier years. Thus, it was quite a coup of image reengineering—as well as of actual engineering—to brilliantly reenergize the brand across all the bases at the end of the century with the felicitous reintroduction and reinvention of the company's most enduring and beloved product, the Beetle.

The New Beetle was designed by the young industry wunderkind J. Mays, a child of Oklahoma by way of Germany, where he headed design for VW and Audi (he has since moved on to Ford). Today, according to *The New Yorker*'s design critic, Paul Goldberger, Mays is the industry's "pre-eminent representative of the current trend toward nostalgic automobile design, which breaks with the practice of the previous generation of car designers, who prided themselves on looking forward, not backward." J. Mays's New Beetle was the world's first truly "postmodern" car, in that it made ironic reference to its original without descending to the dubious decision of slavish reproduction, which would have been a shameless and ultimately worthless exercise in nostalgia marketing. Beneath the familiar shape was a ground-up redesign of virtually every aspect of the original. Among other achievements, the new Bug was rated as one of the safest new vehicles, according to several insurance industry and government reports.

Like Apple's campaign, advertising support for the New Beetle launch (by Arnold Communications, part of Snyder Communications) was deliberately reminiscent of the company's grand old whimsical Doyle Dane Bernbach print ads, which supported the initial product launch in the sixties in a similar atmosphere of refined levity. In the original campaign, VW poked fun at itself with the headline "Nobody's Perfect" beneath an early Bug on a gas station hoist, obviously in for another valve job. Nearly forty years later, a new Bug is shown at a standstill with the headline "0–60: Yes," an honest acknowledgment that the new car was no racing machine. After nearly two decades of drift, Volkswagen rediscovered its core brand values as well as it own voice. In doing so, VW rekindled its relationship with its original core users and also established a new, younger brand franchise.

The Value of Brand Alignment Inside the Company

In the end, all of this emphasis on cracking your brand's genetic code comes down to one clear message:

> *Though it is important to demonstrate consistently to the outside world that you know what your brand is about, ultimately it is even more important first to demonstrate this internally and to continue to do so at every opportunity.*

Mark Twain once sagely observed that one of the best things about telling the truth is that you never have to think about what to say. This enduring statement retains great relevance for any contemporary company, whether it consists of a single free agent or is a global hairball with 200,000 employees.

Grasping core brand truths emotionally as well as intellectually enables employees to understand the value as well as the potential risk of a proposed innovation. An organization that has a low brand IQ across the rank and file is often lethargic and process-driven to the point of vapor lock. Innovators become dispirited after exerting themselves to the limit, only to discover that they were innovating in the wrong area altogether, or that their work undermined the essence of the brand. Old Brand World command-and-control organizational structures that leave all decision making to a select few will not compete well against companies that undertake growth initiatives along strategically defined brand values, which are broadly shared by employees who have internalized them. When all levels of a company grasp the core truth of a brand, there is less friction, dilution, and delay between idea and action. Inspiration replaces frustration and the creative process is unleashed intelligently.

Finally, remember that profit should never be core brand value. Being profitable should be every company's goal, or part of its corporate mission, but as a core value it can be misleading and destructive. Companies can easily become profitable at the expense of their own long-term viability.

One of the best ways to discern between a brand value and a corporate value is to ask yourself this question: Is the brand value in question meaningful to your customer? Will it affect the way they feel about you? Will it make them desire you more than the next company? The last time I checked most customers have mixed feelings about the brands they patronize creating profits at their expense. At Starbucks we had an ongoing program whereby departments competed with each other to decrease costs in some way. Each month the department that had done the best job was provided Starbucks T-shirts with "Starbucks Profit Improvement Program" emblazoned on them. To me, I thought it was odd that anyone would wear such a shirt in public.

Profitability should be a business imperative, an operational philosophy, or a measure of success, but as a core brand value I believe it is fool's gold.

–3–

building brandwidth

Brand Principle #3
(the Spandex Rule of Branding)
Just because you can doesn't mean you should.

"We've really got to do this right."

Starbucks CEO Howard Schultz and I stared fretfully out his office window, which commanded a sweeping view of the cloud-socked Seattle skyline. On any other day the two of us would be rapidly bouncing ideas off each other, discussing marketing strategies, or thinking up some new way to take Starbucks to a higher level. Today was different.

"If we screw this thing up," Schultz said, concern evident in his voice, "our mistake will be visible to millions of people." By which he meant not just our loyal customers but tens of millions of potential customers. "And think of the partners"—the eight thousand Starbucks employees— "who have worked hard to establish our quality standards. What do we tell them if we fail?"

The issue Schultz was so anxiously referring to was a pending agreement with United Airlines, a deal Starbucks had agreed to in principle before I joined the business, but that had not yet been fully signed on to by the top brass at either company. Schultz wanted my judgment in making the final decision. He knew that the deal would pose significant brand implications for what was then a relatively unknown and far from "underground" Seattle coffee company about to go global with a single document. Interestingly enough, the impetus driving this unusual partnership had come from United, which desperately wanted to improve its in-flight coffee service. In their initial proposal, they had candidly disclosed that their frequent fliers were becoming increasingly dissatisfied with the quality of the brew on board. A number of customers had gone so far as to target the on-board coffee as the thing they "most disliked" about flying the friendly skies. More than a few had even paid us the compliment of politely blaming Starbucks for elevating their palates, thus rendering the airline swill unbearable.

Unfortunately for us, we had not yet embarked upon our Big Dig. We were still months away from possessing any meaningful data that would illuminate our brand's standing across a number of markets, product categories, and consumer segments. Data of this sort would have been helpful for evaluating the pending deal. We lacked the essential data points that would have provided us with basic measures of the level of trust in our brands and we knew that attempting to replicate Starbucks coffee quality at 500 mph and 30,000 feet above the nearest espresso machine would sorely test our product.

In 1995 Starbucks was one of the fastest-growing brands in the country, and in some respects its position was analogous to Nike's circa 1987, when Jerome Conlon and I first tried to dig deeply into the Nike brand. Both brands were rooted in the Pacific Northwest, and both were young, explosive potential "category killers"—brands that packed the power to utterly dominate an emerging market. Yet despite those superficial similarities, the two brands were in very different stages of their evolutionary cycles. By the time I left Nike it had become a multibillion-dollar global powerhouse with an enormous reservoir of brand strength. Halfway through the nineties, Starbucks remained a theoretically powerful but still modest concept with less than a 2 percent share of the total U.S. coffee cups consumed. Though early fans of the brand in Los Angeles, San Francisco, Seattle, Vancouver, and Chicago were already carrying our bright white cups with the green logo proudly displayed forward everywhere they went (Starbucks had just entered New York City the year before), the growth potential overshadowed the actual size of the company. Given the comparative fragility of the brand and the fact that we had not fully defined it on our own terms yet, the United Airlines joint venture posed an enormous risk: that the brand would become diluted—or polluted— before it was clearly established. Brands, like people, have but one chance to make a first impression. Ideally, those impressions for Starbucks would occur in its cafés. But the opportunity presented by United—to "sample" Starbucks coffee around the world and lay claim to a specialty coffee category—was worth the risk.

Growth Strategies
Can Be Brand-Friendly

Striking the right balance between the imperatives of growth and the need for ongoing brand preservation and conservation has become the chief challenge of all brand stewards today, from the company CEO on down. Whether companies are start-ups, venerable packaged-goods concerns, or business-to-business services, when growth is pursued for growth's sake, numbers can become tyrants, and they also can become blinding. Retailers, in particular, are inundated with sales figures every day, rendered in a variety of ways that boggle the ordinary mind. It's truly remarkable that any of them manage to look forward, given how often they are forced to look backward. Imagine driving a car at a high speed by looking over your shoulder at where you have been for directional guidance. That image pretty much sums up the paradox that so many companies, particularly in the retail arena, face in confronting brand problems.

For the most part, Starbucks functioned as a retailer. Every day meant new numbers: yesterday's sales measured against those of the same day a year ago, and then the same for the week, the month, the quarter, the year. Then all of it was separated by store, by district, by market, and by region. Starbucks also broke down the data by hour sold and by type of product. Yet these numbers, necessary as they were in the operation of the company, told me nothing about the brand. I wanted to know what effect our meteoric expansion was having on our most loyal customers. I also wanted to know why nonusers were staying away. That was where the Big Dig came in.

It is a mistake to pursue growth for growth's sake. Equally, however, it is wrong to surrender to Ostrich Syndrome, sticking your head in the sand, closing your eyes, and praying to God that change, if it comes, will leave your profits, your customers, and your sacrosanct brand untouched and unsullied. Brand dilution and brand pollution may be two of the deadliest sins of brand stewardship. At Starbucks we faced brand dilution with our expansion; one of the surest ways to make something less special is to make more of it. We faced that in spades. If meeting our store opening targets meant hiring sub-optimal employees, we would dilute the brand at its most defining point. Brand stasis—the result of deep-seated conservatism, risk aversion, or overzealous brand protection—is nothing to be proud of either. Not to do anything to grow and expand your brand's reach can be the worst decision, or nondecision, that you can possibly make, especially if your industry is in the throes of change.

Since the dawn of the twenty-first century, many brands have stubbornly refused to acknowledge massive shifts in the way commerce and marketing take place. Others, meanwhile, have enthusiastically forged forward into new territory. Consider Charles Schwab. Moving heavily into electronic stock trading was more than an enormously smart expansion decision; it forever branded Schwab as a pioneer in the ongoing conquest of cyberspace. Similarly, Larry Ellison of Oracle expended a great deal of personal effort in shifting his company in the mid-nineties to become a Web-centric business. "Web-centric," in fact, became part of the definition of the Oracle brand. An even greater challenge faced Jack Welch at General Electric, due to the sheer volume and size of the company's legacy networks, in making the Internet the sun around which all other planets revolve at that continually forward-thinking and broadly diversified business. All three of these firms have grown at explosive rates without undermining their core, or compromising their brands. The point is that growth can be brand-positive, if it is intelligent growth. And in the brand-building game, as in so much of everything else, God and the devil are in the details.

Whenever a company attempts to broaden its brand—for increased revenues or for profits—it should always be diligent about assessing the impact that additional "brandwidth" will have on its brand strength. This does not mean merely performing some standard numerical calculation. Even after the tangibles have been weighed and the research completed, someone relatively high placed within the organization also needs to look at the plans subjectively and say, "This feels right" or "This just doesn't feel right." When it comes to growth scenarios, you have to respect intuition and common sense as you judge what is appropriate for your brand. If it turns out that you lack intuition about your business or your own brand, you are probably in the wrong line of work.

Close-up:
The Starbucks-United Deal

Back in Brewtopia, the Starbucks-United deal was waiting for my approval. We all recognized that United was an incredible growth opportunity. The proposed venture would gain us worldwide product trial and exposure. We would expose our product and our brand to nearly 100 million United passengers per year, of which roughly half were estimated to drink coffee. But there was a downside: the deal could also pollute the reservoir of goodwill we had built up in the company since Starbucks' founding at Seattle's Pike Place Market in 1971. Part of the Starbucks brand mystique had been the fact that it was not available everywhere. United would put a few miles on the brand in a hurry.

Also under serious consideration at that time was a proposal from Sam's Clubs, an offshoot of Wal-Mart aiming to go up against the BJs and Costcos of the world, to expand sales of our whole-bean coffee through their discount channel. Initially, it had struck our sales people as too good a deal to pass up. The coffee bags had already been printed with Sam's logo; the beans were about to be roasted. Fortunately for us, however, the final commitment to the deal had not yet been consummated, due not to brand concerns but rather to increasing and ominous fluctuations in green-coffee supplies and prices. At the end of the day, that price and supply volatility meant that striking two major high-volume agreements at roughly the same time would create enormous exposure and financial risk.

Both deals promised vast expansions of coffee volume. But the Sam's Club agreement promised only volume, while adding little to the underlying strength of the brand. It would involve significant brand stretch into an unabashedly mass-market platform. Starbucks already had a sub-brand of whole-bean coffee at Costco, related in no small way to the presence of a Costco founder on the Starbucks board of directors. I felt we had enough exposure in that channel already. The UA proposal, by contrast, offered a co-branding arrangement—an association of two independent brands—with one of the finest airlines in the world. We knew that frequent fliers were among Starbucks' best customers. Also comforting was the fact that many flight attendants were loyal customers, since Starbucks had just begun an expansion into major airport terminals. Chicago and San Francisco, two of United's major hubs, happened to be exceptionally strong Starbucks markets. We would go with United, Schultz and I agreed, but only if we could be guaranteed that the brand would not be demolished.

We agreed on the three basic concerns that would have to be addressed before we could strike a deal.

First, we needed to ensure that the product quality would be protected. This was, after all, on one level nothing more than a wholesale agreement. Training our own baristas to deliver consistent quality in a Starbucks-owned café on terra firma was one thing. Asking flight attendants to brew and serve a perfect cup at 30,000 feet while traveling 500 miles an hour through turbulent air was definitely another.

Second, I was especially concerned about United's presentation of the brand, both on board and in its advertising. How would the 70,000 United employee-owners deliver the brand message? Could we retain creative control over our brand in all communications? If not, I had a strong feeling that it would be better to scotch the deal at once.

The third issue was how flight attendants would explain the dark roast and body of a cup of Starbucks. They needed to be able to answer fundamental questions about our coffee that would no doubt arise from the passengers who had never before had anything stronger than Folgers. How many of those customers would lament the loss of the diluted brew they had been drinking for decades in diners, truck stops, and airplanes? At this point most of North America was still drinking coffee made from barely roasted, dirt-cheap low-elevation coffee beans brewed with questionable tap water, filtered through the equivalent of a gym sock, and then left on a burner for hours.

I knew from my own experience that Starbucks coffee, procured from higher-elevation arabica farms and roasted longer, was an acquired taste. It had taken my parents three pots of Starbucks to make the switch. Schultz and I decided that we could hardly make some inevitable but unpredictable degree of product resistance a deal breaker. We had to lead the country away from bad coffee and raise the level of the collective palate. If we didn't, someone else would.

Even after it appeared that United shared our concerns, Schultz was still cautious when I checked in with him one last time before flying to Chicago to begin the negotiations.

"We don't have to do this deal," he said. "Just do what's right for the company. We'll have lots of other opportunities down the road." That would prove to be an understatement.

After two tough meetings in Chicago, both sides hammered out an agreement in the fall of 1995. Starbucks would take its first flight aboard United in January 1996. We received ample quality assurance guarantees and quick exit clauses if we felt at any time that moving forward would mean damaging either brand. Since at that point we could only guess at the potential for loss of brand esteem, we inserted into the contract a clause guaranteeing us the right to randomly conduct surveys on board. We paid particular attention to that subset of passengers who identified themselves as "espresso drinkers" and/or "Starbucks customers" in the hope of understanding the impact on our five-day-a-week latte loyalists. Replacing these customers would be costly, we knew, and we didn't want to lose them in exchange for any amount of brand trial or volume.

A handful of Starbucks executives even secured the right to "flag" brewing machines on board aircraft that were not working properly and take them out of commission, if necessary. As a practical check, in the months that followed the launch, I spent most of my United flights walking around, talking with the flight attendants and passengers, and doing my own research. I'm sure Howard Schultz and every other Starbucks executive who flew United did the same.

On the marketing side of the deal, all systems were also go. We had just set in motion what would in effect amount to our first national advertising campaign, albeit a co-branded one, on the back cover of magazines like *Time, U.S. News & World Report,* and *Business Week.* Television spots would run in all major U.S. markets for the first two months of the launch. The advertising was paid for by United and inspired by United Airlines' longtime brand chief, John Ruhack, who did an excellent job of honoring both brands in the campaign.

The first United print ad said it best: "We Are About to Give Airline Coffee a Good Name." The ad copy listed all the improvements United was making for its customers, and modestly concluded by stating that Starbucks coffee would soon be served on every United flight around the world. The copy had a little kicker of which I was particularly proud. On that first flight to Chicago to review the deal I had somewhat disingenuously queried a flight attendant on her feelings about the coffee she was serving. After grimacing a little, she boldly confided that she had heard that United was going to shift to Starbucks. I feigned surprise. She was genuinely excited about the proposed change. "You have to understand something," she said, whispering while graciously refilling my cup. "We have to drink this stuff, too." Apparently, her feelings about United's coffee were shared by many other flight attendants.

So the last line of the ad copy read simply: "After all, we don't just work here. We have to drink the coffee, too."

Six Methods for
Building Intelligent Brandwidth

1. Co-branding and Strategic Alliances
Starbucks' deal with United represented just one type of joint venture, a co-branding arrangement with potential benefits to be gained for both

sides. Co-branding and other forms of alliances—and dalliances—between brands tend to arise whenever there seems to be a real prospect of obtaining synergies by bringing two brands together. Perhaps the best-known brand co-ventures are movie tie-ins of the sort embarked upon over the years by fast-food companies in conjunction with the release of "hot" Hollywood films. But other examples of co-branding abound in today's universe, particularly in the New Economy, where barter arrangements are far more common than cash or hard-value exchange.

One interesting example of a high-profile co-branding effort that bridges elements of the New and Old Economies was initiated in the summer of 2000, when PepsiCo agreed to promote Yahoo! on 1.5 billion soft-drink bottles and displays at some 50,000 stores nationwide. Yahoo! in turn agreed to promote Pepsi's products on an all-new co-branded Web site to be operated by Yahoo! called Pepsistuff.com. During the August promotion, bottle caps of Pepsi brands contained a code that could be redeemed on-line for prizes and discounts. The value of this co-branding arrangement, in which no cash would change hands between the parties, was clearly vested in the synergies to be gained from linking a terrestrial brand, popular in the youth market, with an on-line brand equally popular with the Pepsi generation. The result was a clear win/win.

In other joint ventures, just one brand is visible to consumers, while a second, invisible, brand usually steps in to help with production or distribution or product design. This was the case when Starbucks launched bottled Frappuccino, a joint venture with Pepsi to produce a cold coffee drink based on a cold Frappuccino drink originally devised by Starbucks baristas in Southern California. Pepsi provided Starbucks with help in product development, production, and distribution.

In an arrangement where both brands are presented front and center, it is likely that one brand will benefit more than the other; they don't always end up as win/win situations. But in the Starbucks-United deal, both benefited equally. If you find yourself on either side of one of these increasingly popular strategic alliances, you should stop before signing anything to ask yourself the following questions about how the partnership will be approached and executed.

CO-BRANDING AND JOINT VENTURE PUNCH LIST

1. Your Brand's Strength: In the minds of your core customers and stakeholders, will this alliance dilute the brand's image and value? Can you measure this? Do you have an adequate benchmark? What

does your gut say about the situation? Do you really need to even research this? And if so, how much will it cost?

2. Control Issues: Do you have adequate creative control over the communications program and the way your brand will be perceived? Who is going to be the chaperone on this date? And if it's the equivalent of a corporate marriage, what does the prenuptial agreement look like?

3. Costs and Benefits: What is the real long-term benefit of attaching your brand to another one? Is it to open valuable new markets that you can't ever open on your own? Or is it just a way to accelerate time to market? Is it to raise the perceived brand image by associating it with a much stronger brand? If so, do you completely understand how your current customers view the other brand? Is it to reduce costs, or is it merely to add revenue? What are the perceived problems that can occur? How will you identify and control product-quality issues that may come up? It is as important to try and visualize the downside here. Know intimately why you are entering into the partnership and be sure everyone on the team knows it, too.

4. Purpose: Is the purpose of the co-branding effort to insert the brand into a new channel within an existing market, or is it to create a new product category altogether (like bottled Starbucks Frappuccino or Starbucks Ice Cream)? Is there any other way to achieve the results that you want? What are the costs in resources and timing to go it alone? Starbucks could have gotten into the ice cream business without Dreyer's but it would have required years of time and millions upon millions of dollars in additional overhead to achieve what we did in a matter of months for a small investment.

5. Measuring Success: What defines the measure of success for the joint venture? What are the key milestones along the way? Where are your exit points?

6. Getting Out: What is the exit strategy? If the alliance is hurting the brand or the business, can you get out, how quickly, and at what cost?

In the case of the Starbucks-United alliance, our chief fears related almost entirely to question 1: In the minds of our core customers and stakeholders, would this plan dilute or strengthen our brand equity? We were fairly confident that linking our name with United's would not provide any great tangible or intangible benefit for the brand. If anything, we faced a very real danger of diluting our strongest asset—our powerful and intimate emotional connection to our core customer.

Questions 3 to 6 left little doubt that United would rapidly expand brand awareness and product trial, the number of new customers, on a scope that could take Starbucks on its own four or five years if not more to achieve. In essence, United allowed us not only to connect all the dots between the major markets of North America but also to effectively create a trial mechanism in major overseas markets as well. Internationally, United had strong routes to Asia with a hub in Tokyo, which in fact became Starbucks' first entry point overseas.

2. Brand Extensions

When *People* spawns *Teen People,* that offshoot is considered a brand extension. In that case, it worked. Such a venture can bring untold new revenues to the home team if done properly, without too much cannibalization of the original property. *People* itself initially emerged from a popular section in *Time* magazine, and was therefore a brand extension in its own right. It, too, was a dazzling success, albeit in the same product category as its parent: mass-market magazines. But there's a limit to how far even *People* can go; I trust that AOL Time Warner will spare us *Really Old People.*

Brand extensions have proved to be lucrative in many different contexts. *60 Minutes* gave birth to *60 Minutes II.* Recently, Gerber decided to extend the enormous reservoir of trust they have developed over decades as the number 1 baby-food purveyor to introduce a new line of products, including infant first aid, under the Gerber brand.

But not all brand extensions work. For every home run like Diet Coke, there are foul balls. Thirsty for a can of pop? How about a can of Pepsi, Diet Pepsi, Cherry Pepsi, Pepsi One, Diet Pepsi without caffeine, or the unforgettable disasters Pepsi Light and Crystal Pepsi? Would you like it in a bottle or can? Would that be a "Big Slam" or the thirty-two-ounce size? Plastic or glass?

If you pursue the growth strategy of brand extension, remember this: *Every brand has its limitations.* Companies have limitations, too. You may be able to independently justify any number of growth initiatives that seem to be in sync with your brand values, but it is quite possible that your brand cannot sustain all of them at one time. One plus one plus one may equal minus two if you don't have the means to execute all of them at the same time.

In the mad rush to leverage hard-won goodwill, some companies stretch their brand as though it were a pair of Spandex shorts over the back end of a rhino. Some of us might look at such a zoological specimen and marvel, "Look at all that brand equity!" Other, more experienced students of brand stewardship would realize that the moment the rhino had to break into a run or sit down, something ugly might happen. Brand fabric can only hold so much within its span. Stretch a brand too far, and sooner or later a tear will form in the fabric. And repairing a damaged brand is a more complicated matter than simply wielding a needle and thread, especially if the fix requires convincing consumers to retry a brand that has repeatedly disrespected them or simply failed to meet expectations every time they bought the product or service.

Another pitfall to avoid is letting manpower or marketing dollars be the determining factor of how far you can go with your brand. Consumers have become fickle about brands they perceive to have grown too fast and transcended their traditional base too quickly. A prime example of this problem is Calvin Klein, who licensed his name to the floundering fashion conglomerate Warnaco and later sued his licensee for deliberately diluting—downgrading—what had been a high-end brand. One of Warnaco's brand crimes, according to Klein's lawsuit, was that it dumped huge amounts of Calvin Klein branded merchandise into discount channels like Costco in order to attain fixed year- and quarter-end financial goals. Warnaco filed for bankruptcy protection in June 2001, before the case was fully resolved. It is no surprise, then, that its distribution practices may have not had Calvin Klein's best brand interests at heart. They were just trying to stay alive. It makes you wonder what kind of protection CK had in place within the Warnaco licensing agreement. Obviously not enough.

In contrast, an example of a brand that expanded rapidly but *without* getting diluted, without suffering a loss of brand esteem, has been Ralph Lauren. At every level and in every channel, Lauren kept tight control of its most priceless asset, its brand. Even when it entered my local hardware store with its line of paints, it did so with the best point-of-sale merchandising and collateral materials I have ever seen for any home product. The mere fact that Lauren planned to update the color palette seasonally, rather than the industry norm of every five or six years, greatly pleased the employees working the paint department. They finally had something interesting to talk to consumers about, something to look forward to each season, and a product that was a massive departure from the boring products they had been saddled with for decades.

The Spandex Rule of Branding bears repeating:

Just because you can doesn't mean you should.

One reason for Starbucks' phenomenal success in a number of risky brand-extension maneuvers has been its unwavering commitment to creating a best-of-class product in whatever category it competes in.

A good example of positive brand stretch is Frappuccino, both bottled and blended in the café. It was born as a result of a persistent suggestion by several Starbucks baristas who had created their own cold blended coffee concoction. Corporate stepped in and developed the product into what we now recognize as Frappuccino. It became a runaway success across the country in the summer of 1995. As a menu item, it was a product extension for the Starbucks retail channel. But the success of Frappuccino was not going to be limited to Starbucks' own store-based retail channel—not if Howard Schultz had anything to say about it.

Shortly before Starbucks began putting blended cold beverages into its cafés, Pepsi-Cola and Starbucks entered into a relationship to create new coffee products for the North American grocery distribution channel. The first effort was a carbonated coffee beverage called Mazagran, which was test-marketed in California in 1994. A niche product that attempted to merge the best qualities of cola and coffee, it never became a mainstream hit, and after a brief trial run on the West Coast it was pulled from the market.

The Mazagran experiment was responsible for one lasting contribution, though: a Starbucks coffee extract developed by Don Valencia, Starbucks' head of research and development. This stuff was like liquid gold, as it had an awesome potential to be infused into any number of real coffee-flavored products. At the very management meeting with Pepsi in which the fate of Mazagran was being reviewed, Howard Schultz challenged the group to consider an R.T.D. (ready-to-drink) version of the already successful hand-crafted café product Frappuccino. Though the new frothy cold drink had appeared in Starbucks cafés only a few months before, Schultz already knew he had a hit. A year later, in 1996, he would announce to Wall Street analysts that Frappuccino would one day be a billion-dollar business around the world—a claim I don't doubt for a minute.

Again, it was Starbucks' R & D genius, Don Valencia, who took the ball and ran with it. Largely because of our ability to leverage the deep product development, production, sales, and distribution resources that Pepsi president Craig Weatherup placed at our disposal within the Pepsi organization, we had a first round of product formulations ready for taste testing in just a few weeks. The results of our initial market tests were dramatically different from those for Mazagran. As Schultz later wrote, "Within the first few weeks of introducing bottled Frappuccino we were selling ten times the quantities we had projected. We couldn't make it fast enough." What was perhaps more important than the volume of sales was the fact that we had conquered a new channel, and this opened the door for more retail adventures in the supermarket and grocery store aisles.

3. Transcending Distribution Channels

Much of the buzz in branding lately has been generated by nontraditional brand extensions that appear to effortlessly leap from one distribution channel into another, as was the case with bottled Frappuccino. In the wake of that success, Starbucks went on to introduce its own branded coffee ice cream, as well as whole-bean and ground coffees, to more than 30,000 grocery stores in North America. Further, Starbucks has also begun selling its own branded line of espresso machines through specialty retailers and department stores, in addition to Starbucks cafés. These are all excellent examples of how to widen an access point and generate relevant new revenue streams that do not jeopardize existing brand equity.

The basic rule in transcending distribution channels is:

In creating brandwidth, always look around your core product category position before looking elsewhere, particularly when taking the brand into a new distribution channel. If you do it right, the new growth will strengthen, rather than dilute, your brand.

4. Transcending Product Categories

A number of fine brands have found ways to profitably enter entirely new product categories through careful leveraging of core brand values. The heavy-equipment manufacturer Caterpillar licenses its brand to the shoemaker Wolverine World Wide, which markets Caterpillar boots. Church & Dwight's Arm & Hammer baking soda brand—a venerable icon if ever there was one—has given birth to a best-selling toothpaste. Two impressive examples of broad yet relevant brand stretch are Ralph

Lauren and Martha Stewart. Both companies moved into hardware—most notably, paint—Lauren from strictly fashion apparel and Stewart from strictly housewares and cookbooks. Stewart, Nike, Harley, CK, and Swiss Army sell watches and sunglasses. These may not be as great a category leap as from cookbooks to latex, but they are major league vaults just the same.

Sony, long an audio and video hardware brand, made several leaps outside its category, including a costly pothole-filled detour into Hollywood film-making, before pulling off a more successful brand detour into computers as well as computer-game hardware and software. In fact, by 2001 Sony's game software and hardware alone represented more than 30 percent of corporate profits. Movies and computer games both lie within the entertainment position, which now lies at the heart of the Sony brand—which once upon a time stood strictly for small-scale consumer electronics.

Not satisfied with making movies, Harvey Weinstein propelled his "hot" Miramax motion picture brand—itself a sub-brand of Disney—into books, music, and magazines, with Tina Brown's *Talk* magazine and its publishing arm, Talk/Miramax Books. Contrary to predictions, the book publishing venture has proved more successful at generating buzz and best-sellers than the magazine, which has yet to enjoy that combination of highbrow and broad appeal that has characterized Tina Brown's magazine offerings to date. Meanwhile, Brown's former employer, *The New Yorker,* sells branded CDs featuring short stories read by its roster of top authors. Everyone is getting into the game.

You've probably seen the attractive lines of toiletries, personal-care products, and aromatherapies offered by the Gap and Banana Republic. Banana Republic now also sells china and tableware. Since its core products are concerned with fashion, aesthetics, and personal appearance, such offshoots make sense. Today there are hundreds of brands in the grooming and personal care product category, and in the future, big brands like Michael Jordan may possess the critical mass to carve out larger and larger pieces of that business.

Eddie Bauer started out in Seattle as a specialty outdoor retailer, but, no longer content to upgrade the interiors and trim for special editions of Ford Explorers and Expeditions, the company now sells furniture and housewares. How well its furniture line will perform remains to be seen, but Eddie Bauer has created a lifestyle brand capable of supporting a broad array of products, and is not one to miss an opportunity: at some

Eddie Bauer stores you may find yourself standing in line in an Eddie Bauer coffee bar.

The original champion category jumper was the Walt Disney Company. It originated as an animation company, then a movie studio, branched out into theme parks, created a Sunday-night television program, and established hundreds of retail stores selling only Disney-branded characters and products based on its creative content. This veritable wizard of branding most recently created a cable channel and one of Broadway's most popular productions, a staged version of its animated feature film *The Lion King*. Most recently, it launched a radio network.

In contemplating brand extensions, particularly category- and channel-jumping ones, the consistent theme must be: build on brand trust. This is the substance that you are seeking to leverage and the critical brand asset that you are putting at risk. Know exactly what you are dealing with. What permitted Ralph Lauren and Martha Stewart to prevail in a product category long dominated by Sherwin-Williams and Benjamin Moore was that consumers not only trusted Lauren's and Stewart's fashion sense, but they also trusted their commitment to quality. Stewart's trustworthiness in this regard was so well known that her brand equity even permitted her to go into a partnership with the discounter Kmart without compromising her brand's core values of good taste at a fair price.

In the case of Sony, it became critical for its management team to grasp more precisely where its brand trust was strong, and where it was not. The powerful Sony brand name added little to the luster of Sony Studios in Hollywood, a place where—much like in Japan—personal relationships mean everything. But when Sony branched out into computers, a half century of goodwill and trust supported that brand extension, within a certain boundary. Notice that Sony quite rightly did not seek to compete toe-to-toe in the desktop PC space with Compaq, IBM, and Dell, but sought to prevail in the marketplace with laptop, notebook, and other portable computers, an area in which its reputation for miniaturization stood it in good stead. Much the same phenomenon occurred when Nike decided to sell sports watches and miniature portable music players for jogging—athletic spaces in which the Nike brand carried a great deal of weight. Recently, the high-end sunglass manufacturer Oakley introduced a line of running shoes, directly competing with Nike in its own space. Interestingly, Oakley announced with great fanfare that its footwear line would not utilize offshore labor to build its products, a direct swipe at Nike with whom it had ongoing legal battles over eyewear design. Less than two years later Oakley quietly announced that it would cease manufacturing its footwear in the United States and that it would have to source its product overseas. It simply could not be profitable any other way. Unfortunately for Nike, the press didn't make much of this concession. Lesson here: if channel leaping means compromising your publicly stated core brand values, think before you leap.

5. Sub-branding

Another increasingly common strategy for increasing brandwidth is sub-branding. This is a newly fashionable term that has enjoyed a great vogue in the marketing arena, yet is nearly impossible to define precisely. The brand-development guru Kevin Keller, who is also a professor at Dartmouth's Tuck Business School, has taken one of the best stabs at it: "The practice of combining an existing brand with a new brand to brand a product is called sub-branding, as the subordinate brand is a means of modifying the super-ordinate brand."

The relationship among sub-brands within a large corporation can be confusing to the best brand marketer. What is the relationship between General Mills and Wheaties? Between RJR and Nabisco? Between RJR Nabisco and Triscuits? Further complicating the issue is the never-ending compulsion of huge companies to mate. What was once First National City Bank morphs into Citibank, which buys Salomon Smith Barney, a brokerage house that was itself the result of a merger of Salomon Brothers and Smith, Barney. It then merges with Traveler's Insurance, which is actually a direct descendent, believe it or not, of the old Continental Can, which some time ago diversified itself of its can-making operations and reinvented itself as a financial services company.

Sub-brands are just as confusing in the media companies. Are CNBC, the cable channel, and MSNBC, the cable channel–Web site, sub-brands of NBC? It would seem so. But MSNBC is also a hybrid sub-brand of NBC and Microsoft, its parents. And what relationship do these offspring bear to GE, the granddaddy brand? Not much, because they are separate brands. If a brand bears no resemblance in name to its parent brand, there is nothing "sub" about it. It's a different concept altogether.

The best way to think about these brand family trees is to reconsider precisely what we mean by a brand. A brand isn't a product. An Oldsmobile Cutlass Ciera isn't a brand, or even a sub-brand. It's a model, just as a Mitsubishi Mirage is a model. Is Mitsubishi the brand? Yes—it just happens that Mitsubishi makes everything from heavy equipment to home electronics. The same questions can be applied to the mega-brands GE, Procter & Gamble, General Foods, and General Mills. In some areas they are still brands, but in other areas they have ceased to be so. For example, GE is very much a brand in the field of medical imaging, light bulbs, nuclear power plants, jet engines, and financing for buying jet engines, as well as consumer electronics or even cars. But the level of resonance the GE mega- or umbrella brand possesses with consumers has tended to dissipate the more it diversifies. Interestingly, although GE continues to please its stockholders by generating, over time, the highest rates of return in modern history, it has become somewhat muddled as a consumer brand. If anything, the GE brand came to be defined by its onetime CEO Jack Welch, who regularly graced the covers of business magazines and newspapers around the world.

The prevailing confusion around sub-branding becomes particularly acute when a gigantic company owns a portfolio of brands. What starts out as a drive to grow revenues through acquisition or merger often nets a flock of brands that have varying degrees of connectivity and relevancy to the "parent" brand. For example, Nestlé controls more than five hundred brands. Some, like Nestlé's Crunch candy bars or Nestlé's Chocolate Chips, keep the flagship Nestlé brand name in the public mind. But how many people know, or care, that Nestlé also owns Carnation, Stouffer's, MJB, Hills Brothers, and Taster's Choice instant coffee?

The main reason to create a sub-brand is to avoid brand dilution, muddying the meaning and associations adhering to the original brand, and to take a big step toward transcending the prevailing image of the parent brand. An excellent example of a successful sub-brand is Lexus. The brand is entirely owned by Toyota, but it has successfully created its own distinct image of luxury in the minds of consumers quite apart from Toyota's core image as a provider of reliable, feisty, but not flashy cars. Thus, sub-branding could be considered the opposite of a brand extension. Lexus was deliberately provided with its own set of brand values, much as GM sought to do with Saturn, which, like Lexus, enjoys its own independent dealer network, brand imaging, and positioning. Ten years after the launch of Lexus, few consumers see the connection to Toyota so clearly. Lexus has become, for all intents and purposes, an independent brand. This is perhaps the ideal outcome for any sub-brand.

Our first true sub-brand at Nike was Air Jordan, a collection of footwear and apparel introduced when Michael Jordan joined Nike in 1984. Its stunning success blinded us to the reality that it can be a daunting, costly, and ultimately frustrating task to try to create an entirely self-sufficient sub-brand from scratch. Despite a few attempts, we never succeeded in replicating the unique and priceless Michael Jordan dynamic. When Shaquille O'Neal and his agent, Leonard Armato, negotiated with us, one of the reasons we didn't sign O'Neal was their demand for a signature shoe and a television campaign that would rival that of all other Nike endorsee campaigns *and air before the first regular season NBA telecast*. Shaquille had just left LSU, and had not yet played his first NBA game, which gave us an incredibly short window to put together a campaign. Even if we had enough time, though, I don't think Nike would have done it, for we then thought that Shaq would not have been able to generate the kind of interest that Michael Jordan had. It turned out that we were right, and our nonsigning became, in the words of Nike's then-president Dick Donahue, "the best deal we never did."

Reebok signed Shaquille O'Neal a few weeks later, quickly absorbing most of its marketing dollars. By doing so, Reebok essentially delivered its women's business to Nike. O'Neal may have sold shoes to young boys but he didn't do much for Reebok's core franchise, women eighteen to thirty-four. Michael Jordan, on the other hand, captivated and inspired a much broader audience and strengthened Nike's entire brand portfolio every time he appeared in Nike advertising campaigns.

The lesson: If your sub-brand is personality-driven, the personality should be consistent with your brand values. It should not undermine or jeopardize fundamental parts of your business.

Nike had trouble replicating the Jordan phenomenon, but we did see a moderate success with All Conditions Gear (ACG), Nike's first foray into the hard-core outdoor arena, competing with brands like Patagonia and REI. We hoped to eventually create sub-brands and businesses that might one day grow into entirely distinct brands in their own right. When that didn't happen, we decided to try to split the difference, and achieve some of the benefits of brand segmentation, by developing groups of products that represented "brand collections," as opposed to "sub-brands."

The collections concept grew out of a realization on the part of management that we had reached a certain limit with the Nike brand, at least with retailers. By the late eighties, retailers had begun to complain to us that they just could not take any more Nike-branded merchandise; they feared that a surfeit of Nike could unbalance the delicate retail mix in their stores. In response to these justifiable complaints, we decided to create a handful of tightly focused collections of shoes, apparel, and accessories, each targeted to a unique consumer segment and attitude. A single sport like basketball might have three or four collections for the various positions and styles of play, while tennis could have two—one for the young at heart and one for the entrenched country club set.

Here's a breakdown of some of Nike's original collections and the thinking that went into them:

Force: Big, heavy basketball shoes for big, heavy guys—forwards and centers. Moses Malone was one of the first (size 22), followed by Charles Barkley and David Robinson. Basic apparel concepts. No frills. Serious gear. Get out of my way. That ball is mine, and that paint under the hoop is my house.

Flight: Lightweight expressive shoes for outside shooters and point guards. Reggie Miller, John Stockton, Gary Payton, and a squadron of high-flying trash-talkers wore these. Stronger fashion statements here. Speed, agility, and finesse. I can float like a butterfly and sting with long threes. And I wanna be like Mike.

Jordan: If God played hoop. Where ultimate physical performance meets art.

Air Raid: Outdoor basketball shoe built for the inner-city blacktop player. Less of a collection than the three above. Initial shoe tied directly to an advertising campaign with Spike Lee: "Mo Colors, Mo Better." Primarily a response to a strong collection from Reebok called Blacktop. (Nike never did well when following; this product proved it.)

Challenge Court: Tennis collection that debuted with Andre Agassi wearing hot pink Lycra underneath denim shorts. Effectively woke up the country club. Ads featured the Red Hot Chili Peppers. Irreverence justified. Girls screamed. Andre had long hair. He dated Barbra Streisand. It got strange.

Supreme Court: On the other side of the net were athletes like Pete Sampras. More conservative attire. Wider access point. The country club allowed Nike back in, but on probation. No screaming teenage girls. Sampras spoke softly but carried a really, really big racket.

Each new collection had its own design, pricing, promotion, and advertising strategy, yet all were unequivocally connected to Nike and its brand values. The commercials were still tagged "Nike," but the product logos were heavily weighted toward the collection icons. Shortly after the launch, it became clear that no intelligent retailer was going to be able to afford to pass on any of Nike's collections. Tom Clarke, at that time

Nike's president, and Mark Parker, Nike's head of product design and development, masterminded the collections concept as a means to provide the retail trade with "digestible chunks" of Nike products while at the same time delivering to the consumer more differentiated and unique products.

6. Acquisition

Occasionally, when a company acquires an existing company, it is a bid to acquire not merely its business but also its brand values. The hope is that some of the new sub-brand's brand values might rub off on the parent company. A case in point would be Chrysler's acquisition of American Motors, a takeover entirely predicated on Chrysler's desire to get its hands on the Jeep brand as a way of revitalizing its own corporate culture. According to Chrysler's Bob Lutz, Jeep and Cherokee products came complete with a culture "that could be likened to the Wake Island Marines—under siege." The decision to connect the Chrysler brand to that of Jeep represented an attempt to burnish the Chrysler brand, which had acquired a wimpy and lackluster image, by acquiring the macho-image Jeep.

Chrysler's timely acquisition of Jeep utterly transformed the culture of the parent company. It helped unleash a new creative process and tremendous growth across the board at Chrysler. In the decade following its AMC acquisition Chrysler introduced more revolutionary automobile designs than any other domestic automobile company.

Interestingly, one of the best examples of a merger gone wrong is the acquisition of Chrysler by Daimler, which before its own merger with Mercedes had enjoyed its own distinct brand identity in Europe. Daimler-Benz, as it became known, went after Chrysler because it was looking for globalization and a wider entry point into the U.S. market. In addition, it was looking for a faltering company that, it hoped, could be turned around with a stiff dose of Teutonic discipline and respect for precision. Unfortunately, the much-vaunted so-called merger of equals turned into a takeover, which turned into a rout for the American side of the business. Slighted in the transition was Bob Lutz, and key Chrysler engineers and designers who had worked so hard to elevate the brand followed him out the door. Lutz's defection early in the process was seen as the canary fleeing the mine shaft. What appeared on paper to be a complementary mix—each brand occupied a different end of the automotive spectrum—ended up being a recipe for disaster. The corporate cultures were too far apart for any real brand alignment to occur naturally. DaimlerChrysler may one day turn into a well-integrated automobile company, but as it stands today, it represents a cautionary tale of what a lack of brand alignment can do to even the most intelligent managements. (And in an intriguing coda to the forgoing events, in the summer of 2001 GM hired Lutz to entirely rethink its design process.)

Acquisitions and mergers often attempt to blend values and cultures, but it is important to respect the fact that brands have distinct genetic codes embedded inside them. Attempts to erase a once-proud brand from the face of the earth by an acquiring parent are more common than successful brand marriages. A case in point would be Snapple, a pioneering brand in the "New Age" drink market, which was acquired by Quaker Oats as a bid to give the parent company a shot of New Age magic. Unfortunately, Snapple was very quickly run into the ground, and became a disaster for all concerned. Brand marriages need to be as carefully scrutinized as any marriage; like so many human couplings, they often fall victim to an excess of good intentions and a shortage of realistic appraisals before the knot is tied.

Three Things to Avoid When Growing Your Brand

1. Never Close Your Eyes

Even for a 140-year-old company like Levi Strauss, newfound growth late in life can feel like hitting puberty all over again. In the late eighties and early nineties, Levi reinvented itself and experienced tremendous success following the launch of Dockers, a breakaway sub-brand that cracked the magical $1 billion mark in less than two years. I suspect Dockers made some of the old-timers feel young again.

But by the summer of 1997, growth in all of its business lines was slowing. The domestic market for the company's core denim products was coming under attack from all sides. Costs were climbing at Levi Strauss's San Francisco headquarters, in part due to its ownership of factories that were operating well below capacity and a corporate aversion to layoffs. As a privately held company, Levi Strauss did not come under the sort of intense pressure that a publicly traded company in its position would have. It was during this period that I was asked by Levi Strauss to give a speech in Carmel, California, to a large group of the company's marketing professionals from around the world. The average tenure and caliber of the conference attendees was astounding. Here, obviously, was a company with a highly developed culture and a tremendous amount of pride in its brands. At the same time, it was clear that these highly intelligent people were not at all clear as to where their beloved brand was headed: Was it to be the face of the future, or a nostalgia trip to the past?

"Levi Strauss has taught me much about branding," I told them. "I can remember spending six-fifty that I made picking beans to buy my first pair of 501s, a full two dollars over what other jeans cost. I was only twelve. Yours was one of the first brands I fell in love with. You have one of the great brands in modern history."

A few months later, on a trip to San Francisco, I dropped in on Gordon Shank, then Levi Strauss's president for North America, to see how things were going. Shank had been one of Levi Strauss's chief brand architects in his long career there. He looked a little tired. "Growth hides a lot of mistakes," he said. "For seven years we could literally do no wrong. Along the way we took our eyes off of what was happening all around us. It embarrasses me to say this, but we did not fully acknowledge the Gap as a major competitor until a short while ago."

For too long Levi Strauss had regarded manufacturers as its prime competitors. In recent years, it had expanded that view horizontally to include brands like Nike. (If any two companies should have had alignment, it should have been those two, for the combination of sneakers and Levi's had been a powerful one for many years.) But had Levi Strauss looked more vertically, toward retail, it would have seen an even more formidable foe in the rise of a new breed of manufacturing retailers such as the Gap. The irony in the situation is that the Gap was itself established on the back of the Levi's brand. For many years it was the primary place to get Levi's, and much of the Gap's "basics" positioning can be traced back to the walls of Levi Strauss denim that once filled its stores.

Because the tables can turn incredibly quickly in today's high-flux, low-loyalty brandscape, it pays for even the strongest and most seemingly impervious brands to continually refresh themselves. Levi Strauss lost at least one, if not two, generations of consumers by not stepping up its innovation and looking at the market more broadly. Levi Strauss did one very smart thing—it created a super sub-brand in Dockers—but then let that success lull it into complacency. It would be as if Nike had created Air Jordan—and stopped in its tracks there, and decided to rest on its laurels.

2. Never Ignore the Effect of Profit Improvement Programs on Your Brand

I once met a gentleman from a very large packaged-goods company while flying from Chicago to New York. We fell into one of those anonymous plane conversations. This one eventually found its way to branding. I did not reveal what I did (I was at Starbucks at the time) other than the fact that I was in marketing. While swapping stories he made an amazing confession about a flagship product that he had worked on for many years.

The product was once the category leader in almost every way. Quality, market share, consumer preference—you name it, his brand was always ranked among the best. In its present form, however, it had weakened and fallen from grace. Between O'Hare and La Guardia he gave me the case history of how this all came to be.

"For eleven straight years," he began, "we made aggressive profit improvements in the manufacturing process. We convinced ourselves that price was important to consumers and we also had profit goals to reach each year. So we created an incentive program for everyone that influenced the cost of the product. We tried just about anything we could, within reason, to get those costs down. And each year we found something that we could do differently or sometimes just do without. I don't think we ever thought any single incremental 'improvement' would seriously hurt product quality.

"But eleven years later," he continued his sad saga, "someone walked into the room with a competitor's product that was, we had to admit, awfully good. So good, in fact, that it made ours almost unpalatable by comparison. Although the other product was more expensive, it was obvious to all of us that we would have no chance with consumers if they were given any sort of real choice between the two. We had diluted our product to a point where the brand could not begin to compete at the level it once owned."

Interestingly, as his company began to "devalue" their product little by little each year, so did most of his direct competition. Because he had been the category leader, everyone else had to make similar changes to stay competitive from a pricing standpoint. I'm quite certain that large retail buyers had an influence on this drive to get costs down, fiercely pitting one brand against another.

The competitor that changed his world? It was a rogue start-up not steeped in the incrementalist method, led by a product visionary by the name of Howard Schultz. While Starbucks has undeniably a great product, it was certainly helped by the fact that its competition was more concerned with improving profits than giving consumers what they really wanted.

3. Never Expect Success in One Area to Guarantee Success in Another

About the time the "Just Do It" campaign was taking off, in the late 1980s, a rival footwear company was experiencing meteoric growth. A business called L.A. Gear, based in Southern California, had shot from zero to nearly $1 billion in revenues in a startlingly short period of time. The management brashly created a new niche in the athletic footwear category with cheap shoes that visually emulated performance footwear, but were fabricated of much poorer quality materials and designed to appeal to teenage girls rather than world-class athletes.

Was there a play for Nike in this emerging market? We wondered, looking on with mounting alarm at what could be the rise of a second Reebok. After all, Reebok's original offerings had hardly been "court-worthy," and yet Reebok had nearly cleaned Nike's clock with the Freestyle. Could Nike stretch its brand to include $29.99 sneakers aimed at young teen girls with no particular sports or fitness activity in mind? Nike mulled over a number of defensive strategies to fend off this growing threat.

At the peak of L.A. Gear's somewhat inexplicable success, I visited their exhibit at the Atlanta Super Show, the annual trade show for the footwear industry. For its exhibit Nike had created a 50,000-square-foot shrine to the world's best athletes and displayed a dozen highly focused product collections, each with its own highly specialized merchandising environment. At a cost of several million dollars, we had created a virtual portable Nike Town in the middle of a convention hall. L.A. Gear, by contrast, had simply set up a stage surrounded by tables and chairs, not unlike what you would see at a sleazy nightclub.

Their show began with a dozen drop-dead-beautiful young girls who appeared to be clad only in trench coats and L.A. Gear sneakers. Not usually one to give a compliment to a competitor, I turned to the buyer next to me and shouted over the thumping disco music, "Interesting visual strategy. You have to look at their feet!"

Just as I was delivering this trenchant observation, the girls flung their coats into the three-hundred-plus crowd of now-whistling, clapping male buyers. The strip act revealed an unusual application of what appeared to be brightly colored dental floss, which covered enough of the tanned young bodies so as to not get any of us arrested. Overlooking the spectacle from a crow's nest above the stage was an L.A. Gear top executive, who bellowed over the noise, "I'm not sure what that has to do with sports but I sure like it!"

However questionable their taste, we had to give L.A. Gear credit: they had developed an enormously interesting brand around a unique set of values that appealed to a significant section of the population. At the height of the pandemonium we witnessed in Atlanta, no one could be sure where L.A. Gear was headed, but they were headed there in a hurry.

Nike's response to this gauntlet's having been thrown down in the women's market was to create two sub-brands of fashion-driven products. For teen girls we created Side One. For young women looking for affordable "athleisure" products we created a brand called "i.e. for Women." Although both lines contained strong products, neither rang true to what Nike had come to represent as a brand. The shoes were not "court-worthy," and die-hard Nike staffers found it hard to get out of bed in the morning, fired up to work on them. They had no cultural roots into which we could tap the way we could with basketball, running, or cleated-shoe sports like football and baseball. Eventually both product lines failed, but not before we made a pitch to Madonna to serve as the "spokes babe" for Side One. That particular meeting began to derail when she asked if Nike would affix to the side of each shoe a couple of Anglo-Saxon words packed with enormous shock value that I would feel uncomfortable printing here, let alone on several million pair of shoes.

So for better or for worse—ultimately for the better—Nike stuck to its knitting and went on to gain the top position in the women's fitness market by creating products and advertising with young women in mind instead of three-hundred-pound centers for the Los Angeles Lakers. We spent the better part of three years bringing it about.

Rather than engage in a glitzy marketing effort, we found some unusual ways to weave the women's fitness initiative into the very fabric of the Nike brand. One year after the launch of the "Just Do It" campaign, Wieden & Kennedy crafted a print campaign to accompany Nike's best product efforts ever for the young women's market. The women's "Just Do It" print campaign was a mix of empathy, inspiration, and empowerment. It spoke to women in a voice that was intimate yet strong, philosophical yet honest. The following year Nike produced an eight-page print advertisement that chronicled the life of any woman. "You were born a daughter," began the series of statements that covered everything from first bras to first boyfriends to biological clocks to gaining acceptance of mind, body, and spirit across the ages. Images of everyday women of all ages were interspersed throughout the text. Nike's voice of authentic athletic performance had acquired a new language that was both visual and verbal. Of all the work we did at Nike, I am most proud of that campaign for its strategic as well as creative brilliance. It proved that creating new brandwidth did not have to undermine the brand's core. In the end, Nike not only hand-checked L.A. Gear but unseated Reebok from its number 1 position in the women's area, its greatest stronghold.

The moral of this story: L.A. Gear attempted to create too much brandwidth too quickly for a brand built on a shallow, fad-sensitive foundation. Nike succeeded in displacing L.A. Gear and unseating Reebok because it created a strategy that was consistent with its own brand values. In so doing, Nike greatly expanded its own brandwidth rather than taking the easy way out and simply cooking up yet another sub-brand.

Smart companies recognize that profitability and brand survival are not simply functions of cutting costs. Growing a company's valuation by shrewd financial management can also quickly reach a point of diminishing returns. For most companies, further budgeting "improvements" won't do what is needed most: significantly strengthen the brand's relevance and resonance with innovative products, transformational distribution strategies, and compelling brand positioning. But be careful. Moving a brand in the wrong direction—or in too many different directions—in the pursuit of top-line growth may end up diluting its value, if not its long-term viability, even if the short-term revenue gains appear to be enormous. Any growth initiative should refresh, rather than punish, your brand.

show some emotion

Brand Principle #4
Transcend a product-only relationship with your customers.

Hogs in Paradise

Some years back, I joined a few friends for several days of fishing and re-laxation in the Florida Keys. Key West lies at the tail end of a very long causeway that connects a string of tiny islands extending some ninety miles into the Gulf of Mexico. In anticipation of the trip, I had formed vivid mental images of our languid arrival at this tropical oasis. Jimmy Buffet music would waft through a warm breeze scented with sun lotion. Palms would sway, and ice cubes would tinkle in tumblers of gin-and-tonics by the pool. The combined stress level of the entire "Conch Re-public" would equal that within one minivan somewhere up North.

Instead, at the heart of this funky little resort town, we stumbled upon a Harley-Davidson rally in full rumble. This was not an impromptu gathering, but an official HOG (Harley Owner Group) event, with no less than five hundred riders taking part. Despite a record heat wave for late September—it was in the mid-nineties with matching humidity—the Harley faithful were decked out in jeans, chaps, and heavy black leathers. But these sweating folks would have it no other way, because they had authentic Harley sweat. You don't wear cargo shorts and sandals when riding a fat boy, and if you do, well, you just shouldn't be riding a hog at all. You'd be better off with a Vespa.

After our first full day of fishing we ended up at a jam-packed seventies-style rock bar on Duvall Street. As a self-confessed brand fool and hopeless observer of human behavior, I was in a target-rich environment, given the mix of tourists before me. Over the din of Loverboy, Foreigner, early Doobie Brothers, Aerosmith, and Lynyrd Skynyrd, I took note of the rivets, World War II–era helmets, boots, and Harley jackets with growing interest, and not a little bemusement.

But something just didn't seem quite right with the picture. For a few minutes, I couldn't put my finger on what was bothering me. Then it hit me: here in the midst of these ostensibly "authentic" hard-core road-hog rebels, too many of the easy riders sported manicured nails, perfect teeth, and expensive haircuts. Some looked suspiciously like antitrust lawyers and brain surgeons.

During the musical breaks, I watched, slack-jawed, a series of tattoo contests in which participants removed their clothing on stage to reveal a wide range of creative Harley-Davidson iconography. During one break, I struck up a casual conversation with a fifty-something hairdresser whose husband, one of the contestants, was proudly displaying his own personal work of art upon his hairy back. They hailed from a small town in Alabama, she told me proudly, and five years earlier had taken a sizable chunk of their savings to buy an American legend on wheels. Clearly, they had never looked back.

With all due respect to the annual Saturn reunion in Spring Hill, Tennessee, I haven't come across any Saturn owners rabid enough to have a Saturn logo tattooed on their butts. This wasn't a display of mere brand loyalty I was witnessing; this was full-scale, 100 percent brand religion. And despite the prevalence of tattoos out there, this brand connection was more than just skin-deep. The last time I'd been exposed to such brand frenzy was when I first observed kids, usually jocks, with Nike swooshes shaved into their hair. Even by 1991, the idea of having a swoosh tattooed somewhere on your body was hardly a new idea; in fact, it was a rite of passage for many of Nike's younger, entry-level hires. But these Nike cult disciples were suburban kids. In Key West, the Harley-Davidson cultists were salaried adults.

Fanaticism has always found a fertile breeding ground among the young and impressionable, whether it involves political ideology or religious extremism. People at these formative ages also have their first experience of undisciplined brand consumption and carve out a unique personal style. In Japan, this love affair with brands typically takes hold

in the college years, when young adults first enjoy freedom from the regimented uniforms of their public school system and are not yet connected
ball and chain to fourteen-hour workdays and neckties.

But in Key West, the born-again Harley-Davidson faithful were grown-
ups. Seeing the composition of that crowd brought the following realization
home to me: *Harley-Davidson had intentionally cultivated a relationship
with consumers that radically transcended a product-only relationship.
People don't just buy a Harley; they become members of a community
bound by an ethos and shared set of values that cross many social and
economic strata.*

HD had succeeded in developing an emotional connection with one
of the most diverse ranges of consumers on the planet. On Duvall Street
that night were blue collars, white collars, and studded dog collars. Just
about the only brand ambassadors not on the premises were clergy,
though I wouldn't have been at all surprised if they had also been represented, incognito. For other lasting evidence of the strength of this particular brand religion, try searching the Web under "Harley-Davidson."
You'll find HOG chapters all around the world posting rally data, information about fund-raising rides for curing diseases, and a thousand individuals' home pages where proud owners display their pride and joy in
polished splendor. There are even a few "Harley Mom" sites.

Today, demand for Harleys, though not quite at mid-nineties levels,
runs so strong that a secondhand late model can cost more than a new
one. Customers remain so loyal that the average age of a Harley rider has
climbed from thirty-nine to forty-four. In fact, the greatest brand challenge facing Harley is that the bike has become too expensive for
younger, less affluent consumers. But rather than dilute the brand by putting out a cheaper model, Harley has purchased a motorbike company,
Buell, which puts a Harley engine on a lighter, stiffer frame, to produce a
vehicle that costs roughly $5,000 less than the average Harley, which
tends to go for $15,000 and up. ("Pull Some G's" is the Buell slogan, a
sly reference, some suspect, to the "G's" saved as well as to the force of
gravity.) Thus, Harley avoided dilution of the major brand while still
choosing a new market segment with a cheaper and materially different
product.

During the nineties, Harley sales roughly doubled what they had been
a decade before, hitting tantalizingly close to the $2 billion mark by the
turn of the century. In the meantime, the Harley mystique has grown so
monumental that even non–Harley owners want to own Harley-branded

paraphernalia, including items as unlikely as jukeboxes. The Harley-Davidson Chrome Visa card boasts more than 100,000 holders, with the sort of demographic profiles that make marketers salivate: average age forty-four, median income $70,000, married with kids with a home in the suburbs. That demographic segment breaks down into two large sub-groups: skilled blue-collar workers with high incomes, and white-collar professionals who view the Harley as a luxury purchase. Few brands straddle these two social segments with the palpable grace and ease that Harley has managed.

But things weren't always so rosy for what, until relatively recently, was a brand on the run. By the early eighties, Harley had seen its share of the "big bike" market slip from over 50 percent to less than 25 percent, as low-cost Japanese competitors like Honda, Suzuki, and Kawasaki bit big chunks out of its core business. Japanese imports threatened Harley's prime position with a strong combination of low price and high quality, and cut deeply into the stretched and stressed loyalty of some long-established customers. The company was in deep trouble, on the brink of closing the doors of its fabled plant in Milwaukee, Wisconsin.

The main challenge to the long-term durability of the brand was that though the company remained popular with its core ridership, its brand imaging had become seriously tainted by a popular impression that its motorcycles were the official bikes of the Hell's Angels. The association with unsavory aspects of the counterculture, fueled by films rang-ing from Marlon Brando's *The Wild One* to Peter Fonda's *Easy Rider* and, most notoriously, *Gimme Shelter,* had fixed the brand in the public mind as being pervaded by an undercurrent of violence, danger, and drugs. If ever a brand needed to widen its access point, it was Harley-Davidson.

By 1982 this once-shining symbol of rugged American individualism felt compelled to appeal to President Reagan's International Trade Com-mission for help. Reagan signed off on a plan to hit the Japanese im-ports with a steep tariff unless they "voluntarily restrained" themselves. The Japanese backed down—lowered their motorbike exports—and even helped Harley retool, reengineer, and generally get its act together again.

By the end of the decade, it was morning again in Milwaukee. Yet in the end, the Harley turnaround had less to do with government protec-tion than it did with renewing the product's appeal to some of the same basic human emotions that HD has been riding for decades.

Decoding Hog Emotions

Since the company's founding in 1903, Harley-Davidson has triggered a number of intense emotions in its customers and in consumers. Among these are the need for escape and the desire for authenticity, rebellion, and (once mainly male) camaraderie. For much of the brand's colorful history, Harley-Davidson enjoyed a relatively focused consumer base: antiestablishment, loud, obnoxious, irreverent, and, on occasion, criminal. It appealed to the maverick and the outlaw in all of us with its promise of the freedom of the Old West and the uncharted future that lay ahead on the open road. This set of associations generated an undeniable emotional power, but it had a weakness: these emotions ultimately carried too many negative connotations and were quite frankly too immature to appeal to anyone but the most devoted customer.

For much of the past century, the company failed to transcend its narrow customer core and tap new revenue streams. Harley's big turnaround came when the brand began to carefully connect—and reconnect—to a broader set of emotional needs than those experienced by hairy road warriors named Buck or Straight Shot. As the company prepared for the fight of its life to simply stay afloat in the sea of imports, it became a poster child for two other emotions, sympathy and empathy. Americans of all stripes, types, and colors could sympathize and—often to their dismay—empathize with the plight of an aging American manufacturing icon that had lost ground to imports.

Emotional potency gives the proud owner of any great brand opportunities for leverage. Let's take a moment to review in greater detail some of these potent feelings.

Belonging

Right at the top, I'd put *belonging*. We all want to belong to something larger than ourselves. This is a core human value ranked toward the top of the hierarchy of needs created by Abraham Maslow. The human desire to belong to a larger group is so deeply embedded in our primal tribal histories that for any brand to fill this need in its customers, particularly across a wide socioeconomic swath, is a notable victory. What does it mean to feel as though you belong? In this context, it means that the mere possession of a product can make consumers feel as if they are somehow deeply connected to everyone else who owns that product, almost as if they were together in a family.

But the concept of "brand belonging" extends beyond the mere ownership of products, and is equally relevant when the relationship is more about service or simply shared values. A group like the Navy SEALs has its own brand ethic. The same principle applies to impassioned equestrians, Giants fans, or devotees of handmade wooden boats. In the presidential realm, consider George W. Bush, who hails from Texas, a powerful and recognizable brand unto itself, given that Texans' state pride borders on the fanatical. It should also be noted that George W. is an integral part of the Bush family brand.

To appreciate the strength of the motivation to belong, consider the fact that one of the most often cited reasons for job dissatisfaction in the workplace is not pay or position, but rather not feeling a part of the process and being recognized as part of the team—any team. People who believe they are on the outside looking in are both unhappy and unproductive and it is usually just a matter of time before they leave for another job. This drive is so essential that it bears additional emphasis: *We all want to belong to something larger than ourselves.*

Longing

Closely related to the need to belong is the emotion of *longing,* which is sometimes called yearning. In practical marketing terms, it means that you, as a consumer, hope that someday *you too* can become part of some great brand's saga. In marketing, this is called "unrequited demand." The easiest way to create unrequited demand is to avoid overproduction and keep the entry price of your product high, which is the time-honored strategy of luxury brands like Porsche, Mercedes, Cartier, or Tiffany. This concept is at work in limited editions of all kinds, including fine art. A sense of scarcity creates value and is often but not necessarily a function of price.

Abandoning an "unrequited demand" strategy in the unrestrained quest for growth can be costly. In 1996 and 1997, Nike decided to broaden its product line and distribution base, particularly in the area of apparel, and saturate the market with swoosh products. The so-called swooshification of the planet eventually caught up with the company in 1998, when supply outstripped demand and its error become obvious. The problems were soon translated to Wall Street. It would be nearly three years before Nike brought its inventories back in line with consumer demand, by which time the stock price had tumbled by roughly 40 percent.

Rugged Individuality and Freedom

The near-universal desire for greater personal freedom, and the more particular American quest for rugged individuality, are what we might call *cultural emotions*. These feelings draw upon a nostalgic appeal for a particular culture and are often felt more strongly by those outside the culture than those inside. Brands ranging from Marlboro to Ralph Lauren, Guinness, and Gitane cigarettes have tapped into these yearnings. They are the reason that L.L. Bean clothing proved enormously popular with the brand fanatics in Japan, and why all of Hong Kong seemed to be in love with "big" quintessentially American brands from Calvin Klein to Nike to McDonald's.

Connecting a brand to a timeless human emotion or to a specific cultural dynamic is not simply a matter of picking superficially "appropriate" music for a commercial or a corporate video. Nor can it be achieved by signing up a popular celebrity or capturing readers' or viewers' attention by making them laugh out loud (although I recommend that most brands find a way to do that from time to time, particularly in the pursuit of poking fun at yourself, which helps to make your product and brand seem less remote from the life of the average consumer). But remember: a genuine emotional connection must be intrinsically relevant to what your brand stands for, to those unique physical and emotional needs you deliver, and to what you believe at your core to be your timeless values.

Human Emotions for the Ages

As mentioned earlier, one of the most useful sets of insights available to marketers for understanding the role of emotions in human psychology is Abraham Maslow's hierarchy of human needs. The relevance of Maslow's theory to brands and branding is that too many products are pushed at consumers through blunt and often clumsy appeals to only the most basic needs. A starving person thinks and dreams about food, and little else, just as a dirty person yearns for soap and a chilly person wants a sweater to keep warm. A more skillfully marketed product will appeal to emotional states ranked higher on Maslow's scale of human needs that, Maslow argued, all people feel.

THE NEED TO FEEL SAFE

The need for physical security is felt most acutely by adults during emergencies or in periods of disorganization in the social structure, such as widespread rioting, terrorism, or civil unrest. Security is a drive that is also felt especially strongly by parents of children—a need that was skillfully addressed by Volvo, automotive security blanket to the world.

THE NEED FOR LOVE, AFFECTION, AND "BELONGINGNESS"

According to Maslow, people need to escape loneliness and alienation, to give and receive love and affection, and to have a sense of belonging. Of course, this need is met most directly by family and friends, but it can also be met by the feeling of belonging enjoyed by the Harley-Davidson bike owner at a rally. Kodak appeals to this feeling with its ads depicting family moments, as did AT&T in its pre-breakup days with its classic line "Reach out and touch someone."

THE NEED FOR ESTEEM

People need a stable, firmly based, high level of self-respect, and respect from others, in order to feel satisfied, self-confident, and valuable. If these needs are not met, the person feels inferior, weak, helpless, and worthless. The status and self-reward conferred by luxury brands such as BMW, Montblanc, or Perrier-Jouet address this need for esteem.

THE NEED FOR SELF-ACTUALIZATION

Maslow describes self-actualizing people as those who long to be involved in "a cause outside their own skin." This is a critical and extremely powerful need, one met for centuries by institutions like the church and its related spiritual activities, by traditional community organizations, from the Red Cross to the Community Chest, and by nationalist, patriotic, and revolutionary causes. All of these outlets for this deep and abiding need still exist, of course, but it has often been noted—most often disapprovingly—that in today's consumer-driven universe, at least part of this need to become self-actualized is pursued through the purchase of material goods. Even the most world-denying ascetic (or the most worldly hedonist) would probably agree that some portion of the human need for devotion to a cause that "actualizes" is sometimes attempted through a relationship to a branded product or service. Speaking as one who has seen firsthand the power of a brand unleashed, there is no brand on earth that can deliver the top of Maslow's pyramid. The best that marketers can do is to respectfully acknowledge that the need exists.

Decoding Emotions at Starbucks

In the early years at Starbucks, the commodity nature of coffee led to a certain degree of creative tension, which divided those who believed that the company was in the food-service business and those who thought the company was in the business of lifting spirits one cup at a time.

In truth, Starbucks is in both businesses. It will always involve some aspects of the food-service industry, because the heart of its business is serving coffee, often with food, in coffeehouses. But for Starbucks to have defined itself as a food-service business in strictly the same terms as a chain of fast-food outlets and offering discounts, promotions, movie tie-ins, bonus packs, and kids' meals would have been an enormous mistake. This was not entirely obvious to fresh management recruits who came to the company straight from the fast-food juggernaut offices in Chicago, Miami, or Tokyo. By then, Starbucks had already developed a connection to something deeper and more culturally rich than any burger joint could hope for: the venerable tradition of the coffeehouse. Howard Behar, one of the driving forces behind Starbucks shortly after Howard Schultz gained control of the company, once told me: "A burger joint fills the belly, but a good coffeehouse fills the soul."

Emotive Brands at Work

No company possesses the ability to create an entirely new emotion, although I think Microsoft has come close. Sometimes when I use their products I feel this strange blend of joy and loathing. Joy because the products are often so easy to use, and loathing—although that may be a bit strong—because they have become so ubiquitous that in an interconnected world we are left with little choice but to use them.

Still, the entire range of human emotions is out there to be tapped as opportunities for augmenting and enriching brands. We're given a pretty standard set of emotions when we're born—we all feel joy, shame, sadness, insecurity, horror, surprise, pride, self-confidence, and sympathy, to name a few. How we grow and uniquely evolve and the environment in which we develop determines how and when which emotions are expressed in our daily lives.

Did Nike create the feeling that an eight-year-old boy gets when he scores his first goal in soccer? Is Nike responsible for the feeling a runner has when finishing her first marathon? Did Nike engineer the means by which endorphins are released into the bloodstream? Did it invent the feeling of guilt that you may have about not working out more often? Did it program the fear of having a heart attack at the ripe age of forty-two?

Obviously not. What Nike did do—so well that in the process it built itself into a multibillion-dollar brand—was skillfully tap in to the wide range of emotional rewards that are uniquely relevant to sports and fitness. None of these emotions are unique to Nike products, but the company found ways to say both explicitly and implicitly, "We know how that feels and we know why it's important." Nike simply became a *protagonist* of the emotional and physical rewards of sports and fitness at a time when its competitors were dancing on the head of a pin by selling consumers little more than newly designed cushioning systems.

Did Harley-Davidson create the feeling of escape from responsibility? No, that primal emotion goes back to the time one of our cave-dwelling ancestors intentionally took the long way home. Did Harley-Davidson invent the fulfillment and bonding that comes from the camaraderie of traveling with friends and relatives? Nope. Nomads on camels probably wrote the book on that one, albeit in a more quiet and plodding way.

Great brands find relevant ways to tap the emotional drivers that already reside deep within each of us. Powerful emotional currents exist as part of the human condition. Human beings are in fact the most complex emotional concepts that God has created. Great filmmakers recognize this, and tell stories in a way that deliberately strikes a powerful emotional chord. Great films make you think and they make you feel. They can make you belly-laugh and they can make you cry in the dark of a movie theater and sometimes both in the space of mere minutes. Great brands, if they are consistently good, accomplish this year after year, decade after decade, and sometimes for more than a century.

Some Respected Emotional Drivers

Did American Express create the feeling of security and safety that a respected credit card or financial service provides? Did Prudential? Allstate?

Did Visa create the fear of not being able to pay for a meal when entertaining someone? Or did American Express Traveler's Checks?

Did Intel create the sense of accomplishment that comes from owning bleeding-edge computer technology? Or did Apple? IBM? Palm?

Did Apple create the sense of empowerment felt when personal creativity is unleashed by technology? Steve Jobs has come closer than anyone else to defining that feeling, but he certainly was not responsible for that emotion.

Did Volkswagen create the joy of simple, affordable transportation? Or was that Honda?

Did Coke instill the pride Americans feel about their country? Or was that Chevrolet?

Did Mercedes, or Montblanc, Godiva Chocolate, or Rolex, create the human need for self-indulgence? Or was that Starbucks?

Did Barnes & Noble create the timeless search for enlightenment or the simple escape that a great book provides?

Did Levi Strauss create the value of timeless, utilitarian, unpretentious style? Or was that the Gap?

Did Hallmark create the need to show love or be loved at Valentine's Day? Or was that 1-800-flowers?

Did United Airlines create the need for bringing friends and families that have grown apart back together? Did United foster the feeling of sadness that befalls a working mom who finds herself 2,000 miles away from her young child? Did it create the joy of a reunion among friends and family? Or was that MCI?

Kodak and Disney

Two of the world's most beloved brands—beloved because they have so successfully attached themselves to the nexus of emotions surrounding the idea of family—are Kodak and Disney. Did Kodak create the feeling young parents get when they see their toddler learn to walk, or create the rapture of watching a small child bury its hands in its first birthday cake, or the pride that accompanies that child's high school graduation? Of course not. But it was one of the first companies to align itself with all of these rewards. Making good film and implementing a great processing system are key factors in the company's success, but by themselves, they are purely product-oriented attributes that carry precious little emotional value.

In fact, Kodak management's own emotional investment in chemical processing and celluloid film blinded it for the longest time to the prospect of digitizing the same data, and making the transition to a fully digital consumer imaging system. That finally happened, but rather than being out in front, Kodak ended up playing catch-up to its competitors. If everyone at Kodak headquarters in Rochester, New York, had understood early on that they were not in the film and chemical processing or printing paper or camera business, but in the memory-storage and story-telling business, that transition would have come sooner, and easier. The brand is about capturing the times of your life, not the particular equipment or processes that permit that to happen.

Did Disney create the tender moments of reading a small child to sleep at bedtime or taking children to their very first movie? Did Disney develop the need for a small child to clutch a stuffed animal? Did Disney instigate the concern parents have about protecting their children from carnival culture? The answer, again, is no. It simply became a respectful protagonist for the magic of family life, and has brilliantly attached itself to the unique emotions that reside in the child within all of us. Along the way it built an unprecedentedly successful global brand franchise around these feelings.

Guinness: Places of the Heart

Some brands establish a powerful connection to an aspect of a culture defined by a country or a geographic region. Guinness is a good example of this. Besides forging a link to all things Irish, it is connected to an age-old institution: the Irish pub. The Guinness Irish Pub giveaway contest, which gives a traditional Irish pub to the winner of a contest in which contestants are tested for skills ranging from poetry writing to pint pulling, taps in to a strong emotional connection to Ireland that, surprisingly enough, extends far beyond those bound by Irish blood. A large number of entrants in the increasingly popular contest possess no known Irish roots. Guinness discovered that the idea of running a pub in Ireland had less to do with being or feeling Irish than it did with a desire for escape, to live in a beautiful place, and to do something on your own terms.

The contest brilliantly trades on the oral and written rituals of the Irish community by insisting upon a strong literary effort in prose or poetry as a first hurdle for every entrant. Only winners of the preliminary literary part of the contest are invited to Ireland to participate in the next phase: the performance piece, in which contestants are judged on their

ability to pull a perfect pint. And only after they can demonstrate that ar-
cane skill are contestants judged on their ability to instill the sense of
community that is a hallmark of a great publican, who is often a prac-
ticed storyteller and performance artist. In every sense, the emotional
connection to Ireland is both broad and deep: to poetry, to performance,
to literature, to music.

The creativity on the part of the marketers here was to recognize that
Guinness could benefit from tapping in to the cultural idea of belonging
to the ancient tradition of being "Irish" without appearing exclusive.
Guinness is as much a state of mind and place as it is a drink.

PepsiCo: Emotions and Necktie Products

In the early sixties, Tom Dillon, the CEO of BBD&O, then Pepsi's ad
agency, wrote a white paper to his client Pepsi in which he referred to
Pepsi Cola as a classic "necktie" product, i.e., "If you looked at a man
and saw what kind of necktie he was wearing, you could tell whether he
was conservative or outgoing." A soft drink was a necktie product, because it too served as an indicator of personality and style. (By the late
sixties, this notion would have been laughed out of the boardroom—an
indication of how quickly cultural shifts transpire today.)

Armed with this key insight, Dillon hit on the then-radical idea of
moving Pepsi Cola's marketing away from talking about product attributes and focusing on the consumer. It wasn't easy to differentiate among
the various colas by taste, texture, or other physical characteristics, so it
turned out to be far more effective to develop a personality around the
emotional style of a person who would choose a Pepsi over a Coke.

The image of the "Pepsi Person" that the agency formulated was that
of an individualist, a bit of a maverick, young in spirit if not necessarily
in age. This idealized image of the Pepsi consumer formed the basis for
the "It's Pepsi, For Those Who Think Young" campaign, which in turn
was the direct conceptual ancestor of the now-classic "Pepsi Generation"
campaign, one of the most powerful of all time. The point of both campaigns was to define the "Pepsi Person" as youthful and carefree, in contrast to presumably conservative, stodgy Coke drinkers. As a basic human
need, who among us doesn't want to stay young at heart?

PepsiCo (Again): Just Dew It

More recently, PepsiCo has taken a leaf out of its own book and once
again scored big with teens by cleverly resuscitating its tired old Moun-

tain Dew brand and aiming it at cool young dudes and dudettes. These "Gen X" and even "Gen Y" consumers display more than a healthy dose of cynicism toward conventional marketing. In order to reach them, Mountain Dew marketing efforts have brimmed with the sort of boundless high energy and thirst for fun that have connected with teens in a generation-defining manner not seen since the Pepsi Generation.

In something of a self-conscious reprise of that campaign, Mountain Dew teens were portrayed as having a contemporary, slackerish, disaffected emotional style more reminiscent of the Seattle grunge movement than of the surfin'-safari hijinks of the Pepsi Generation. But these alienated teens show a surprising willingness to believe in something that believes in them—even a product like a soft drink that once sold itself as a hillbilly potion.

Mountain Dew cannily expanded on its campaign by sponsoring ESPN's X (Extreme) Games, a freestyle Olympics, if you will, that actually resembles a Mountain Dew commercial. One Mountain Dew marketing maven refers to the X Games as "aspirational," in the sense that even those who don't actually slip and slide over the cliffs themselves enjoy tapping in to the "extreme" emotional spirit of the brand. Where Pepsi connects to the young at heart, Mountain Dew targets the wild at heart.

Snackwell's: A Mother and Child Reunion Is Only an Emotion Away

RJR Nabisco's lower-fat snack-food brand Snackwell's learned the value of emotional drivers when it abandoned a 50-cents-off coupon to drive sales—the old transactional trick—in favor of establishment of a bond between its products and women's lives (though the *New York Times* labeled this a "treacly" bond).

"Women don't want a transaction," explained Terry Preskar, a Snackwell's senior business director. "They want a relationship. We wanted to build a relationship that would really drive deep loyalty to the brand." As a relationship builder, Snackwell's created a paperback journal to be given to any purchaser of two boxes of Snackwell's products, which mothers and daughters could fill out together in time for Mother's Day. Branching into the nonprofit realm, the company forged an alliance with Girls Incorporated, an Indianapolis-based organization whose motto emphasizes making girls "strong, smart and bold."

Snackwell's also called in the futurist and trend spotter Faith Popcorn, whose research confirmed that "consumers may still want coupons, but what they really want is a meaningful connection to the brand." The company chose to focus on the mother-daughter theme because they found that it resonated powerfully even among women without children. "There was such strong support there because every woman is also a daughter," said Ms. Preskar. "They have tremendous heart for making things better for the next generation."

Montblanc: An Emotional Write

Norbert Platt, the CEO of the pen, watch, and luxury goods company Montblanc, was recently interviewed about his brand's emotional resonance with consumers. "Montblanc," he concluded, "is about passion and soul. . . . As the world keeps winding up, we unwind. Technology has created a need to step back and take a deep breath. Our corporate philosophy is 'de-acceleration,' a cyber-backlash. Consumers crave things that preserve a moment."

How did Montblanc ensure that this brand message was conveyed in its marketing and promotional efforts? They decided to "become known for our visionary support for culture and the arts," Platt explained. The company created a corporate cultural foundation to "encourage intellectual enrichment." They spearheaded a campaign to increase worldwide arts patronage. They became founding sponsors of the Philharmonia of Nations, a dream initiated by Leonard Bernstein to promote world peace through music.

"I wanted people to feel passionate about our brand," Platt says. "This may require them to voice their opinions. In the heat of debate, they may go over the edge, even antagonize peers and superiors! That is okay! I want people to be emotional and sometimes even irrational. This furthers creativity, new ideas, and future-oriented thinking."

MasterCard: Priceless Emotions

Many people in the service industries have a hard time accepting that their "products" rely on emotional connections with consumers. What, they ask, is the emotional depth of the relationship of a credit card holder to his or her preferred brand of card? Thin and tenuous at best, for the most part. But American Express built its success on the momentous discovery that a tiny sliver of plastic can convey a great deal about its holder to others, and touch nearly every level of Maslow's hierarchy (only to find its success continually eroded by fierce competition in the field). Maslow's most basic need, for security, is clearly provided by any credit card, because it rests on a bond of trust between merchant, buyer, and bank: no actual cash has to change hands, because all three parties can "trust and verify." It also conveys security to the consumer because if it is stolen or lost, the loss will not have the same adverse consequences as it would if cash were lost.

The original Amex gold charge card showed that even the color of the plastic can convey social esteem and the inclusiveness of membership in a club. I can certainly recall feeling excluded when, rushing for a flight at an airport in Asia and holding my gold card, to gain admittance to an American Express lounge, I found that admittance was restricted to holders of the *platinum* card.

Yet viewed from another perspective, the relationship between a card holder and card provider remains by its very nature transactional. Recently, MasterCard imbued its plastic with an explicit emotional connection when their advertising agency, McCann-Erickson, conceived what it called its "reality-check theme": "The best things in life are free. For everything else, there's MasterCard." This was developed into a series of spots that explored the theme of "priceless" moments that occur around events in which the MasterCard can be used. In the campaign a series of transactions are shown, inferring that they were charged to the credit card. At the end of each commercial something occurs that is far more valuable than a hot dog, a Coke, or tickets to a ballgame: the time between father and son, for example.

The "Priceless" campaign was credited by one industry observer with "adding an emotional content to a product normally devoid of emotion." For the Asian market, a "priceless" moment translated as an expensive round of golf culminating in a "hole-in-one with a witness." A Latin American version depicted an awestruck young boy meeting his favorite Formula One driver. The tag line: "Stopping [the boy's heart] at three hundred miles per hour—priceless."

The "Priceless" campaign struck such a strong emotional chord with consumers that Joseph Tribodi, MasterCard's VP for global marketing, was thrust into the role of a global Dear Abby. He's been receiving letters and e-mails daily from people all over the world suggesting their own private "priceless" moments as the basis for future spots. That degree of engagement between a consumer and an ad campaign is rare indeed.

Nike: Forging Emotional Ties with Women to Expand the Business

Appealing to strong emotions is generally a powerful strategy, but it can also entail running risks, if the emotions elicited by a campaign are not the ones the marketer intended. One aim of the "Just Do It" campaign was to broaden Nike's appeal to women. But in attempting to reach beyond our core audience, we made one creative decision that badly backfired.

One of the first "Just Do It" spots to air starred Joanne Ernst, an exceptionally fit and attractive triathlete. In the spot, Joanne verbally challenged viewers to stop trying to decide what to do, be it weights, running, cycling, volleyball, or basketball, and instead urged them to "Just do it!" Unfortunately, in a series of quick cuts between Joanne sitting on a locker-room bench with a towel around her neck and a blur of her sports activities, she repeated the line so many times that it felt like a nail was being driven into your forehead. And then, after the Nike logo was flashed at what seemed to be the end of the commercial, she suddenly reappeared on the bench and added with a wry smile, "And it wouldn't hurt to stop eating like a pig, either."

That last line was unscripted; Joanne spontaneously delivered it to director Joe Pytka for fun, as an out-take. But I think she believed, like most of us, that exercise can only do so much. The comic relief that the line provided saved the ad from coming off as too high-pressure and self-serious—or so we believed.

The morning after the first airing of the spot, I walked into my office a little before 8 A.M. "You have some important calls to make," my assistant said, the concern obvious from the tone of her voice. "You really have to call this lady right away," she said, handing me a message slip. "She's so upset I can't even understand what she is trying to say." I was dumbstruck, still blithely confident that we had just hit the marketing equivalent of a grand slam.

I immediately dialed the number, and between sobs, a woman told me that she had just buried her fifteen-year-old daughter, her only child, who had died from an eating disorder. "Please don't do this," she begged. "You have no idea who you are talking to with those commercials. You are hurting people. People are dying because of the negative imagery companies like Nike project."

For several hours afterward the phones lit up as every disorder organization on the planet demanded my home address. But toward the end of the day we noticed another thread in the backlash: lots of women simply hated the ad for reasons that had nothing to do with bulimia or anorexia nervosa.

To determine exactly what kind of emotional connections we were making, we immediately fielded focus groups in three U.S. markets. The groups represented three different segments of the female population: young ultra-athletes, twenty-five to thirty-four years old; twenty-five-to-forty-four-year-old casual fitness participants (women who worked out once or twice a month); and twenty-five-to-forty-four-year-old seriously overweight, inactive women.

The results were astounding at first, but upon reflection made perfect sense. Dedicated young female athletes who had the luxury or commitment (many were fitness or aerobics instructors) to spend several hours every day chiseling their bodies loved everything about the ad, and they saw absolutely nothing objectionable in it. On the other end of the spectrum, the sedentary nonathletic respondents thought the spots were obviously not aimed at them, and most of them found the commercial funny.

But the women in the middle, the largest group of potential female Nike customers the brand could ever hope for, universally rejected the ad. In their world, there was little time for dedicated exercise. Most of them either worked long hours in a demanding job or spent every minute of the day on the endless and thankless duties of a stay-at-home mom. To these women, the ad made Nike seem completely out of touch with their concerns. We seemed openly disrespectful of the "real" world that they lived in. We were, in their eyes, insensitive jerks. Frankly, they weren't far off.

These focus groups provided the inspiration for what would later emerge as one of Nike's most successful print advertising campaigns, an emotionally charged production that we appropriately called "Empathy." The ad received the Stephen Kelley Award twice, the highest honor for any print advertising in the world. The message was inspirational rather than aspirational; it promoted empowerment and self-esteem through sports and fitness. For that heightened sensitivity to the women's perspective, we had to thank both the advertising agency and the angry women in those focus groups in Chicago, Boston, and San Francisco.

Left to its own devices, the athletic core at Nike still occasionally forgets the other 98 percent of the population when approving advertising. One particularly egregious example occurred during the 1996 Olympic Games in Atlanta, when Nike broke a campaign that stopped even me in my tracks.

"You Don't Win a Silver, You Lose a Gold" was the tag line, a slogan hardly destined to win over soccer moms and Little League coaches around the country, or anyone else who believed in the notion that winning was secondary to playing the game. "It's the way Olympic athletes talk to one another," was the defense from a friend of mine who wrote the tag line for Nike. That may or may not be true, but I don't think it's how the majority of the television-viewing public wants to view their athletes up on the medal stand.

A few years later, Nike made an even more serious blunder. On October 26, 2000, the *Seattle Times* ran the headline "Nike Pulls Another Ad, Issues Another Apology" over the following story:

> For the second time in a month, Nike has withdrawn an advertisement and apologized to those who found the material offensive. The magazine ad spoofing the dangers of trail running was withdrawn after complaints it insulted the disabled. The ad promoted Air Dri-Goat trail running shoes and claimed they would prevent the pictured runner from slamming into a tree, "rendering me a drooling, misshapen, non-extreme-trail-running husk of my former self, forced to roam the Earth in a motorized wheelchair." "We have a long and diverse record of supporting disabled athletes and we're extremely and sincerely apologetic," Nike spokesman Lee Weinstein said. Ad agency Wieden & Kennedy also produced the Nike TV commercial that showed middle-distance runner Suzy Favor Hamilton fleeing a chain-saw-wielding maniac in a parody of horror films. The commercial was quickly yanked after complaints flooded TV stations.

So What's the Lesson Here?

Effective brand building requires making relevant and compelling connections to deeply rooted human emotions or profound cultural forces. Brands that establish themselves within the larger incredibly complex fabric that we call life will set themselves apart in a more meaningful way. Great brands understand the need to respect both the physical and emotional needs of consumers. Establishing an emotional connection with a broad range of consumers does not protect you from gaffes or lapses in judgment. A negative emotional response, even if it is only confined to a small segment of the audience, can be just as strong as a positive one, if not more so. And thanks to the growing scrutiny of the media toward large corporations, small mistakes can become major debacles. A hard-earned bond of trust that may have taken years to build can be broken in an instant. If you are successful in establishing a relationship that is more than skin-deep, respect the person that invited you in. And always remember, there is a very fine line between love and hate.

No matter which marketing vehicle you use, be it a network television commercial, a radio spot, your own Web site, fliers on a telephone pole, or an interactive ad somewhere on the Web, the most powerful and lasting benefit you can give a customer is an emotional one. Physical benefits are the necessary currency of exchange—the transactions, if you will—that by themselves can be quite unremarkable and pedestrian no matter how great your products are. Great brands transcend great products. They respect the timeless human search for people, places, products, and services that are relevant and compelling. Consciously or not, we seek experiences that make us think, that make us feel, that help us grow, and that enrich our lives in some way. Wherever possible, make your brand a part of that process.

brand environmentalism

Brand Principle #5
Everything matters.

In 1995, after signing on with Howard Schultz to help manage the Starbucks brand, I underwent the training program required of all new Starbucks employees. And that means everyone, regardless of job description. Whether you're a part-time eighteen-year-old college student or a thirty-eight-year-old corporate exec, like I was, you are obliged to attend a course at Brew U, where you are seriously steeped in the ways of the company: its values, its history, its culture. Unlike many other corporate training sessions, however, the Starbucks course does not impart the kind of abstract, irrelevant learning that gets quickly forgotten, like calculus. This institution of higher learning teaches a skill most graduates will never forget—they learn, for once in their lives, how to brew a decent cup of coffee.

The dozen or so coffee illiterates in my particular group spent some twenty hours together, spread out over several days, learning the ways and means of Starbucks. (As an officer of the company, I had the even higher honor of subsequently traveling the country, working behind the counters of a randomly selected group of Starbucks stores over the next several weeks.) In the core program, we learned how to time the perfect espresso shot (18 to 23 seconds) and how to steam milk without scalding it (best to keep it under 175 degrees). We performed the centuries-old technique of brewing unfiltered French press coffee, using very coarse grounds with water just off boil, steeped for precisely three minutes.

In addition, Starbucks taught me and all the other green beans a thousand pieces of information that most people wouldn't dream of contemplating when ordering a cup of coffee. But the company understands that each and every bit of knowledge and every lesson, however major or minor, is equally critical to the fate of the brand. One of my personal favorites is a program called "Star Skills," an exercise that helps aspiring baristas maintain a Zen-like mental state and warm smile behind the espresso bar at 7:19 in the morning, when they're caught short-handed and faced with a line of twenty-three precaffeinated, not-quite-humanized customers. When my training was completed, though, the single most remarkable thing I took away from it was the knowledge of how coffee beans behave once they're roasted. They behave, in fact, *a whole lot like brands.*

Let me explain.

Why Brands Are Just Like Coffee Beans

For a better-than-average Starbucks coffee bean, the roasting process, like war, can be hell. One day they're hanging out in a tropical breeze in Sumatra or Kenya, and before they know it their little gray-green husked backsides are thrown into a very hot, swirling, stainless-steel roasting machine thousands of miles away. The darker Starbucks roast profile means the beans are processed a while longer than most roasters dare, but—and this is critical—they are not burned.

Bear with me here a little longer as we follow our bean. It next finds its way into a bag that is eventually opened in a Starbucks store and poured into a drawer or bin. Once there, it has one week to be ground and used or it gets sent to a local charity. Why so short a life span? To preserve its intense aroma. The roasting process removes so much of the moisture from the bean that it tends to absorb everything in its path: whatever odors are in the air, for hundreds of feet in any direction, get sucked right into the bean. It's hard to satiate roasted coffee beans. They're a lot like Imelda Marcos in a Nordstrom shoe department.

Odors and coffee beans are especially bad bedfellows, since most of what you "taste" when you drink coffee is made possible by your sense of smell, as opposed to your taste buds. Don't believe me? Hold your nose and take a sip. Coffee that has absorbed the odor of, say, cigarette smoke or scrambled eggs won't be the best cup of coffee you've had in a while. For this reason, Starbucks was one of the first retail establishments in North America to ban smoking. Of course, health issues were involved, too, but it was more for the sake of the coffee. Odor-protected coffee simply tastes better.

So what does all this have to do with brands?

> *Brands, like coffee beans, are highly sensitive sponges that absorb whatever is around them. And they don't discriminate between the good, the bad, and the ugly.*

This dynamic is especially true of brands that are highly desired and widely respected for their exclusivity and unique sensibilities. Brands like Gucci and Tiffany, for example, do everything they can to avoid pedestrian presentations. Similarly, cheap brands do everything they can to rub up against great ones and take their place on the shelves of the better stores, so as to bask in reflected glory. This is also why mass retailers lust for premier brands.

What Is Brand Environmentalism?

No brand steward worth his or her salt can ignore the fact that brands absorb all impressions, negative and positive, whenever and wherever they spontaneously occur. This means that the "environment" in which a brand exists is wherever that brand is discovered or discussed, not just where a corporation desires it to be. Brand environmentalism is about more than just how the brand looks at the retail level. It used to be that this was really all that most companies worried about, apart from advertising and a tightly conceived notion of public relations. But it's not just about point-of-purchase anymore.

> *Brand environmentalism means accepting the responsibility to protect your brand and present it in the best possible light whenever and wherever it may be found.*

Great companies look beyond the point of sale and go deep within to examine such once-considered-irrelevant elements of their businesses as their corporate offices and the factories that make their products. They undertake a major effort to ensure that the press completely grasps what it is that they do, and how and why they do it. They leave nothing to chance. They no longer merely dump their products or services into the marketplace and then let them fend for themselves. Instead, they act as the brand's chaperone. They control whatever they can and they do their best to influence the rest.

It used to be that "presentation" was exclusively the task of the re-seller; today, great brands exert as much influence as possible over every possible contact point with customers. Some provide branded "show-rooms" that augment the traditional distribution platform. Nike Town is just one example of this approach. Other brands are both a branded product and retailers of their own exclusive product line; this is true of the Gap, Banana Republic, and Old Navy, all of which are Gap divisions. Others, such as REI, an outdoor enthusiast's retail nirvana if there ever was one, distribute their own brand of clothing and equipment alongside hundreds of other branded products. Nordstrom is another "tweener" of sorts, a retailer that is increasingly selling more of its own branded prod-ucts such as NOL (Nordstrom's Own Label) or sub-brands such as Fac-cionable (which it distributes exclusively) in a mix that includes other prestige brands.

Brand environmentalism has long been one of Starbucks' greatest strengths, and nothing you see, smell, touch, taste, and hear in its stores is an accident. There is no serendipity here, and nothing left to coinci-dence or chance when it comes to the customer experience. Dave Olsen, Starbucks' chief coffee guru, circumnavigates the globe several times a year in search of the world's best coffees. Part scientist, part philosopher, part Indiana Jones, Olsen is an observant, well-traveled, humble man.

Once, on a coffee safari to East Java with Dave, I asked him what was most important to Starbucks. What was the brass ring? Was it the coffee, was it the store, or was it the people? He thought a moment and em-phatically answered, *"Everything matters."*

As we walked in the predawn light to a coffee-drying facility on the flanks of a volcano near Jember, it occurred to me that Olsen had distilled the entire company and the brand itself into just two words. It was re-freshing to hear someone who worked endlessly to procure the world's best product take the broader view, when many companies are content to take refuge behind their products' features and benefits as their reason for being.

Olsen's concise view of brand preservation could serve as good advice for any company in any industry. It precludes any selective perception from the corporate perspective and forces closer scrutiny of all influences on a brand. For brands that live and die at retail, this advice is mission-critical.

To summarize:

> It's no longer acceptable for companies that distribute through retail channels—or any channel—to simply ship their products and then assume that the world around their product or service is a factor that can be safely ignored.

When (and Where) Brand Environmentalism Pays the Greatest Dividend

Brand environmentalism is a critical value for any organization, but face it, creating a nice display for an irrelevant, undesirable product will hardly be a productive exercise. There is only so much lipstick you can put on a pig.

> *Brand environmentalism means undertaking a commitment to constantly improving and safeguarding the integrity and associative value of everything that surrounds the brand in all phases of development: where it is conceived, where it is made, where it is seen, and where it is sold. It means leveraging every opportunity to tell a more complete, more consistent, more unique, and more compelling brand story.*

Let's quickly review here some of the core brand-development concepts that we have already discussed, which should all be embraced for brand environmentalism to achieve its greatest effect.

1. Crack your brand's genetic code and understand the core values and the experiential qualities that reside in or near your product or service category. What is the timeless story that you are telling?

2. From that bedrock understanding, select growth strategies (e.g., additional products, services, and markets) that develop organically from and enhance your brand, as opposed to diluting or fragmenting it. There may be other products or services that complement your brand and that may be especially useful in creating a more completely enriched presentation of it. Starbucks sells a broad range of useful and beautiful items for the kitchen, from espresso machines to cups to stainless steel con-

tainers. Nike now sells watches as well as MP3 players, all designed with the athlete in mind—not to mention more than a few sports bras every year.

3. Great products and services are the most fundamental building block for any business. But great *brands* are created to transcend that foundation and respect or meet emotional needs that customers may have. Customers walk into a coffee shop looking for a little inspiration or rest. Either way, great music adds to the experience. The coffeehouse also fills a social need for many people. Starbucks works hard to make its customers feel welcome and to provide an inviting place to visit, if only for a few minutes. (I like the notion of Starbucks as an energy company, fueling the body and the soul.) Clearly identify both the physical and emotional benefits of your product or service. For brand environmentalism, the emotional side of the brand ledger is a tremendous palette from which to paint. But remember: strong products and services allow you to take branding to the next level and establish a deeper, more emotional relationship with customers. Never take your eye off the product.

Brand Bravado in Brewtopia

Shortly after returning from Starbucks boot camp, I signed up at a health club not far from Microsoft's corporate campus in Redmond, Washington. Ninety-five percent of the club members were Microsoft employees, since membership came as a job perk. On any given day, I was one of the few people on the treadmills that did not know the first thing about writing code. (More to the point, I was one of the few people there who didn't *care* if I ever wrote code.)

One morning I headed to the men's therapy pool after a workout. I discovered the Jacuzzi filled to the brim with eager young Microserfs all gathering around someone who looked vaguely familiar. Seeing no space in the Jacuzzi, I entered the steam room, from which—despite its door being closed—I couldn't help but overhear a voice occasionally boom over the muffled sounds of group hydrotherapy.

My ears pricked up when the voice began to blast apart the emerging direct-retail strategies of a number of high-profile brands, including Nike and its Nike Town strategy.

Since just about everything I was hearing seemed misguided, I took the opportunity to slip into the hot pool directly across from the source of this diatribe, which at closer range I recognized to be Steve Ballmer.

Ballmer was then and is now Bill Gates's right-hand man; today he's president of Microsoft. As Ballmer continued to bellow, he eyed me warily. I had never laid eyes on him before, and I'm pretty sure he was thinking the same thing about me.

Unable to withstand Ballmer's scrutiny any longer, and equally unable to resist telling the emperor he wasn't wearing any clothes, I introduced myself as the new marketing strategist at Starbucks. I also told him I'd been at Nike when its retail strategy took shape and was part of the corporate task force that put it together. "With all due respect," I said, "I think you're missing the point of what Nike was trying to do. It wasn't just about getting into retail sales."

With that I began to tell the story of Nike Town. To his credit, Ballmer permitted me to speak for several minutes, even when my account openly contradicted much of what he had said. Everyone around the tub sat in silence as I imparted the naked truth. . . .

Flashback: The Nike Town Story

Early in 1988, Nike had grown increasingly entangled in an acrimonious relationship with its largest retail account, the Kinney Corporation (eventually to be redubbed Venator; both firms were successors to the now defunct Woolworth's). Kinney owned Foot Locker, Lady Foot Locker, and Champs, three retail chains that combined represented more than 20 percent of Nike's business. As Kinney quickly evolved into a retail gorilla, penetrating virtually every shopping mall hung out in by teenagers, it began to flex its newfound muscles and dictate terms to its suppliers, wherever and whenever it saw a potential advantage for itself. The consolidation of the retail universe, which had seized hold of just about every retail category from groceries to tire dealers, had at long last begun to affect sneakers.

Kinney made matters worse for us at Nike by refusing to buy more than a smattering of Nike apparel. Apparel was a brand extension that represented, for us, a critical step in our strategic plan to diversify out of athletic footwear as the only real means of generating meaningful long-term growth. Our growing reliance on Kinney for survival made us uneasy; their growing reliance on *us,* as consumer demand for our products began to soar, drove them up their Astroturf-lined slat wall.

The relationship reached its melting point after Phil Knight broke off discussions with his counterpart in the Woolworth Building in New York. Kinney wanted to be treated far differently than any other Nike account, something that rubbed Knight the wrong way. At its heart, Nike was more interested in selling to local, long-established specialty athletic stores. They had been the first to buy Nike. Knight remembers his friends. In past years, when Nike was not as strong a brand, Knight might have worked harder to forge an amicable resolution to the mounting tension. But Kinney needed Nike, and rather than work around the clock to placate them, Knight decided to try a new tack: play hardball.

He summoned his senior lieutenants to a meeting with the principal intent of discussing development of a two-pronged, potentially contradictory retail strategy. One included the Kinney Corporation in Nike's future; the other did not. "I want to know how to make love to them if I have to," Knight said, "and I'd also like your best thinking on how to replace one thousand retail storefronts if need be. Frankly, I'm not sure which is worse." In the case of the latter scenario, Knight urged us not to exclude any idea, from concept shops in department stores to free-standing Nike-only stores.

Under the skillful management of Steve Nichols, director of strategic accounts and Nike's point man on the Kinney account, we were ultimately able to avoid retail Armageddon while proceeding with our plan to tentatively stick our toes in the brand-retail waters. Our first effort: a 23,000-square-foot retail laboratory in Portland, Oregon, that we dubbed Nike Town, which opened in 1989.

Nike Town Portland was an immediate success, and a few weeks after the opening, it was clear we would have to build an even bigger store the next time around. Despite this, it was also clear that the most important feature of Nike Town was not its *size,* but its retailing *mix.* Unlike Foot Locker and other more conventional athletic-wear retail outlets, Nike allocated as much square footage to its apparel as it did to footwear. At Nike Town, we displayed all of the company's posters, bags, hats, sweatbands, you name it—if it wore a swoosh, it now had a home. At the time, this was considered a high-risk strategy since it could signal that Nike was going to get into the retail business and jeopardize its current distribution system. But since the store was in our own backyard, few paid much attention to it.

A year later, we opened Nike Town Chicago on Michigan Avenue. It was a 55,000-square-foot immersion into Nike's brand values that began as soon as a customer grasped the swoosh-shaped door handles. Within a few months Nike Town Chicago became the number 1 tourist attraction in the Windy City, an honor it held for several years.

To the uninformed, it appeared that we had designed Nike Town simply as a brand showcase for consumers. But in truth, the stores were intended as much to showcase our approach to the 10,000 retailers in North America who sold our products—to give them a demo of how to effectively sell our products. In both the Portland and Chicago Nike Towns, sales of apparel and accessories combined ran roughly equal to those of footwear. This was in stark contrast to our position in the conventional retail channel, exemplified by the Kinney stores, in which Nike was lucky to get any of its non-footwear swoosh-bearing items placed. Even Nike posters started flying off the shelves faster than we could print them. The Nike Town experience gave us strong ammunition with which to approach our retail partners and explain that on our own turf, at least, our campaign to diversify out of the footwear ghetto was a considerable success.

The Nike Town experience contained two complementary messages:

1. There was enormous latent demand out there for Nike brand products of all varieties.

2. The best way to satiate that demand was to tell the Nike story more completely and far more creatively than any retailer had before.

The most surprising thing about the Nike Towns was how soon they began generating some serious cash. This was an utterly unexpected development, considering that all the products on display were sold at full retail value; we did not want to upset our traditional retailers. The stores were as much theater as they were retail, with lots of open space, expensive fixtures, and creative lighting. We then shared this data with our major retail accounts, who, though initially skeptical, soon saw the light and began to buy and showcase a more complete Nike presentation of both footwear *and* apparel collections.

From that "strategic inflection point" onward, Nike's apparel business shot from an unprofitable $250 million business to a profitable $2 billion annual revenue stream in just a few years. In addition, through events like postgame shows, in which local radio stations would interview Nike athletes on-site from a Nike Town, the brand became part of the community.

The lesson of this story of high-stakes brand environmentalism: we seized control of the way the world viewed our brand, one store at a time. And in the process, we opened up new revenue streams, solidified our brand image, and by our example changed the way Nike would be sold by retailers around the world.

In short, we protected our coffee beans.

And now, back to the hot tub in Redmond.

Microsoft Town?

My story now told, I awaited a reply from on high. After a few pensive moments, Mr. Ballmer stood, wrapped himself in his towel, and finished off the conversation with one brusque sentence: "Retailing software is totally different. Our strategy is simple: we've got six linear feet of space at Wal-Mart."

Now, to be scrupulously fair to Ballmer, Microsoft was under little pressure to change its retail strategy in order to protect its products or profitability. In fact, most of what the company sells can now be downloaded from the Internet, something that Ballmer was obviously aware of back then. But it struck me that Microsoft still desperately needed to step in and define its brand more intimately, because it desperately needed to close a growing emotional gap with its customers, a key step that the brand had so far assiduously avoided. Most everything Microsoft does is carried out through third parties. Even its customer service support is outsourced. And though that may be great for its bottom line, it's just not great for its brand.

Unfortunately for Ballmer and the rest of the team at Microsoft, while we were sitting in that Redmond hot tub the Justice Department was taking depositions from Microsoft's competitors. It wasn't long before the company became embroiled in the preliminary stages of the long-running litigation that culminated in Judge Thomas Penfield Jackson's ruling that Microsoft constituted an abusive monopoly. Since that ruling, although a federal appeals court has questioned Penfield's recommendation that the company be broken up, his finding that Microsoft's business practices were inherently abusive and monopolistic was upheld on appeal.

Monday-morning quarterbacking has never been my strong suit. But it has often occurred to me in the half decade since our health club encounter that by so steadfastly ignoring the notion of developing a "retail strategy" and by confining the brand to a narrow identity with the city of Redmond, Washington, Microsoft may have missed a chance to create a stronger emotional connection with its consumers. This emotional connection might have stood it in good stead when it faced legal challenges.

If I had been at Microsoft, I would have encouraged the company to open the first Microsoft showroom in Washington, D.C. I would have invited educators, politicians, and nonprofit organizations to software seminars. I would have placed dozens upon dozens of high-powered PCs on the showroom floor, where people could try them, some of whom would probably be experiencing the Internet for the very first time, thanks to Microsoft. It could have been called "Windows to the World." And I would have suggested that Microsoft commission the services of top designers to create an all-enveloping environment that made technology more accessible and more human. I would have seized the high ground and demonstrated how computer technology—with Microsoft in the vanguard—is changing the world for the better. And I would have done everything I could to demonstrate the "soft" in Microsoft.

Four years and volumes of Justice Department testimony later, I was having lunch at the Bellevue Athletic Club with Scot Land, a Seattle venture capitalist and former Microsoft executive. We were discussing the sad, confused state of brand development in the technology sector, when a woman who had been sitting near us approached our table and asked whether we were "with the company."

"I couldn't help but overhear your discussion about branding," she said, glancing not so casually down at the paperwork spread out before us on the table. "There's nothing more important to us right now than branding. It's about all we talk about these days."

I replied that we were not with "the company," as she put it, and explained that we were just a couple of friends waxing poetic on the subject.

"Well, take my card anyway," she insisted. "And please, feel free to call me anytime."

I glanced down at her card after she left and nearly burst out laughing. Her title? Director of strategic brand planning for Microsoft, probably a new position. Talk about too little, too late.

Case Studies of Brand Environments: The Good, the Bad, and the Ugly

Every brand exists in an environment that is critical to its success in the marketplace, whether it has a strong retail presence or not. A law or accounting or consulting firm's offices are an integral part of its environment, in addition to its letterhead, its logo, its dress code, and the voice and tone of the receptionist. Dave Olsen's phrase "everything matters" means *everything*—not just the most obvious physical features of a retail environment. That's the easy part of the job. The tough calls come along when the meaning of "environment" becomes as expansive as possible, encompassing literally everything that a company might be able to control when showcasing a brand. In the course of my career as a brand architect, various situations have arisen that have helped shed light on a few key "brand environmentalism issues." Herewith, a few brief case studies:

Shell Oil and Starbucks: Don't Overlook the Restroom

At a think tank for Shell Oil, I was asked by the CEO to consider ways that the company could elevate itself above the commodity nature of the gasoline industry. In the ensuing discussion, a number of great ideas were thrown out. My suggestion: Improve the cleanliness and overall quality of every Shell station restroom. The average motorist is unlikely to be able to discern the quality of gasoline, but anyone can discern the quality of a gas station's restroom; it's easy and immediate. If you have small children, this is an important criterion when picking a place to fill up. Unfortunately, given the nature of the gasoline business and the role of independent operators, providing consistently clean restrooms with freshly supplied paper towels, quality tissue, and breathable air was not necessarily a claim that any gasoline company could confidently back up. Still, in my own experience, Shell does seem to pay more attention to this feature than do others nowadays.

Sometimes brands compromise their integrity, knowingly or unknowingly, when they try to cut costs. Part of Starbucks' stellar success has been its ability to contain or even reduce expenses without undermining or seriously threatening the integrity of the brand. It's not perfect in this respect—no one is—but it ranks among the best. Like many companies, Starbucks holds regular profit improvement meetings that are designed to keep everyone's eye on the bottom line in their respective areas. At one of these, a young bean counter from the finance department made an elaborate presentation which suggested that the company go to single-ply sheets of toilet paper instead of two-ply rolled paper in every Starbucks store in the system. The savings would be considerable, he insisted.

Before I could respond a question was raised. "Won't people just use more of the single-ply sheets?" asked one executive in all seriousness.

"We factored that in," came the equally serious reply. "As you can see in
our assumptions, we have projected that there will be a thirty-one percent
increase in the number of individual sheets or panels used, but since they
are single ply, we will still be way ahead on cost."

This was my first such meeting, and I was stunned by the dialogue. As
the presenter took us all through tables of numbers and projections, I
turned to one of the executives seated next to me to see if I was the only
one who thought the conversation was a bit bizarre. "It seems a little
strange," I remarked to him, "to invest enormous sums of money to redesign and upgrade the stores and then stock them with the kind of toilet
paper found in discount gas stations. Is this for real?" Fortunately, during my sanity check the management team came to its senses and voted
down the proposal before I had to weigh in.

My counsel on subjects like that is very straightforward:

> *When thinking about ways to cut costs, begin in areas that customers*
> *cannot readily see, touch, smell, or hear. Then work back from there.*
> *And above all else, be consistent across all customer contact points.*
> *You are only as good as your weakest presentation—or your restroom.*

A cost-cutting measure like changing long-distance carriers is a safer
place to go than toilet paper. Consolidating the cleaning supplies to fewer
suppliers is another option, assuming the products perform as well. Even
the lighting fixtures can be reconsidered, assuming that the quality of
light is not fundamentally affected. In the case of a retail store, walk
through a typical customer transaction and see what customers spend
most of their time with.

- Feel what they feel.
- See what they see.
- Hear what they hear.
- Smell what they smell.

Begin with the quality of the door handle, the cleanliness of the glass in
the door, the clean and uncluttered foot path to the counter, and finally
the counter itself, which is, after all, where customers place their hands
and write their check or place their cash or credit card.

And don't forget the restroom.

Minding the Store—Wherever It Is

Good brand environmentalism isn't always a question of minding an *actual* store—it can be any store or point-of-sale location where branded products are sold. Only a few companies have the resources to create their own retail platform; for those that don't, their brands must be aggressively protected through every point of distribution. When Oakley, the manufacturer of high-quality eyewear and thermonuclear protection, discovered that Costco had somehow intercepted a shipment of slightly defective product destined for sale overseas, it sent employees or representatives into every Costco store to buy up every pair and had them promptly destroyed. It is highly likely that Oakley also investigated the process whereby the product got into Costco's hands in the first place.

Is it any wonder that brands like Estée Lauder have endured and developed so strongly? For decades these brands have defined the standard by which in-store brand presentation is controlled. Their relationship with specialty retailers like Nordstrom is legendary.

When Disney found that a European distributor wanted to create a Disney Channel on the Continent that would occasionally feature programs that in the States would be R-rated, Michael Eisner had no hesitation about pulling the plug on the deal.

Brands must chaperone their products all the way down the distribution chain to the end user. But not all brands do this effectively. Why is it that all Ford dealerships essentially look like Chevrolet dealerships which look like Toyota dealerships? Apparently, the automobile industry doesn't care enough about brand differentiation to make it work where it matters most. As a result, consumers step inside large boxes made of tilt-up concrete walls and lots of cheap industrial carpeting. Why, then, do these same companies hold their advertising agencies' feet to the flames and demand campaigns that set them apart from their competitors and "break through the clutter"? (There—I was hoping to write this entire book without saying that, but forgive me, they aren't my words.)

The Rings Around Saturn

In the automobile industry—a vast wasteland of very uninspired brand environmentalism—one domestic brand, Saturn, took a different tack. "When GM first launched its Saturn project in 1985," my friend John Yost, then a principal at the San Francisco boutique agency Hal Riney & Partners, recalled, "we were brought in two years before the first cars came off the line to help to conceptualize and configure an entirely new sort of car and brand experience for GM." At the time—and this was a sign of GM's mounting desperation in the face of the Asian onslaught—GM was even willing to back a project as quirky or threatening to the status quo as Saturn. And it was a further sign of GM's desperation that it was willing to approach Hal Riney & Partners in San Francisco, a famously creative agency, at an early stage in the planning process to help bring the concept to fruition.

"I couldn't help thinking," Yost—who would later help found another innovative creative agency called Black Rocket—remembers with a smile, "about the strong parallels to Russia converting out of the Soviet system. Inside GM there were certain key individuals who played a sort of Gorbachev role, ushering in the new ways of doing things knowing full well that this posed a potential threat to their own power. And then there were powerful senior people who quietly wanted Saturn to fail. Saturn's ultimate success was an indictment of their entire careers, of their traditional ways of doing things."

Business is truly the same all over the world, no matter the prevailing political or social system: the out-of-the-boxers are always fighting the in-the-boxers. Although Yost rightly insists that credit for launching the Saturn cannot be given to any one individual, he praises the then CEO of GM, Roger Smith, with bucking a great deal of criticism to steadfastly support "the one idea he had in desperate response to the failure of the system around him."

Still, the obstacles were numerous and predictable. At one of Yost's first meetings with Saturn's newly appointed sales and marketing team (made up almost entirely of refugees from Saturn's parent company, GM) he was given the results of a $150,000 consumer research study.

On the basis of reams of costly research (by now, you must know how I feel about the value of traditional research) the team presented their two top names for Saturn models: the Aura and the Intrigue. It took all of Yost's sense of tact not to gag or crack up, possibly endangering the entire project. As gently as possible, he and his colleagues at Riney sought to explain that these two names sounded like traditional old GM monikers—"full of hot air and signifying nothing."

"Where is the great brand revolution conveyed in those names?" he asked. This heretical question was met with silence from the group. They hadn't considered such a peculiar perspective. After huddling for a little while, Yost and his colleagues suggested something so simple and straightforward it was truly a breakthrough: "Why don't we call the two cars the Saturn Coupe and the Saturn Sedan. Period. End of story." It was Saturn's simplicity and common sense that were revolutionary. The names of the models should be consistent with that.

The "creative" team from GM was dumbfounded. But Yost and his team stood their ground. "You've been saying no bullshit, no hype, keep it simple," Yost reminded them. Yet even after accepting the names, the old-schoolers couldn't resist "trying to focus-group it up." Fortunately, the research came back overwhelmingly positive.

Remarkably enough, the boys from GM (there weren't many women in this group, Yost recalls) next tried to do the same thing with the design of the supposedly "unique" Saturn showrooms. They hired expensive architects who were given the explicit goal of conceiving of a "definitive design of the future for an automobile showroom." They spent $500,000 to build a model of their out-of-the-box new showroom "concept." After it was completed, they cordially invited the team from Riney to take a look at it and give their reaction. "They didn't want any input for the design," Yost recalls. "It was finalized and all signed off on. We were just supposed to give them the old rubber stamp." The folks from Riney found their courage and came back with the bad news. "It's not warm, it's not inviting, it's not comfortable, it's offputting. It looks like a giant erector set."

To Yost's surprise, this time the GM team weren't defensive about it. They said, "What do you think we should do?"

"How about starting out by bringing in some plants, something alive, if not kicking," came the reply. Of course, as Yost generously points out, "it took guts on their part to bring in the agency at all, particularly so early in the planning process. That in itself was real out-of-the-box thinking within the buttoned-down environment of GM."

Saturn succeeded in breaking the traditional mold of automobile marketing, in which product design and advertising account for 90 percent of the result. At Saturn, thanks in part to the Riney team, *everything* mattered.

How Prestigous Brands Survive Downscale Retail Environments
RALPH LAUREN PAINT

Of course, not every great brand needs a "unique" or even costly brand environment in which to shine. I can well remember the first time I encountered the Ralph Lauren paint brand in a mass-market hardware store. Even though we have already discussed the Lauren brand earlier, it bears revisiting here. For starters, it was certainly the best retail presentation of a paint line that I had ever seen. The catalog had the production qualities of a well-executed annual report. And where most paint companies introduce a new color every five or six years, Lauren was set on introducing new colors every season. The retired painter working in the store that day was ecstatic about the new product line.

But still, you had to wonder: *Why* on earth would Ralph Lauren risk tarnishing or polluting his brand—commonly associated with wealth, privilege, fine fabric, and aristocratic traditions—by placing it one aisle away from toilet plungers and motor oil? I think that one answer lies in Lauren's unique genius in understanding the inner mind-set of the Lauren consumer, who is in fact appreciative and sensitive to issues of authenticity and is not merely a captive of simple snobbery. Lauren could be said to have grasped the essential value of reverse snobbery—that to be associated with the nitty-gritty world of hardware was not really downscale but in fact partook of the nostalgia appeal of the general stores of olden times. In those general stores, clothes and rope and nails and shoes and paint would all be sold together, and nobody considered the mix in the slightest way demeaning.

A further motivation behind Ralph Lauren paint was Ralph's growing dissatisfaction with the conventional paints available to his stylists to color backdrops in advertising or catalog photo shoots. Every season, his new clothing and linens would lean toward a particular color palette. And Lauren is known for his eye for color. By offering paint hues with names like "Candlelight Silver," "Buffalo Creek," "Nantucket Yellow," and "Workshirt Blue," he executed a skilled crossover from his fashion apparel line to an entirely new category: fashion hardware.

MARTHA STEWART HOME

A similar sensibility, a crossover aesthetic that transcends traditional categories of "upscale" and "downscale," pervades the innovative venture launched by Martha Stewart in partnership with Kmart. The canny juxtaposition of the "upscale" Martha Stewart Home line of housewares, linens, and accessories and the retailing everyman Kmart—the marriage of the upscale with the downscale brands—has proved as exciting as it was controversial. Stewart didn't simply flop an item here or there in the store: she approached the project as a coherent brand collection. The retail chain Target is aiming to pull off a similar trick by hiring the postmodern architect Michael Graves to design a line of house-wares from tea kettles to spatulas to carving knives to flatware to pots and pans.

In both cases, two upscale brands succeeded in using what would in con-ventional terms be considered downscale environments to enhance their images, not tarnish it. They did so by transcending the confines of the tra-ditional categories of "discount" and "luxury," and by simultaneously demonstrating that "popular" need not be synonymous with "cheap." Quality is the watchword of both brands, in the hardware store or Kmart as in the most exclusive retail environment. And in both cases the brand stewards are the name brands themselves, Ralph Lauren and Martha Stewart—sensitive individuals who have the savvy and the self-confidence to prove that a "brand-positive" environment can happen in the most unexpected places. They left little to chance as they seized the opportu-nity to convey their brand values across new product categories and markets.

Starbucks' Skunk Works: Reinventing the Coffeehouse

When I joined Starbucks, one of my first projects was to help with a complete redesign of its cafés. To drive the efforts, Starbucks recruited the former Disney creative executive Wright Massey as its new VP for store design. Wright's first request of management was that they create a space within which he and his team might better contemplate the Star-bucks environment of the very near future.

A classic "skunk works" was established on one of the unfinished floors in the Starbucks Support Center building in Seattle's SODO (South of Downtown) district. A motley crew of more than a dozen writers, art directors, graphic artists, and interior designers would call this pretty un-conventional spot home for the better part of two months. I visited Massey on my first day at Starbucks, aware that this would be one of the most important projects for the company. Unfinished doors had been placed on rough wooden sawhorses and were being used for tables. Words and images were drawn onto bare walls, creating a sort of graffiti that helped capture both the brilliant and the bizarre thoughts of the day. (These walls would later provide inspiration for the multilayered murals that you see in many Starbucks cafés today.)

The design initiative had four primary areas of exploration:

1. *Dig* deep within the brand and cut no corner in communicating a respect for the art and science of coffee, as well as what made the Starbucks interpretation of the five-hundred-year-old coffeehouse tradition unique.

2. *Learn* whatever was useful and relevant from the cookie-cutter fast-food restaurants in terms of efficiency, ergonomics, and cost savings while avoiding cookie-cutter design solutions. Because Starbucks was by then opening a store a day, it needed speed and efficiency as well as creativity. Still, we could not afford to be entirely predictable like a McDonald's or a Taco Bell.

3. *Create* a more expansive palette on which Starbucks could draw. The strategy here was to provide a much wider range of design elements that could be applied to meet the needs and requirements of a specific location. A Starbucks on a college campus would have to look and perform differently than a grab-and-go Starbucks on the ground floor of a sixty-story high-rise office building. A catalog of design features—Wright would later call it a "kit of parts"—would one day soon have to work in Topeka as well as Tokyo, in a 5,000-square-foot grand café at Astor Place in New York City and on a tiny latte cart at a summer music festival in Portland, Oregon. Starbucks could no longer take one light fixture, one piece of casework, or one display case and assume that it would work everywhere. That was a fast-food-company approach. Rejecting this solution, however, exposed us to potentially higher costs—a pitfall that made the fourth area especially challenging.

4. *Reduce* store construction costs by at least 25 percent. In the trailing twelve-month period, Starbucks had experienced runaway construction expenses that could, if allowed to continue, break the company financially.

The inherent conflicts in our mandate were both apparent and daunting:

Elevate the brand while cutting costs. Become a master at mass customization. Move like the wind but pay attention to even the smallest of details. Make it appealing to the customer but make it work ergonomically for the employees. Make it so simple to build that a café could be put together virtually anywhere, and in weeks rather than months.

The pace and intensity of the project created difficult moments for many on the team, several of whom quit midstream, buckling under the intense pressure to do the impossible. Every week, another six stores were being built from the old design template—stores that would then have to be retrofitted once the project was completed. But Massey had the drive of a Patton, a trait that proved essential to the project.

To help stimulate Massey's group, we shared with them the initial consumer insights that we had gleaned from our "Big Dig" into the world of coffee. Jerome Conlon, then Starbucks' head of consumer insights and another Nike alumnus, shared my belief in the value of brand mythology—that every brand has a timeless story to tell somewhere deep within it. In the case of Starbucks, we already had an ingredient to work with besides the coffeehouse itself. The Starbucks logo bears the image of a Siren, a mythical being whose song was said to drive sailors mad with desire. The name "Starbucks" came from Herman Melville's *Moby-Dick;* Mr. Starbuck was Captain Ahab's first mate. Nautical themes were clearly an area to be investigated. Even Starbucks' whole-bean coffees were rich in opportunities for storytelling. The coffee-growing countries of Sumatra, Java, Ethiopia, Kenya, and Sulawesi were fertile grounds for imagery.

One of the most fascinating design exercises was with the logo itself, which presented us with a unique opportunity to mine the mythology surrounding the Siren, or "the White Goddess," in poet Robert Graves's terms—the ancient female deity who, in the view of some scholars, predated the classical Greek gods. The goddess angle was another one of Conlon's ideas and he quickly offered it to the design team for inspiration. I suggested that we let the Siren break free of the round Starbucks logo that had kept her contained for so long, and let her have a little fun. Given her storied and seductive nature, I knew that granting her a get-out-of-jail card would be an interesting creative exercise. A week later, six new "Siren" logo extensions had emerged, each with its own name, so that we could identify them for usage in different environments. One of my favorites: "Bad Hair Day Siren." That wasn't one for the coffee mugs, but it was another icon, another character, in the Starbucks brand story.

Eight weeks after they moved into the skunk works, Wright Massey and his team delivered more than enough material to open several thousand new stores. Not only that, they provided a tool kit that would make it possible to quickly remodel existing stores. And by careful design and hardball vendor negotiations, average store costs were cut by 20 percent. The design project was also expanded to include all facets of Starbucks packaging so that everything, including the new products Starbucks would soon be selling through the new grocery channel, would connect back to the brand.

Today, whenever and wherever you intercept the Starbucks brand—on a bag of whole-bean coffee, a pint of coffee ice cream, a bottle of Frappuccino, a bar of chocolate, or an end-aisle display in a grocery store—you will encounter a coherent design vocabulary. Embedded within every new coffee label, every new image wrapped around an insulated coffee tumbler or imprinted on a ceramic mug, lies a special visual and graphic language that will serve Starbucks well for years to come.

The Gap: From Retailer to Brand

Ironically, the Gap, a company destined to beat Levi Strauss at its own game, began as a place to sell Levi's jeans only, in an environment otherwise devoted solely to records and tapes. Over time, the Gap evolved into a Levi's discount house, saving Levi's the toil and trouble of having to dirty its pristine hands with discounting. Only after the Gap had been around for quite a few years was Mickey Drexler (who later became CEO) recruited from Ann Taylor to revamp the chain's image and appeal. Under Drexler, the Gap gradually transformed itself into a brand in its own right, and in time, a global power brand to reckon with. Drexler accomplished this by taking complete control of his own brand imaging and positioning, from determining how the stores looked and how the products would be designed right down to determining what kind of salespeople would work the floor.

The company that had started out selling Levi's jeans ended up leaving Levi Strauss behind. The major decision that allowed this transformation to go forward was Drexler's controversial commitment to cutting himself off from his major supplier: the Levi Strauss Company. A potentially disastrous decision, it proved to be one of the savviest moves Mickey Drexler ever made. As the Gap began to source its products overseas while keeping tight control over the manufacturing and design process, Levi Strauss continued to own and operate its own factories around the world. Levi Strauss clung to the aging "vertical integration" business model in which some companies not only assemble their own products—rare these days—but even sometimes grow their own raw materials on land they own. By the mid-nineties, fixed assets like factories began to look like liabilities to most companies scrambling to find ways to reduce costs in an increasingly competitive global marketplace. By the late nineties Levi Strauss had shut down more than a third of its manufacturing capacity. This occurred not only because the factories employed expensive labor (some factories were located in the United States), but also because the company proved unable to revamp its own facilities as rapidly as an outside contractor could. Any cost for retooling or upgrading was a cost Levi Strauss had to bear completely.

Some who have worked with Drexler have dismissed him as a consummate "control freak," but the desire to control everything is consistent with the concept of brand environmentalism. If Drexler is a control freak, then so are Ralph Lauren, Martha Stewart, Howard Schultz, Steve Jobs, and Michael Eisner. Looks like good company to me. It's a great trait when they are right. Of course, when they are wrong, as happens from time to time in any industry, they can be exceptionally wrong.

Drexler's controlling nature led him to make another momentous and potentially disastrous decision that only a true maverick could have pulled off. He bucked industry wisdom and developed the bulk of his advertising in-house. The Gap may have spent only a fraction of what Levi Strauss did on advertising media in the late eighties and early nineties, but because of its tight control of both in-store and mass-market communication, it developed a single, clear brand voice that became quickly recognizable. It was also quite unlike most apparel advertising.

"I wanted a different vision of advertising," Drexler later recalled in a revealing interview in *Fortune* magazine. "Before, every ad this company placed had been promotional. Every TV ad said, 'Levi's on sale.'" That down-and-dirty approach rankled the more refined sensibilities of Drexler. "I thought that what should drive this business is the top five percent—the people with taste," he explained. "We had to create our own brands and control our product. Good taste is a rare commodity in America. Everything is a concept; no one piece can be separated from any other piece."

Initially Drexler didn't intend to go his own way with advertising. He invited a number of ad agencies to give presentations, but none of them "got it." Like Phil Knight and Howard Schultz, Drexler was far from impressed by what passed for advertising among the traditional agencies. He recruited a former colleague from Ann Taylor, Maggie Gross, to handle all of his work in-house. Gross later recalled that she didn't consider herself an "advertising" person, but rather a "retailer." "We started from the merchandise, not from some great idea for an ad," she observed. "We're in a business where gut reactions are much more important than focus groups."

This same sensibility—and a vision of the ideal evolution of an underutilized brand—was central to the Gap's at the time much-maligned 1983 acquisition of Banana Republic. Many hardened fashion-industry veterans ridiculed this move, because to them Banana Republic could represent nothing more than a hackneyed house whose safari-theme clothing, once briefly in vogue, now seemed absurdly old-fashioned and Indiana Jones–esque by the mid-eighties.

They all laughed when Drexler picked up Banana Republic—where the rhino wall trophies used to leer down at row upon row overstocked with camouflage suits—for a song. But no one was laughing when, by 1995, BR had aggressively remerchandised its entire clothing line and moved boldly into personal-care products, which positively radiated a more refined sensibility, one that was rapidly transforming Banana Republic into a high-end, preppy upscale version of . . . the Gap.

Such a seamless weaving of two separate brands into a symphonic whole was a masterpiece of brand segmentation. It avoided the desperate perils of excessive brand stretch while permitting the Gap to remain casual in contrast to Banana Republic's increasingly "urban" appeal. In time, the launch of Old Navy filled in the gap—so to speak—at the low end, so that the Gap wouldn't be forced to go downscale in order to fend off the inroads being made by Wal-Mart, Sears, JC Penney, and the other fashion discounters.

Where Drexler and his staff truly excelled, setting a high standard of performance throughout a highly competitive industry, was in their ability to gracefully refresh their brands, to keep them from getting stale or tired or dull. The Gap takes great pains to ensure that its look doesn't get dated—heeding the cautionary tale of the first death of Banana Republic—by constantly updating its inventory and image. Banana Republic, for example, has broadened its brandwidth by selling a high-end line of home furnishings.

Simultaneously, part of the reason the Gap has succeeded as well as it has is that for every aggressive fashion statement it makes, it also strives for timelessness, for classicism, and avoids being too trendy or fashionable. This sort of stability provides consumers some degree of comfort in a world otherwise swept by often-disconcerting change. Sure, the Gap is not perfect. It may stumble, but over the years it has done an amazing job of honoring its core brand values of simplicity and affordable style.

Big Blue Gets Cool
Under the leadership of its president, Louis Gerstner, IBM has developed a far more refined brand aesthetic and design sensibility (thanks, I

suspect, to his own marketing background) than it had in the past. Prior to Gerstner, the company had conceived a clumsy campaign for the IBM PC starring a character who resembled Charlie Chaplin. The exploitation of a long-dead slapstick comedian to promote a computer was generally perceived as a lame attempt to personify a brand in dire need of aesthetic refinement—not to mention the infusion of some human personality. The sleek cube called Macintosh, the product of a Steve Jobs–inspired "Manhattan Project" at Apple, had already set a new standard for a product, the computer, that was rapidly becoming a commodity. While the Apple struck most people as "cool," it was also regarded as simultaneously warm and intimate, even personable.

When Lou Gerstner took over IBM, one of his first decisions was to name Ogilvy & Mather as IBM's sole advertising agency. This ended an era in which the brand and aesthetic message of the company had become hopelessly fragmented as a result of several creative shops exerting influence over IBM's once-coherent if stodgy brand image. With its move into the PC end of the business, IBM had to speak to consumers with one clear voice and in a way that it had never had to before as a mainframe operation. No longer were its customers corporate information technology officers. IBM was evolving into a different brand, one that the "average" consumer would be encountering in a computer store and in every advertising medium. Brand schizophrenia could no longer be tolerated.

The trademark and corporate visual-image consulting firm of Lippincott & Margulies began a full-scale makeover of IBM's long-unfocused and out-of-date brand identity. The study conducted by L & M, entitled "The Spirit and Letter of IBM," resulted in the creation of a clear, consistent, and understandable brand identity in customers' minds. L & M wrote in its advisory report that "brand attributes and the way they are expressed must be closely linked. Companies that present a clear, cohesive, distinctive, and relevant brand identity can create a presence in the marketplace, add value to their products and services and may command a price premium." The result was a much-improved image campaign oriented around a tag line that truly made sense for the new Big Blue: "IBM. Solutions for a small planet."

The campaign supported a much more design-influenced line of products, featuring the sleek new ThinkPad notebooks, which rivaled and even topped Apple's best efforts in the rarified realm of taste, concept, and style in the laptop category. The stark matte-black Aptiva desktop was likewise an improvement in its time.

IBM's new corporate image found its way into every aspect of the IBM operation. Even segments of its business that had very little overlap with the consumer side fell into line as one more slightly different but integrated shade of blue. IBM is a complex and diverse company with a quarter million employees spread around the globe and across countless business units, divisions, and departments. Guided by the strong hand of Ogilvy & Mather, and under the leadership of CEO Shelly Lazarus, IBM began to present its diversity in shades of blue. Diversity was good, as long as it was connected in some way to the core brand. If there were such a thing as a brand environmentalism award, I would have given it to IBM around 1997. The company that had at one time become a symbol of all that was wrong with corporate America had within a few short years come to embody all that was right.

Taste Goes Technical at Guinness

Protecting a brand environment is often more than tweaking visuals, especially for foods and beverages. It may mean ensuring that products are consistently presented in a fashion that shows off the brand at its best. The Guinness Brewing Company (now a division of the food-and-beverage giant Diego, the product of the recent megamerger of Guinness and Grand Metropolitan) goes to great lengths to preserve its brand environment by obsessively protecting the distinctive taste of draft Guinness drawn straight from the tap at the pub.

Guinness regularly refers to its popular beverage as "the Blond in the Black Dress," and treats it with abiding respect. So important is it to the company that its signature product be presented in a forthrightly pub-like manner that the company long refused to issue its classic black stout in cans. But by 1994, its in-house Environmental Protection Department (my phrase, not theirs) had produced a clever little widget in the bottom of a can, which explodes when the can is opened. This releases nitrogen gas that simulates the pressure of the draft keg, and lends a can of Guinness stout opened anywhere in the world its trademark creamy head and distinctive "mouth feel." Here is a case in which committed brand environmentalism inspired a full-scale technical innovation.

To ensure that pubs offering Guinness on tap don't let their pipes clog, and that bartenders and publicans don't forget how to properly pour a pint of stout, Guinness employs a global army of "draught specialists" to drive all over the world sampling random pulls of Guinness pints. This is in some respects remarkably similar to the training Starbucks gives its baristas to foster customers' sense of home and belonging anywhere in the world where Starbucks pours its coffee.

As more and more brands go global, serious training in the ways of "brand environmentalism" becomes ever more critical to maintaining and preserving core values. Conflicted presentations destroy brand trust. The pressures of expanding into international markets are unavoidable once a company and its brand grow to a certain size. But the inner feel of a brand, its essence, its tone, its sensibility, is often—like Guinness, like Coke, like Montblanc, like Virgin Atlantic—grounded in a given culture or even region. The abiding challenge is to forge a global entity that respects what is unique about each country it operates in while also respecting the timeless values of the brand that define it.

Raiders of the Lost Lobby at Universal Studios

Several years ago I walked through the lobby of Universal Studios' corporate office in Los Angeles, a square black building near the entrance to the Universal back lot, and was completely dumbstruck. There was an unsettling absence of any of the creativity, style, and storytelling that one would expect from one of the world's largest and most successful entertainment companies. It was an extremely large room with a brace of security guards posted at one end, in charge of the obligatory sign-in sheets on a clipboard. Its high-ceilinged space was more than two thousand square feet of cold, hard, and sterile empty air, a corporate black hole that could easily have been mistaken for the lobby of a very large mortuary, lacking only the bouquets of flowers left over from the last funeral service. Now that I think about it, I can't recall seeing a single plant, either, or a note of music to be heard. There was no life, no vitality, no inspiration, and no attempt to acknowledge what business Universal was in. I thought we had made a wrong turn.

Just a few feet away stood Universal's back lot, the world's largest collection of soundstages filled with right-brained creative spirits. A little farther up the hill was Universal's answer to Disneyland: a theme park with rides, theaters, and hip restaurants complete with guided tours of the Universal facility. It's a good thing the tour did not include the black box that housed the executives, for its message might as well have been "We are big, we are old, we once had money, we have no style, who the hell are you?" Buildings can communicate if you listen hard enough.

Curiously, on another corner of the Universal property were located the corporate offices of Steven Spielberg, Jeffrey Katzenberg, and David Geffen's DreamWorks SKG. Spend two minutes inside the lobby of the studio that Spielberg, Katzenberg, and Geffen put together and you'll see how an entertainment company should present itself. No detail was spared to create an environment that feels more like a hip bed and breakfast in some Southwest paradise than a corporate office. Perhaps it is meant to be reminiscent of what the area looked like a hundred years ago.

The DreamWorks approach seems to be signaling a change on the horizon in corporate America. Companies big and small are beginning to realize the benefits of the increased employee retention, ease of recruitment, and greater creativity and productivity that can result when employees feel appreciated and inspired by the environment around them. Universal has since remodeled its headquarters and even changed the dress code for the corporate office—but only after the brand found itself on the brink of Armageddon.

Corporate Headquarters as Brand Environmentalism

But the real challenge for any company is not simply to create a nice place to work but to seize the opportunity to create an environment that embodies the core values of the brand both explicitly and implicitly. Brand statements should no longer be limited to advertising, annual reports, and employee handbooks. There is no place more important to communicate those values than in front of every employee (or customer) every day.

Scott Wyatt helps lead one of the world's most successful architectural firms, NBBJ, which designs everything from sports stadiums to hospitals to corporate offices. In the case of the corporate office, the value of a well-designed building is enormous, Wyatt, the company's CEO, explains. "A great workplace is like a powerful memo from the CEO to every employee every day that reminds them what business they are in and that they are an important part of that business." Unlike some architectural firms that have a particular "look" which is present no matter what the project, NBBJ designs around the core values of the client, those qualities that set them apart and are integral to everything they do.

"I sometimes think much of what we do is brand architecture," he remarks. From my own experience I agree with that assessment. Wyatt's credentials at NBBJ and at his prior firm include three companies I worked with while they underwent a complete transformation of their corporate offices: Cole & Weber Advertising, Seattle (an Ogilvy affiliate and my first advertising job out of school); Nike's world headquarters;

and the Starbucks Support Center in Seattle. In the case of Nike, Wyatt's team helped to forge a hip, sleek, remarkably calming environment in which the sometimes frenzied passions of the inhabitants can be played out. It is a vast court or field of ideas and decisions that offers an on-site sports pub, a number of gymnasiums, a world-class jogging trail (of course), and roads and buildings named after Nike spokespeople and other sports heroes.

The Nike headquarters also radiates a quiet, Zen-like, "in-the-zone" quality reflective of the early Asian influences of the company (when it was partly Japanese funded) and of the calm that the founder, Phil Knight, believes can be critical to reaching the most difficult decisions.

The Starbucks Support Center in Seattle projects a different vibe; the corporate headquarters is a warm beehive of activity that is the next best thing to a coffeehouse—a hundred times the size of the largest Starbucks café. Gathering places called "neighborhoods" are sited throughout and offer comfortable furniture and soft lighting. And no matter where you are in the Starbucks Support Center, you are never more than a few feet from a state-of-the-art espresso machine.

Final Thoughts on Brand Environmentalism and Retail Business

In the nineties, many brands that had become completely reliant on traditional third-party retailing for the distribution of their products began to get into the direct-retail game themselves while attempting simultaneously to maintain their traditional retail relationships. Some developed a complementary direct-mail catalog business, which in most cases transitioned to include Web-based retailing toward the end of the decade. Others, like Disney and Warner Brothers, took the concept perhaps a little too far. By 2001 both companies had expanded their "showroom" stores to so many markets that they began to lose business from traditional retailers such as department and toy stores. I suspect that by the time Disney opened its five hundredth store most retailers may have concluded that Disney didn't really need them anymore. After a while, the presence of a Disney or Warner Brothers studio store in a shopping mall in Anywhere, U.S.A., had just about as much appeal as a Planet Hollywood restaurant.

Brands that have traditionally relied on third-party retailing—which is most of them—must be careful with company-owned and -operated storefronts. Besides irritating your most profitable revenue base, you can also go broke in your quest to create your brand "theater" in far-flung markets. Perhaps Nike Town offers the example of the right balancing act. With just a handful of locations in North America and a few overseas, Nike has kept the concept fresh and unique, and is obviously not going to replace its traditional retail partnerships anytime soon. What Nike Town did achieve, however, was far more important than any sales the stores have generated. It changed the way 20,000 third-party retailers around the world buy, display, and sell its product.

Manufacturers don't have to create many stores to get one of the greatest benefits of direct retailing: immediate customer insights. With only a few stores, Nike was able to ascertain—for the first time since Phil Knight began selling shoes out of the trunk of his car—immediate feedback as to what sells and what does not. It was able to probe the desirability of items that retailers did not want to carry. What began at Nike Town has now been expanded to include Nike.com, where the company can present low-volume "probe" product concepts or limited-edition items. This enables the company to experiment with products without having to build tens of thousands of pairs to fill the retail pipe for a large retail customer. Anything can be explored. And as the trend toward mass customization continues, platforms such as these will be invaluable to large companies hoping to create a wider array of unique, low-volume products.

Gain clarity of purpose before you elect to step into retail on-line or off-line. Are you going to completely replace your present distribution net, or try to affect the way others retail your product by demonstrating a new approach, like Nike Town? Or is it for the sake of customer feedback? Or is it to sell slow-moving, discontinued, or blemished products that are creating problems for your best accounts? For many manufacturers, outlet stores have represented the first step toward a direct-retail business. Whatever you do, be clear in your objective.

One final note. The moment you open your first retail "branded" store, whether a brand showroom or an outlet store, cut no corners in hiring and training store personnel. Anything that happens in those stores is a direct reflection on your brand. There is no middleman to blame. Your store employees are brand ambassadors to the public and for many, if not all, of your customers, the only employees of your company they will ever meet in person. As computer manufacturers such as

Gateway and Apple enter the retail market, I suggest they follow in the footsteps of Starbucks in its early years. It's not just about the product. It's about what happens around the product. How are all the senses of the customer engaged? How clean is your restroom? When you create a three-dimensional home for your brand it is a direct handshake with your customers. Remember that nothing is trivial or insignificant, and that nothing can be ignored.

brand leadership

Brand Principle #6
All brands need good parents.

Brand Parenting in Silicon Valley

In the spring of 2000, just as the bottom had begun to fall out from under the tech sector, I spoke at a conference sponsored by a prominent Silicon Valley venture capital firm, the Barksdale Group. Jim Barksdale, the firm's famous founder, had left a flourishing career at Federal Express in the early nineties to join Netscape. By most accounts, this early Internet browser company was among the businesses that were instrumental in ushering in the IPO madness in the summer of 1995 that continued pretty much unabated—and without a great deal of logic—for nearly five years. The irony did not escape me that just as the first downward turn in the stock market's "irrational exuberance" (as Alan Greenspan so memorably described it) was starting to be felt, I would be standing before a room full of people who had put the high-flying high-tech ball into motion in the first place. Now that it was showing signs of slowing down, they were suddenly looking beyond the strictly technological realm for answers to a whole host of problems.

In the audience were representatives of a number of start-ups that the Barksdale Group had helped to fund, and for which, even at that late date, it still had high hopes. I had been invited to impart whatever wisdom I might have to offer these emerging business leaders on the suddenly popular subject of "digital branding." The entrepreneurial outfits represented that afternoon ran the gamut of industries, business models, trajectories, missions, and challenges. Some were freshly minted; others on the brink of an IPO; a few had recently gone public. The one thing that all of them had in common was that they wanted to grow into great brands, and they were looking to me for guidance to that end.

It was easy to see from the determined faces in the room that everyone present was under enormous pressure to deliver—yesterday, if not sooner. There was no kidding around here, no idle chitchat. The ominous phrase "near-term profitability" had made its belated debut in the Internet business lexicon just a few weeks earlier. At the close of my pitch—which you won't be surprised to hear was not unconnected to the basic concepts I've discussed in this book—I could sense that I had given them advice that would require a bit more effort on their part than they had expected. I could hardly blame them for their anxiety. Everyone in business looks for short cuts; it's only human nature. In the Internet sector, the problem was even more acute. This group, no different from any other gathering of New Economy visionaries in Palo Alto that day, didn't even have time for short cuts. Hours were like weeks in their hyperaccelerated world of business.

But I was not there to deliver what they wanted to hear, and instead laid out the unvarnished truth as I saw it. I told them that what they were now facing was no different from what parents face with a newborn child. Though many in the room were obviously too young to have families, I decided to stick with the analogy anyway. "It takes years, sometimes decades, to build a great brand," I stressed. "You have to protect it, nurture it, instill positive and enduring values within it in the hopes that it will be productive, desirable, and welcome wherever it goes."

I went on to tell them that if they did their jobs right, their brands would one day make them proud, as I was of Nike and Starbucks—children with a lot of parents, but in whose upbringing I had certainly played a nurturing role. I chose not to go down the path of explaining what happens when brand parenting fails. Death in the dot-com world had already become a lot swifter and more jarring than in the not-dot-com world. This group didn't need visual aids to see potential disaster looming around the corner.

When I finished, Mike Homer, the former marketing chief for Netscape, spoke up from the back of the room. In an industry barely five years old, Homer was something of a legend—a young, eccentric, and battle-scarred one. "That's a neat analogy, that parenting thing," Homer observed dryly. "At Netscape, I saw my child born [Netscape's IPO], sent off to war [with Microsoft], and then sold into slavery [acquired by AOL] all in less than five years. That was loads of fun."

The room fell silent. Many pure Internet plays, particularly in the B-to-C (business-to-consumer) space, had mistakenly believed that great brands could be created in a matter of months, given enough funding, high-IQ people, and marketing funds. Most of these would-be brands had emerged as shallow, undeveloped, noisy creations, prematurely thrust onto the stage like three-year-olds in business suits interviewing for top jobs at *Fortune* 100 companies. Unfortunately for them (and their investors), brand building requires more than television advertising, "viral" marketing, banner ads, or e-mail campaigns. It takes far more than a war chest of venture capital, a fat Rolodex, or a heady infusion of public funds. Great brands take steady guidance, the long view, uncompromising values, and products or services that are relevant, compelling, and profitable—and time. And as demonstrated in the previous chapters, great brands also need to define themselves in terms that transcend the product or service and resonate with consumers on a more personal and emotional level. Great brands leverage something that is inescapable for any company: its own human qualities, which are an outgrowth of the people who drive the company.

Once More, with Feeling

Brands are imperfect and forever flawed concepts because they are ultimately and inescapably human creations. It is people who bring brands to life, people who reinvent them, people who manage them, and people who sustain them. And it is people who drive brands into confusion, chaos, or worse. This chapter is about the human side of branding, about the positive and negative influences that people have—intentionally or unintentionally—on their brands, just as parents do on children. Whether it is the CEO, the marketing chief, the ad agency, the board of directors, or the most recently hired entry-level employee, people shape the company and the core values of the brand. Their values *are* its values, no matter what the corporate mission statement says. As such, a brand is only as strong as the weakest personal point within an organization.

As brands evolve over time, they absorb the environment and karma of an organization, not unlike the way children are influenced by the place they call home. Both brands and small children thrive in an inspiring, learning, caring environment where they are appreciated, respected, protected, and understood. Small children are influenced by the values and behaviors of their parents as well as by those of their friends. It is no different with brands, which reflect the company they keep and the values to which their company subscribes.

Organizations must instill values and behaviors that are not only positive but also consistent, that enable the brand to endure economic hardships, unpredictable consumer trends, and shape-shifting organizations. No matter how many employees come and go, the brand and its values should remain one of the constants in any organization. How well the brand survives management turnover is directly related to how effectively the core brand values have been seeded, integrated, and passed on throughout the company.

One of the greatest problems affecting brands today is the high turnover in brand-sensitive positions. Too many short-term brand "parents" can create a troubled child. There is no history, no acquired learning over time, and mistakes are repeated needlessly. It takes time for anyone in any company, in any position, to completely understand their brand. Companies would do well to minimize turnover in CEOs, marketing directors, advertising directors, research directors, and chief product designers.

Another affliction worth mentioning is the problem of too many brand parents. Imagine a child raised by twenty different people with conflicting values, backgrounds, skills, and agendas. Some brands have multiple product or marketing chiefs with little or no leadership at the brand level. In these companies the brand is a ward of the corporate state. No one is deeply connected to it and few assume any real responsibility for it. It is defined by its parts, and never its whole. Marketing funds are allocated to separate product or business unit silos, each with their own interpretation of what the brand is and how it should be presented. Companies that are organized this way often have several advertising agencies, each with a "piece" of the brand. Besides the obvious lack of synergy, companies that are organized this way usually end up schizophrenic and conflicted. Customers see different values, different personalities, and different styles within the same brand. It is especially hard to build trust with such a company. Remember how great brands take each product and division of the company as chapters in a larger brand story?

In light of all this, it becomes only reasonable to ask:

Who is *your* brand picking up around the office?

Where is the brand leadership?

Who is accountable for ensuring that the brand has one voice and one set of values?

Front-Line Employees as Brand Leaders

Great brands have leadership at the top and in the trenches. It is everyone's job. But some brands, in particular retailers and service companies, are especially dependent on the front-line employees who come face-to-face with the customer. In companies like these, dedicated employees engender brand trust and foster brand loyalty better than any marketing program, whereas bad employees can easily undermine a brand that took years or even decades to build. Retailers worry constantly about this, as well they should.

Howard Schultz knew that store-level employees would have a crucial impact on shaping his brand when he took control of Starbucks—all five stores and a handful of employees—in 1987. Part of Schultz's vision was to procure, roast, and prepare by hand the best coffees from around the world. But Schultz also set out to create a company that respected its employees by offering full medical benefits for part-time employees and stock ownership for everyone in the company, no matter how many hours they worked. Potential investors told him that he was crazy, that he was creating unnecessary and costly overhead. But Schultz pressed ahead, unfazed by the naysayers, and convinced that employees who felt respected would develop customers who felt the same way. Schultz was as intently focused on creating the best employee training program anywhere (described in chapter 5) for the same reason. Between creating a top-notch benefits package and a first-rate employee training program, Schultz felt sure he would be able to attract and retain the highest-quality people. He was right. During the most critical growth period for Starbucks, in the mid- to late nineties, Starbucks had the lowest turnover rate of any restaurant or fast-food company in the world.

It became apparent to all of us on the Starbucks management team that what was most important to Starbucks was not actually in the cup, as great as it was. The most significant element was the person holding it—as it passed from the employee who procured and roasted the coffee beans, to the employee who prepared the beverage, to the customer who walked out the door with it.

Schultz's vision of a company that was a rewarding place for both employees and customers was not the product of some management conference or business book. He took his inspiration from his determination not to repeat the poor treatment his own father had received from employers who did not provide benefits or reward hard work. To any would-be brand steward I highly recommend Schultz's own book, *Pour Your Heart into It*. In the book, you will learn in detail just how his personal values provided the foundation for the Starbucks brand.

Brand Leadership Within the Giant Hairball

Perhaps the greatest brand challenge for the successful company like Starbucks is the growth of a large bureaucratic organization, called by some the "corporate hairball." This "hairball" concept was coined by the late Gordon McKenzie in his *Orbiting the Giant Hairball,* a quick, colorful, and comical read that illuminates the dilemma many large companies face when balancing the need for unbridled innovation with the need for process and conformity.

In his magnificent mini-opus on the perils of business bureaucracy, McKenzie chronicles his experiences as a creative guru for Hallmark Cards, a huge corporation in America's heartland. During his thirty-year career, McKenzie saw the company grow into a large, sometimes dysfunctional mass. As an artist, he rebelled against the pressure for conformity and the introduction of the kinds of cookie-cutter management processes that seemed inescapable for a company that size.

But McKenzie's real problem lay in his own success. He had done so well at Hallmark that he was promoted into management and away from his real passion, developing cards and working with creative people. Before long, he became depressed and tried to quit. Rather than accept his resignation, though, his boss gave him the chance to create his own position. McKenzie seized the opportunity and established a role in which he and other professionals in his position at Hallmark could "orbit" the organizational hairball as needed. His new job—his official title was "creative paradox"—allowed him to overcome what he saw as one of the primary failures of hairball culture, which he describes in the following passage from his book:

> With the increase in the Hairball's mass comes a corresponding increase in the Hairball's gravity. There is such a thing as Corporate Gravity. As in the world of physics, so too in the corporate world: *The gravitational pull a body exerts increases as the mass of that body increases*. And, like physical gravity, it is the nature of Corporate Gravity to suck everything into the mass—in this case into the mass of Corporate Normalcy.
>
> The trouble with this is that Corporate Normalcy derives from and is dedicated to past realities and past successes. There is no room in the Hairball of Corporate Normalcy for original thinking or primary creativity. Resynthesizing *past* successes is the habit of the Hairball.

For the reasons that McKenzie so aptly illuminated, hairballs, I humbly submit, are as bad for brands as they are for cats. Unchecked hairballs drain the passion right out of the people who create, nurture, and grow the brand. Of course, hairballs don't seem to bother everyone. Some people actually find them comforting, for they are often as predictable as they are safe. (These are not the kind of people who pack everything up and start their own business or join a start-up.)

A central theme of McKenzie's is the ways in which traditional business structures and processes have been designed to mitigate risks and discourage diverse thinking. In his view, creativity is often purged right out of the institution, much the way most schools educate the imagination right out of children by the time they turn ten, by which point they see everything in terms of black and white, right or wrong. Unfortunately, creative talent thrives in the subjective middle. Conformity to conventional thinking and regimented process comes at the expense of unbridled innovation and a healthy passion for change.

Most organizational hairballs are the result of a constricting command-and-control school of management, which was described by Monsanto's chairman, Robert Shapiro, in his fine foreword to *Flash of Brilliance* by Warren C. Miller.

> Everything about the traditional corporation—from the design of its offices to the volumes that described its procedures—delivered a single, overpowering message: "The company is very big, and you are very small—follow orders and you won't get hurt!"

No wonder words like "management" and "administration" described what people at the top of the standard hierarchy were supposed to do.

No wonder that "control" was the watchword—because deviation from established processes posed dangers, not opportunities. No wonder that the way for people to succeed was to imitate and please their seniors.

No wonder that information was hoarded, and controlled, as the currency of power. . . . Centralization of information, authority, and control is rapidly becoming a suicidal practice. As is a control-oriented culture. As is uniformity and conformity in senior management ranks.

The increasingly frequent calls for businesses to depart from past process is another indication that the traditional organizational structure may not be suitable for the future. Whether they affect public or private organizations, hairballs inevitably replace intimacy, spirit, creativity, transformational thinking, and speed to market with anonymity, politics, analysis paralysis, incrementalism, and a slothlike pace that borders on glacial. They also make it difficult for one distinct, compelling, and consistent brand personality to take shape and survive. For all the above reasons, large organizations present a unique set of challenges to those that must shape and protect brands. In the large company, brand leadership and alignment must be present from top to bottom. The chief executive must lead the brand by example, and every member of the organization must walk the brand talk. It becomes the main job of the CEO or CBO (chief brand officer) to resolve the inevitable contradictions in brand positioning that happen in the large, diverse organization.

The Inevitable Yin and Yang of Branding

After many years of doing service in the working world, you're by now familiar with the players. There are two forces at work in every business. One force is dominated by hyperlogical, spreadsheet-packing process freaks; the other, by intuitive, often unpredictable, free spirits. This is nothing more than the left-brain (logic) versus right-brain (intuition) battle that has raged ever since humans first organized to hunt down the first woolly mammoth. The fact that God designed the human brain this way, creating two different lobes and infinite variations of balance between them, is proof that at least He or She has a half-decent sense of humor.

The conflict between the left and the right brains will last for as long as humans walk the planet and pundits argue about the return on investment for a Super Bowl commercial. There will always be those with an overdeveloped left cranial sphere, who prefer the concrete, tried, and trusted; and there will always be those who prefer to view the world in a more emotive, less tangible, context, who are driven by the more imaginative right side of the cranial sphere. Consider the metaphors that illustrate this dichotomy:

LEFT BRAIN	RIGHT BRAIN
Linear—yin	Creative—yang
Dark	Light
Tangible	Abstract
Logical	Intuitive
Incremental	Transformational
Rigid	Random
Process Theory	Chaos Theory
Mathematics	Art
Function	Form
Control	Influence
Vanilla	Jamocha Almond Fudge Swirl
Microsoft	Apple

Why is this division so important within a business context? Because the balance of left- and right-brain thinking within your organization will profoundly influence its nature and hence what kind of brand it builds. Few humans are exclusively 100 percent left- or right-brained, although we have all met a few who we suspected came close. Being "full tilt" one way or the other would doom you to the life of either an absolute geek or a wacko artiste. Organizations that have well-defined separate "lobes" need talented interpreters, which is why consultants like me—experienced cranial surfers who are not politically aligned to either camp—are in such demand.

Personally, I'm more comfortable in a room full of writers, architects, and art directors than I am when surrounded by number crunchers. In my experience, gifted creative people make connections between disparate concepts faster than anyone else. They're able to think on different levels simultaneously, sometimes taking wild tangents on a moment's notice, which is inherently entertaining. Unfortunately, they are equally prone to throwing tantrums and spending all your money to try out a never-ending stream of ideas.

Linear geniuses, on the other hand, can fix on one issue, one project, or one process and stay on it as long as it takes to get all the tangible and quantifiable evidence needed to make an informed decision. Where the creative person is most comfortable making a decision purely on gut or intuition, the linear talents must use their heads in the logical pursuit of more supportive data.

> *This is why, in any worthwhile organization, both left- and right-brain thinking must not only coexist, but enrich each other in order to achieve balanced and enduring brand excellence.*
>
> *Friction between the camps is inevitable and important. But that friction needs to be productive. Achieving this requires a culture that respects all talents and is able to build bridges across functions. In my experience this happens most often when the CEO has experience in both camps. It is a little-known fact that Phil Knight, one of the most insightful and creative chief executives I have ever known, taught accounting before starting Nike.*

Left to their own devices, the linear yin and the creative yang are unable to sustain themselves. Too much creative exploration without solid financial processes can destroy a company. And a company with the world's greatest financial wizards will eventually fail without the creative inspiration needed to continually reinvent itself. No one can stand still anymore. Equally important, change just for the sake of change can also be dangerous. Thus, both approaches are dependent upon each other for survival. This centuries-old explanation of the relationship between two spheres is described in *The Encyclopedia of Eastern Philosophy and Religion* (Shambhala, 1994).

> The Great One produced the two poles, which in turn give rise to the energies of the dark and the light. These two energies then transform themselves, one rising upwards and the other descending downwards; they merge again and give rise to forms. They separate and merge again. When they are separate, they merge; when they are merged, they separate. That is the never-ending course of Heaven and Earth. Each end is followed by a beginning.

In business, an exquisite balance must be struck between yin and yang; one must not be allowed to become dominant. No brand ever achieves perfect balance, but brands that overemphasize one side of the brain to the detriment of the other inevitably derail.

Apple Computer's decline-and-fall-and-rise-again saga in the 1990s presents a near-perfect picture of how a once-great brand nearly self-destructed because it fell prey to an acute imbalance of the forces of yin and yang. The whole disaster was set in motion when the historically right-brained culture of the company (embodied by Steve Jobs and Steve Wozniak) was overrun by an infusion of left-brained traditional marketers led by John Sculley, who had previously held a high position at PepsiCo. Sculley and his coterie were brought in by Apple's board of directors with the specific mandate of teaching the irreverent adolescent brand how to behave like a grown-up and become a more efficient company. In truth, under "the two Steves" the company had undoubtedly become lopsided in favor of right-brain thinking (intuitive), to the detriment of Apple's bottom line. But in a desperate attempt to redress the balance, the new regime shifted the company too far to the left and stifled the creative culture that had resided at the heart of the company. While moving to cut costs and seeking to impose discipline on what had been an increasingly dysfunctional organization, they ended up smothering the creativity that had made Apple Apple.

Steve Jobs's masterpiece up to that point had been the Mac—but after Jobs's irate departure and Sculley's accession to the throne, no successor to the Mac was launched. The Mac was simply improved and refined, incrementally over time—the spirit of revolution that had motivated the creative forces at the company was overwhelmed by a gray-flannel ethos. As a result, the company foundered under Sculley as it had in the last days of Jobs, but for different reasons. First was an excess of creativity and lack of discipline. Sculley cracked the whip and made the trains run on time, but he cut off the rich air that creativity needs in order to breathe. By the time Steve Jobs returned in the late nineties, there wasn't much Apple left—just a near corpse in grievous need of resuscitation. Once back in control, Jobs reconnected Apple with its boldly creative values. The results were almost immediately made available to consumers: the candy-colored iMac, the sleek G4, large flat panel screens, and the Titanium PowerBook. All combined radical styling and flash with technological innovation, the very values that Apple had exemplified until Jobs's departure. And to be fair to John Sculley and to Apple's board of directors, in the interim Steve Jobs had matured. He returned as a more seasoned—and reasoned—leader.

Herding Cats

If it is ultimately the people in a company who shape brands, it makes sense to ensure that they are motivated, happy, and supported by whatever means necessary so that they can accomplish great things. This is especially true in the creative areas of business, where concepts must be created from thin air and often under intense pressure. It is easy to break concepts down and see how they work. It is a far more difficult task to invent entirely new ones, drawing novel connections between disparate ideas.

I believe that the fundamental personnel challenge facing big companies today is that there are very few good cat herders available. In my experience, managing creative people is a tricky task, roughly akin to herding cats. I can't claim to be the first to employ this abused analogy, but I find it a particularly valid one.

I first confronted the task of managing creative people as a young agency account executive. Like anyone in my position, I had become quite proficient at my client's business. I knew it upside down and inside out and back to front. I had researched everything in sight, and spent countless hours working on marketing plans and mapping out essential growth strategies. Despite my efforts, however, the client, the newly hired president of the Washington Apple Commission, one of the world's largest produce commodity brands, wasn't pleased. He wanted more input into our creative process.

One day, out of the blue, he announced that he thought that there should be a new tag line for his brand. Not only that but he had just stumbled upon a perfect replacement himself. Actually, the new tag line had sought him out while he was sitting in the Seattle Kingdome at a Seahawks football game. He happened to notice the name of an apparel company on the exposed tag of a T-shirt draped on the broad back of some beer-guzzling guy wearing blue and green face paint sitting in front of him. He thought the name was "kinda catchy" and strongly suggested that we present it at the next board meeting as the foundation for a new advertising campaign.

Not having anything better to offer at that precise moment, we told him that we wanted to think it over. Once he left the office, a mixture of panic and resentment set in. Clients are not supposed to come up with brand positioning lines. It was all hands on deck for the next two weeks.

If we couldn't come up with something better, we would find ourselves in the humiliating position of having taken inspiration from a T-shirt.

After one week had passed our creative team had nothing significant to show for its efforts. We began having brainstorming sessions after work with pizza and beer. With two days to go, we were still stuck. Then, the very next morning, I had one of those ideas that can only happen in the shower, somewhere between the shampoo and conditioner. I had the perfect positioning line, and I could now save the agency from certain ruin.

At a few minutes after 8 A.M. I burst into the office of Michele Stone-braker, the creative director working on the account. We had always respected each other, and I thought she would welcome some help in this late hour on her most important account. She had barely taken the first sip from her tea, however, when I violated the first rule of herding cats: I made a very direct creative suggestion.

"Well, I've got it," I blurted out.

"Oh?" she responded politely, stirring her tea. Then she squinted a little, and smiled pleasantly as she prepared to watch me make a total fool of myself. She obviously had been here before. "So what have you got?"

"The tag line," I replied smugly.

God be my judge; to this day I cannot remember what the line was, but I proceeded to tell her how my idea could work across different campaign elements, and how I was certain the client would like it, and how it—

She threw me out of her office. Actually, she took hold of my shirt-sleeve, escorted me to her doorway, and said something like, "Thank you very much." And that was that.

Later that morning I related the story to my boss, Clark Kokich, who immediately laughed. "You've got a few things to learn about creative people," he told me, twiddling the cord to his office blinds, something he liked to do as he stood staring out the window while one of his protégés sat at his conference table, absorbing his wisdom. "Don't take this wrong, but creative people are a lot like sheep," he said. (Obviously, this was in the days before the cat metaphor became the dominant one.) "Your job is to get them to the gate but you can't force them. You need to nudge them a little. Ever see a sheepdog work?" As he asked this he began to stretch out his arms and swivel his upper body from left to right and then back again, looking more like a beginning skier navigating a series of turns than a sheepdog in action. "You have to give them little bits of information one piece at a time, in the general direction toward where they should be going," he continued. Then, bringing his arms closer together with his hands almost touching, he added, "Eventually, they discover the open gate for themselves. And then they've got it!" he cried out exultantly. "And now," his voice lowered, "your job is done and you have to get the fuck out of the way."

At this point he turned and grinned at me. "And one other thing," he said. "Don't ever take credit for anything you do. Creative people don't work for money, like we do. They work for *recognition*."

As it turned out, the agency came up with a great line for the client, "The Original Health Food," and developed a print campaign that received some of the highest marketing and advertising awards in the country. By the time I joined Nike, I was pretty good at herding cats. In my very first meeting with Nike's agency's founder, Dan Wieden, I noticed a large piece of white paper with enlarged black type pinned to his wall. It simply read:

> *CREATIVITY*
> *CAN NEVER BE*
> *ORGANIZED.*

It troubled me at first, though I didn't mention it to Wieden. Then in my head I added a few words that made all the difference for everyone involved in our collaboration over the ensuing seven years.

> *AT LEAST IT*
> *SHOULDN'T*
> **FEEL** *ORGANIZED.*

The Value of Loose Briefs

One of the barriers preventing organizations from reaching their highest creative potential and instilling innovation within their brands is the way in which the creative staff—be they product designers, copywriters, architects, or consultants—are briefed and assigned work. Briefs are used throughout business, from law offices to the halls of global corporations to research labs. And for the most part, they are usually bad. Often the briefs are too tight, mired with executional details and loads of "success factors," "hurdle rates," "action plans," and the like. In effect, they can become tourniquets stanching the flow of creative ideas within your business unit. If your briefs don't allow for movement or some latitude you'll eventually go numb.

A great creative brief has three attributes. It is . . .

1. *Concise*—No more than two pages, one if you're really good.

2. *Tight*—Containing two separate focused statements, of where the business (or category) and the brand are today and where they must be tomorrow in order to achieve success.

3. *Loose*—Let them figure out how to get there.

If the last two attributes sound like a contradiction in terms, read on. A good brief *tightly* defines the particular situation (opportunity, threat, new product concept, current brand image, etc.) as well as the desired *outcome*. But a good brief should also be loose in the sense that it leaves most of the executional details up to the people who are actually doing the executing.

Most companies would do well to spend more time visualizing the desired outcome of a marketing plan or campaign and not to burden the creative team with a hundred creative suggestions that are invariably executional in nature and, as a result, confining. Recognizing that some of the greatest ideas exceed traditional budgetary thinking—one of the most confining aspects of any brief—you should be open to "wild card" ideas that exceed the brief in some way, so long as the team also delivers concepts that address the task in the brief.

Roughly 20 percent of Nike's best advertising was not what was expected from the agency. Some of the very best ideas, while recognizing the specific task at hand—be it a new product or category—also connected it to a timeless and powerful brand value that resonated more deeply with customers than any single product ever could. Other times the creative concept supported the product task but leveraged it as a means to strengthen an aspect of the brand that we knew from our brand insights to be weak.

Companies and their creative agencies must never lose sight of the brand as they go about their tasks. It should always be present. Nike did not see the marketing process as either product- or brand-focused, though clearly there were some venues like the Super Bowl that pushed us to think as broadly about the brand as possible, given the audience. Many companies break marketing budgets into two neat buckets, brand

and product, and inevitably leave few resources to do anything for the brand after all the product assignments have been met. This attempt to establish some sort of division between brand and product doesn't work. It's not the way customers look at products. They don't separate the brand from the product. If anything, the brand looms larger than the product in the purchase decision. Think Coke.

Great brands weave themselves into everything they do, no matter how small, no matter how targeted it may be. But achieving this is a lot easier if the briefing process allows the latitude needed to connect something new with something timeless like the brand itself. *If the job is done right, creative resources won't feel constrained by the briefing process, but instead will be motivated by it to think more broadly and in ways that a client simply cannot.* Too often we strive to only *inform* when what we should really do is *inspire*. Write a brief that *you* would like to receive if the tables were turned. Demonstrate confidence and enthusiasm for the project. Think big and don't meddle.

The Changing Role of Marketing in Brand Stewardship

The premise that brand building and brand stewardship is basically a creative project directed by humans who have human strengths and failings raises the obvious question: Who, finally, is *most* responsible for the brand? On one level, brand building is everyone's job. But on a deeper level, someone must take responsibility for sweating the really tough brand decisions every day, for seeing to it that the brand is viewed in its entirety and not just as some division or aspect or function of it.

Once upon a time, for better or for worse, the marketing department fulfilled this function, and its leadership went unquestioned. But today, "marketing" can involve a wide range of functions, depending on the organization. In some companies it includes product design, research, and development. In others it is limited to advertising, point-of-sale, and retail marketing programs such as cooperative advertising. Some companies place PR within the marketing department. Others assign all brand controls to marketing, while still others create a unique strategic planning executive, who works closely with the CEO or chairman. Some companies centralize marketing as one function; others decentralize it by business unit, by product category, by retail channel, or by consumer type (men versus women, for example).

The rise of on-line business has led to some even more complex configurations. Often three different departments are assigned to develop Internet strategies: Marketing handles the corporate Web site; Sales, Direct Response, or Supply Chain Operations creates the e-commerce platform; and Management Information Systems handles all networking solutions that use the Internet, hosts the recruitment aspect of the corporate site, and installs the intranet. In other companies, the marketing people aren't even allowed in the same room as the IT or MIS department. Still others let Marketing run everything.

Marketing, I submit from the above evidence, is too often a mess. And as a consequence, most brands are as well. No matter how marketing ends up being positioned within a company, this much is certain: there is a critical need for definitional clarity regarding its role. The best definition I've ever heard of marketing is this one:

> **Marketing is the process by which resources are brought to bear against opportunities and threats.**

As a former chief marketing officer, I would like to propose that we all agree that marketing should be considered, first and foremost, a *catalyst for action*. A marketing department should be a fast-moving, responsive organization that can execute a thousand details flawlessly and quickly. It should also provide the grease in the wheel that helps things go round, to maintain forward momentum on all fronts, while ensuring that the initial objective remains in focus.

The longest window for any marketing plan should be twelve to eighteen months. Traditionally, marketing plans have had twelve-month windows, but few of them end the year looking anything like the plan that was initially prepared. Product development may have a significantly longer window, as is the case in the automobile industry, or shorter, as with software. Given the unpredictability of most markets, I suggest that 75 percent of what a marketing team does should be planned. The remainder should be brought into play in response to market shifts, or the emergence of a new opportunity or challenge, when the best-laid plans just don't apply anymore. Companies that don't anticipate such events end up executing ineffective plans, because that is all they planned for. Great marketers plan for the unexpected.

Make Someone Accountable for Brand Synergy

Everything you do with your brand—every piece of paper, every ad, every press release, every product, even the music that callers hear when placed on hold—must connect consistently to your brand values. For some companies, especially highly decentralized ones, creating and managing such connective tissue can be an enormous challenge because no one person is charged with brand unification; no one is minding the store. Brand cohesion does not happen by serendipity. It needs to be engineered. During its halcyon years, Nike had only one advertising department and one design center. Every product, every piece of packaging, every hangtag, every annual report, came through Nike Design. It also used a single agency to drive the core of its advertising program around the world. That may not sound terribly unique, but the fact that it was a small twenty-three-person shop in Portland, Oregon, when the "Just Do It" campaign was conceived is a bit unusual. In the years that followed, the Wieden & Kennedy agency grew to become one of the world's most successful. For Nike, it meant we had a great brand partnership that would enable us to develop a consistent brand voice everywhere we went. It wasn't without its problems, but the brand alignment it delivered was well worth the pain.

The Role of the CEO in Brand Development

In the halcyon days of "brand management" in the 1950s and '60s, most companies had a pretty clear idea of what business they were in, how their products and services would be created and distributed, and how profits would be realized and allocated. The development cycles for products, technologies, and brands were often measured in decades, not the months or weeks we sometimes see today. Thanks to a booming population and what appeared to be an endless supply of new markets opening up overseas, a never-ending supply of new consumers allowed companies to make mistakes with their brands and still survive. The job of communicating with consumers was also a straightforward affair. For most companies, the chief brand steward was the CEO, who had a direct relationship with the advertising agency, usually at the CEO level, and took a keen interest in all facets of marketing. Most CEOs, particularly in the service and packaged-goods industries, came up through the marketing ranks.

Today, the average CEO in every industry runs a more complex operation than his or her predecessors. Most large companies have become global. Many are expanding into new product categories every year, either on their own or through an acquisition. Unlike their predecessors, many of today's CEOs rose through the ranks of finance, operations, or production or logistical functions. With that background, they often lack the instincts and experience to understand the slippery gray area of image, positioning, and brand soul.

Compounding the problem is the phenomenon described above of placing the bulk of brand control within marketing functions that are rapidly becoming decentralized or are being forced down into middle management layers. This may place certain processes closer to the end user, but it also tends to eclipse the broader brand view needed to discern the interrelationships between business, market, or consumer segments as well as potential conflicts in positioning that could undermine brand trust. In response, more and more companies are searching for a solution that allows for the decentralization of marketing resources and at the same time respects the limited cycles available from the CEO.

The Chief Brand Officer

A new position has emerged in business that can strengthen the company-wide brand-development process. I call this position the chief brand officer (CBO), and it is one that a few companies have already created. The precise responsibilities of this job differ from business to business, but here are the principal duties of this manager:

THE CHIEF BRAND OFFICER REPORTS DIRECTLY TO GOD.
If not God, at least the next best thing: the CEO. The brand is often the most important asset of the organization. Since it knows no boundaries, don't put it in a silo somewhere three levels away from the person calling all the really difficult shots.

THE CBO IS AN OMNIPRESENT CONSCIENCE.
The chief brand officer has a pretty straightforward job: to champion and protect the brand—the way it looks and feels—both inside and out-

side the company. This is not a brand identity cop armed with corporate design guidelines. This person is responsible for brand integrity and must be an integral part of key brand-development decisions wherever they occur. Anything that can profoundly affect brand integrity—for example, a joint promotion with another company, a major advertising campaign or public relations thrust, or the decision to create sub-brands—should be within the purview of this person. Even aggressive pricing and profit-improvement initiatives should not be developed without the CBO's involvement.

As I have said countless times already, the brand is the sum total of everything a company does. But as companies become more complex and fragmented, it is virtually impossible for the ultimate brand champion, the CEO, to be part of so many processes. Think of the CBO as a brand conscience who is accountable to the highest echelons of the company but woven into the fabric of the larger organization as a brand guide. This person is not responsible for the financial integrity of the business— the profit-and-loss centers should still reside within individual divisions—but instead is responsible for brand integrity. One measure of this person's success is the degree to which the employees of an organization understand the brand and its values. It is the CBO's job to create brand disciples across the organization. The brand should be important to everyone in the company, but over and above that, it must be incredibly sacred to the CBO. This person must be willing to put his or her job on the line for the sake of the brand.

THE CHIEF BRAND OFFICER IS AN ARCHITECT.

The CBO not only helps build the brand, but also plans, anticipates, researches, probes, listens, and informs. The CBO sees the business on both its macro and micro levels and is a great observer, careful to preserve or sharpen intuitions, rather than simply plug in data. Working with senior leadership, the CBO helps envision not just what works best for the brand today but what can help drive it forward well into the future.

THE CHIEF BRAND OFFICER DETERMINES AND PROTECTS THE VOICE OF THE BRAND OVER TIME.

Though the CBO may not have the authority or responsibility for individual products or services, he or she can be accountable for brand-critical and corporationwide activities like advertising, positioning, corporate design, corporate communications, and consumer or marketing insights. Where marketing may have a twelve-month view or less, the CBO looks two or three years out. Strengthening a brand takes years; altering its course can take longer. Bringing aboard a new agency and developing it into a great business partner and asset of the brand also takes years. The revolving-door aspect of most advertising and marketing positions limits the effectiveness of most external marketing resources. For this reason, I don't advise companies to look at this position as a training ground for other jobs. Find a great CBO and keep him or her as long as you possibly can.

Brand-Development Reviews

Whether your organization has appointed a CBO or not, or has even defined a brand-development process, one thing that you can do immediately is establish a small team of executives to meet periodically to take stock of where your brand stands through regular brand-development reviews. In most companies, this might require a quarterly one- or two-day session. For any company contending with the stresses of rapid growth, rife with conflicts that can dilute the brand, I suggest monthly three- or four-hour sessions to get things on track. No matter how often you have such a meeting, here's a good punch list of five issues to address during the brand-development review.

1. REVIEW BRAND-SENSITIVE RESEARCH AND INSIGHTS.

Examples of such data include brand strength monitors (if you have one), brand audits (internal and external assessment of brand strength and image), and results of focus groups that may have occurred. Less formal material like personal observations and "gut feelings" that are troubling someone in the executive team are also fair game here. Any sort of reaction should be discussed in these meetings. Sinking feelings are not to be felt alone. If research is showing signs of weakness in a particular area, this group should address how to dig deeply enough to understand the root cause. Findings are reviewed at the next available meeting and the cycle continues. This meeting is not to review the business and wade neck deep into sales and profit numbers. It is purely focused on the health of the brand: where it is strong, where it is weak, and where it must create greater relevancy and desire.

2. REVIEW THE STATUS OF KEY BRAND INITIATIVES.

A brand initiative is a strategic thrust to either strengthen a weakness in the brand (one Nike example: "Get the edge back with teen males") or to exploit an opportunity to grow the brand in a new direction (Starbucks' joint venture with United). Brand initiatives change the way the brand is viewed by your customers. Changing your long-distance service is not a brand initiative; that is a profit initiative, and none of your customers will be aware of it when you do it. Opening a Nike Town, on the other hand, represents a strategic evolution into new territory—in this case, a move from wholesale into retail—and an aggressive effort to change the way the brand is communicated in all retail stores.

3. REVIEW BRAND-SENSITIVE PROJECTS.

Relevant areas here include advertising campaigns, corporate communications, sales meeting agendas, and important human resources programs (recruitment, training, and retention) that profoundly affect the organization's ability to embrace and project core brand values.

4. REVIEW NEW PRODUCT AND DISTRIBUTION STRATEGIES.

As part of the brand-development process, any new projects of significant size that affect how the brand is viewed should be examined against core brand values. A few examples:

- Licensing the brand to penetrate a new market more rapidly
- Forming joint ventures to develop new products or brands
- Expanding distribution to nontraditional platforms such as large-scale discount retailers
- Developing lower-priced products that may affect product and brand integrity.

5. RESOLVE BRAND-POSITIONING CONFLICTS.

Any inconsistencies with the brand image should be flagged here—not eighteen months later in the market. Conflicts naturally occur within large organizations that have any level of decentralization or multiple profit-and-loss centers, which tend to view sales-generating tools such as advertising differently. This group must review and resolve conflicts such as inconsistent brand positioning across channels, business units, or markets.

The Danger of Cultural Drift

Shortly before I left Starbucks in 1998 to return to writing and consulting, Howard Schultz walked into my office with an exasperated look on his face. He had just come from somewhere inside the heart of the emerging hairball in Brewtopia.

"Did you know that Management Information Systems is the most expensive department in this company and that we have more people in Human Resources than any other department? Do I even need a large MIS department?" he asked. "I don't even know what most of those people *do*." Starbucks was in the midst of overhauling its information technology platform, no small endeavor, and the conversation took place before companies began to aggressively outsource many of their IT requirements. We had dozens of consultants in the building at any given moment. Schultz's concerns weren't entirely financial. He was also worried about the fabric of the corporate headquarters as it began to change with the dramatic influx of specialists who had never worked a day in a Starbucks store. Some of them didn't even drink coffee.

Just a few years earlier, Starbucks' corporate HQ, which they called the Partner Support Center, had been a place where store managers and field managers, most all of them former baristas, advanced after achieving success at the retail level. Now, Starbucks was hiring hundreds of specialists from the outside, many from management positions at Burger King, McDonald's, Taco Bell, and other fast-food chains. When I joined the company, we made fun of those companies. Now, just three years later, and as a direct result of our success in growing the brand, we had been forced to recruit from them. We needed people who had practical experience with riding a restaurant rocket, hiring a thousand people a month, and watching costs ferociously. But bringing them on staff also meant changing the culture of the company, and in doing so changing the heart of the brand.

I knew the aliens were among us when, in the course of a retail business review session, it was suggested that Starbucks remove the small "short" cups and introduce a larger, whale of a beverage container that would be more profitable. The largest size Starbucks had at the time, sixteen ounces, was a grande. What would we call the larger size? Mucho grande? About this time the soft-drink brands were moving to "Big Slam" and "Big Gulp" beverage sizes, some of which were so large that they could not fit into any beverage holder I know of. The person offering the idea, who came to us from one of the fast-food players, distributed sheets of numbers around the room which supported the idea. It would be more profitable, yes, but what would it do for the single espresso drinker who liked one ounce of espresso with seven rather than eleven ounces of milk? The taste is quite different. By our own research we knew that some of our best customers (nearly 15 percent) drank more pure, smaller espresso beverages. One of the purists from the Coffee Department became quite upset that we would even consider such a notion. Always one to find a humorous way to point out the obvious or to resolve a dilemma, I offered a suggestion.

"If we remove the smaller cups we'll have to take out a large newspaper ad announcing the decision so people won't be confused. The headline will read, 'We've dropped our shorts to make more money. Hope you don't mind.' What do you think?"

Starbucks decided to keep its shorts behind the bar, though at the time of this writing they are not listed on the menu board anymore. You have to ask for one. The bigger cup? It's called a *venti*.

The Goal: Brand Leadership on Every Level

Brands need leadership from within and at every level. They need great CEOs who not only understand the yin and the yang of brand building but who also can create a culture in which diverse skills are respected and balanced. CEOs also need someone who can navigate across the company, surfing all the product and business silos, so that he or she is closely connected to those critical decisions that have a profound effect on the most sacred corporate asset, the brand. Brands also need champions at even the most entry-level position. Retailers must recognize the value of inverting the traditional corporate pyramid so that the greatest number of employees—the front-line employees—have the greatest impact on customers (think Nordstrom and Starbucks).

One day my wife, Sammi, came home from her job at Nordstrom's corporate headquarters and showed me one of her latest projects. It appeared to be an oversized postcard with an image of a handful of employees on one side and a simple piece of copy on the other. It read something like:

> *As an employee of Nordstrom all we ask is that you use the best possible judgement at all times.*

"What is this?" I asked.

"That's our new employee handbook."

That was all there was—back in the mid-eighties, before Nordstrom

created the same several-hundred-page three-ring human resources policies binder that most companies have today. Sammi went on to tell me
how Nordstrom's salespeople were the most valuable to the company,
and how everyone else—including the CEO—was there to help them
provide the best experience possible. Nordstrom brand leadership was
delivered at the point of sale, not on television or in an annual report.

In the New Brand World, companies that aspire to distinguish themselves above all others must spare nothing in their leadership efforts to
make everything tie together, to make everything they do a refreshing extension of something timeless and valued, and to do it where it matters
most—even if it means turning the entire enterprise upside down.

branding and the corporate goliath

Brand Principle #7
Big doesn't have to be bad.

When the retail book giant Barnes & Noble announced in November 1999 its intention to purchase Ingram, the largest book wholesaler in the United States, Amazon.com issued a statement to the press. After expressing his hope that Ingram, which had filled more than 58 percent of Amazon's orders that year, would treat his company "just like any other independent bookseller," Amazon.com's CEO, Jeff Bezos, ominously noted, "Goliath is always in the range of a good slingshot." To which B & N promptly responded, "Barnes and Noble Inc. is amused to read Jeff Bezos' quote in which he describes himself as an 'independent bookseller.' Well, Mr. Bezos, what with market capitalization of some $6 billion and more than 4 million customers, we suppose you know a Goliath when you see one. . . . Might we suggest that slingshots and potshots should not be part of your arsenal?"

To which Amazon replied, simply, "Oh."

The irony of these allegations was that both Amazon.com and B & N had already attained Goliath status in their respective industries. I use the word "respective" here intentionally, for I would maintain that the two companies are today in fundamentally different industries: B & N is a bookseller striving to catch up to Amazon.com in the on-line universe, while maintaining a massive brick-and-mortar presence. Amazon.com, by contrast, hopes to become—to quote any number of Wall Street analysts—"the Wal-Mart of the Net." For Amazon.com, selling books was just a starting point. In fact, less than a year after the Ingram exchange, few analysts were pitting the two against each other any longer: Amazon.com, and its brand, had evolved into a broader-range business. Barnes & Noble, meanwhile, had rescinded its offer to buy Ingram, amid speculation that it had backed off from a deal that many in its own industry viewed with considerable trepidation.

Dueling Perceptions: Will the Real Goliath Please Stand Up?

Though the two companies ultimately possessed different goals, different channels, and different strategic spaces, there was one area in which both were willing to take off the gloves and throw a punch, and that was in the battle of perceptions. For both Barnes & Noble and Amazon.com, the struggle to become the largest and most powerful player in a given niche was counterbalanced by a justified concern over being regarded as "excessively" powerful in that niche. In the commercial equivalent of Teddy Roosevelt's famous injunction to "Walk softly, but carry a big stick," smart companies have grasped the need to balance the will to dominate an arena with the strategically indispensable goal of avoiding being perceived as a bully. Smart companies recognize that in the marketplace, perception *is* reality, no matter how right or wrong that perception is. An incorrect perception needs to be corrected quickly. This issue of image pertains to all companies, regardless of actual size—it's the perception of market dominance that matters. A corner store that deliberately lowers prices to absurdly low levels just to undercut the competition can be considered predatory, even if it's just a mom-and-pop shop.

The bigger a business grows, the more subject it becomes to scrutiny—and not just from the Justice Department and other antimonopoly regulators. The media also get you under their microscope. And the bigger a company gets, the harder it becomes for it to defend itself against charges of being too big, too aggressive, too dominating. The paradox here, of course, is that in nearly all financial respects a "strategic competitive advantage" is considered a good thing. But the advantage stops at the battle of perceptions, where Goliath status can be a negative. As a society we love to champion the little guys, the underdogs, until they become so big and successful that they appear to be hurting the next little guy, the next underdog—even if simply by "removing their oxygen," as one dominant software company was reported to have planned to do to a competitor just before the U.S. Justice Department came after it.

For most of the century, large companies have generally had the ability to block the distribution of smaller competitors' products, and thus their entry into the market as well as the information consumers desired, such as instant comparison pricing. They have also been able to secure easy financing for expansion. Those factors in combination added up to gaining a "strategic competitive advantage." Bigger *was* better and size mattered. But today, largely due to the advent of new technologies, new entrants into the market have got a cleaner shot than ever before at dislodging entrenched market leaders from their perches. A small company can field a new technology as easily as a large one, and change the rules of the game. This is called "disruptive technology." In the case of the Web, big traditional companies that dragged their feet into what is often referred to as the New Economy became particularly susceptible to upstarts. The David of the twenty-first century now totes a high-tech slingshot, and he's not using it to launch stones. Even in the midst of the New Economy correction, the ease of entrance into markets made possible by changing technology continues to sharpen what has become known as "the attacker's advantage."

Today, emerging companies take no pride in the number of additional square feet their organizations may require in order to grow or simply maintain a position. The smartest have found intriguing ways to leverage networking technology and mobile computing to expand services without increasing costs. *Fast Company* magazine made its mark by gazing admiringly not at industry Goliaths but at the rising stars, the little engines who believed that they could, the wild-eyed visionaries who saw a future that had little resemblance to current business traditions. In the New Brand World, passionate refugees from the big corporate hairballs are striking out and striking back with their own bright ideas, unencumbered by bureaucracy and politics, inspired by change, and driven by the conviction that they can create a better product, a better company, and a better brand.

One such company, particularly at its inception, was Yahoo!. Its deliberate irreverence—that exclamation point—conveyed a sense of transgressing the traditional boundaries of what it means to be a business. In the summer of 1998, when I first met Karen Edwards, chief marketing officer for Yahoo!, the company was just approaching a magical threshold when it hired its nine hundredth employee. That was not a big number by big company standards, but in the Internet category, having a thousand people on the payroll is a very big deal indeed—a "strategic inflection point."

At that time I asked Edwards to describe her greatest challenge. She didn't hesitate. "I'm most concerned about becoming the Goliath of the Internet," she replied. "This is an industry that is by definition *anti-big*. We have to keep our culture intact while growing at a rate few companies can fathom."

In the preceding eighteen months, Yahoo! had amassed a market cap of more than $20 billion. Along the way, it had become a Goliath of the Internet, alongside AOL and Amazon. Yet Yahoo! had been able to accomplish all that without saturating the landscape with retail stores or the signage that goes with them, or turning off the sort of concerned citizens who become alarmed when any one company appears to be monopolizing the consumer landscape. IBM has more than 200,000 employees worldwide. Yahoo! achieved a dominant position in its field with roughly 199,000 fewer employees, yet was still concerned with the perception of being seen as a behemoth in its own field. Or was, until the stock market came to its senses in the spring and fall of 2000. By October 12, 2000, Yahoo! had given back all the gains it had made since the day I stood in Edwards's office two years earlier. Unfortunately for even a success like Yahoo!, its sheer size made it a prominent target—right alongside Amazon.com—when the market turned. Being big is fun on the way up, but it can be high-profile hell on the way down.

At Starbucks, we were first accused publicly of being a Goliath in 1995. Despite our then microscopic share of the U.S. coffee market, we began being portrayed in some communities—it started in Berkeley, California—as a greedy, caffeinated Antichrist. According to this alarmist view of our power position, we were poised to suck all that was good out of every community we entered. In the fall of 1995, I paid a visit to a suburb of San Francisco where the battle lines had been drawn.

In this bucolic bohemian enclave across the bay, community activists had been protesting a planned opening of a Starbucks store and had invited the media to witness a demonstration. In a spirit of "open debate," the press had been invited by a handful of local merchants who hated and feared Starbucks to participate in a discussion on the issue of the Starbucks invasion. I flew to San Francisco and met with our opposition. In the course of our discussion I found that few in the audience understood what Starbucks had to offer, or how Starbucks differed from other "chains." During an interview I was asked to explain some of those differences. I mentioned the full medical benefits that Starbucks offers to half-time employees and stock ownership for all employees, regardless of how many hours worked. "It surprises me," I pointed out, "that a community as progressive as this one would rather have businesses that don't offer these benefits to the people who work here."

At that point the journalist interviewing me turned to a protesting shop owner standing beside him and asked him, point-blank, if he offered similar benefits packages to his part-time employees. He stuttered and fumbled and admitted that he offered no such packages. Suddenly, I was no longer the target of dirty looks from the crowd. Instead, the journalist who had been questioning me turned his attention to a fresh target—the unfortunate local shop owner who had taken his part-time labor for granted.

Dancing with Elephants

When a company becomes just too big in the eyes of some customers—a perception typically fostered by special interest groups and bolstered by the press—it inevitably faces the public relations problem of how to deal with the perception of its size. What to do?

My suggestion: *Teach the elephant to dance*. Make him a welcome neighbor. Teach him compassion. Make him laugh at himself. Make him humble. Make him pick up after himself. Show him how to use his superhuman strength for good. More and more we are seeing big companies step up and take this advice, but in fact it's a good strategy for any company, regardless of size, to pursue. Here are a few examples of substantial steps that several large companies, struggling with this issue, have taken to "teach the elephant to dance."

• Phil Knight and Nike joined a coalition called F.L.A. (Fair Labor Association) formed by human rights groups, colleges, the U.S. government, and private companies to alleviate global sweatshop conditions, one of Nike's most brand-negative public perception concerns. Companies whose factories are in compliance with the F.L.A. labor code are entitled to sew an "F.L.A." label into their clothing. Member colleges and universities have agreed that their logos will be applied only to F.L.A.-approved products.

- Gibson Guitar, Chiquita Banana, and a host of other companies have agreed to be certified by nonprofit groups like the Rain Forest Alliance, so that their products and services can be reliably guaranteed not to result from processes that despoil the rain forest for private gain.

- Ford Motor Company, which depends upon sport utility vehicles for much of its profits, concedes that SUV's are the source of serious energy and environmental problems. It pledges to seek technological solutions to these problems, while searching for viable alternatives that can replace elephantine vehicles such as the Excursion.

- Amazon.com has joined forces with the writers' organization PEN to offer the first PEN/Amazon.com Short Story Award.

- When the food giant Unilever moved to buy Ben & Jerry's Ice Cream, Unilever co-chairman Niall FitzGerald arrived for a meeting with Ben & Jerry's top brass wearing a knapsack on his back and proceeded to "talk for three hours about all the sustainable agriculture activities that they had," according to Ben & Jerry's CEO, Perry D. Odak.

Some might argue that the underlying intent of such activities is simply a cynical desire to "hide the elephant," and this has a negative connotation, pulling the wool over people's eyes, or doing tricks with smoke, mirrors, and lights. A prominent example of "hiding the elephant" occurred when AT&T launched a supposedly small, renegade dial-around phone service called Lucky Dog. The corporate ownership was listed in very fine print on the margins of the promotional advertising. The hope here was that gullible consumers would think that they were somehow "beating the big boys." This is what is known as a "stealth" brand. As we become a more open society with information of every sort readily accessible, a society where corporate karma begins to matter more, such dubious branding practices are likely to become increasingly less effective.

The critical difference between "hiding the elephant" and "teaching the elephant to dance" is one of basic honesty. "Hiding the elephant" is, at bottom, a smoke-and-mirrors trick, a piece of cynical manipulation. "Teaching the elephant to dance," on the other hand, is a way of lightening up a heavy corporate image load—to convey to the public that being big is not necessarily the same thing as being bad.

The Corporate Comb-over

One of the most disturbing things that some big companies do in attempting to shape public perceptions is to strain to project an image of themselves through their advertising that often doesn't ring true back at the office. If you're in need of a little "Pontiac Excitement," something tells me you won't find it at corporate headquarters in Detroit. It's embarrassing to watch large businesses desperately manufacture hip imagery to compensate for something they lost a long time ago. Their strategy is like that of the guy who went completely bald on top but combs what is left of the hair above his ears, which he has grown out as long as he can, right back over his head.

Although many of them believe that we don't notice what is going on, the ruse is obvious; the same goes for companies. We are coming into an age of full disclosure, thanks in large part to the Internet. Consumers are looking for the real deal. They are looking for substance, not hype; honesty rather than hypocrisy. Companies that are comfortable within their own skin will do well. Companies that lack the confidence or the honesty to reveal themselves openly, to take pride in what is most natural for them, will have difficulty in the years ahead. The days of the corporate comb-over are numbered. A rebellious, innovative spirit that is genuine and comes from the heart of a big company is both rare and invaluable. Nike was able to blast through the size problems that would have throttled most companies who rely on teens, particularly teen males, for their core business because no matter how fast it grew, it remained true to its inner core. Nike advertising was a high-powered expression of an insanely creative, consumer-focused company that placed authenticity as its highest brand value. And if you're wondering what the source of that attitude was, look no further than Phil Knight. Knight built a company that in many ways is simply a reflection of himself. This often happens when founders stay with a company and guide it personally through its trials and tribulations. The same is true of Richard Branson at Virgin.

Phil Knight was to a considerable degree inspired by one of the first athletes Nike sponsored, Steve Prefontaine, dubbed the James Dean of running. Before Pre's untimely death in 1975, he had run up against what he considered stiff and restrictive athletic institutions like the American Athletic Union (AAU) and the International Olympic Committee. "Pre was a rebel from a working-class background, a guy full of cockiness and pride and guts," Phil Knight recalled to the author Donald Katz, who was writing a book about Nike called *Just Do It*. At Nike, we unconsciously worked with those very values as our touchstones, as a foundation for our brand mythology.

Nike's first sponsored tennis star, Ilie Nastase, was one of the first true "bad boys" of tennis, at a time, the seventies, when tennis was still heavily dominated by good boys. In 1977, Phil Knight was sitting in the stands at Wimbledon when he realized that the appropriate successor to Nastase was John McEnroe. In Katz's words, the young McEnroe "exuded an inconoclastic attitude that both conformed with the Nike view of things and abutted strikingly the subdued norms and conventions of a tennis establishment that had effectively packaged the sport for elite consumption."

By the late eighties, as Mac's career began to crest, we made a bet on Andre Agassi, who with his long hair looked more like a rock star than a world-ranked tennis player. Andre embodied the emerging notion of "rock-and-roll tennis." And the thrilling opportunity that this oxymoron presented to us was a little like placing a golf ball on a tee in front of Tiger Woods. We swung hard and had serious fun. It was, as we often liked to say, *irreverence justified.*

Getting Beyond Cool: Product Purism

Many companies, even as they grow large, still aim to be seen as hip and cool. Laudable a goal as this might be, I've never been a big fan of the quest for "cool," because experience has taught me that pursuing this elusive marketer's dream often represents a classic case of putting the cart before the horse. In this one arena, I tend to side with the product purists, who subscribe to the belief that the product itself should dictate a great deal of your brand attitude. If your product is boring or doesn't meet customer expectations, there's no point in trying to make it *appear* cool with expensive advertising or promotions. It's not productive to get hung up on being perceived by the young as cool and hip, because this particular demographic subset, as noted, is negatively sensitive to marketing messages cynically pitched at it.

Nike didn't set out to become cool or hip—much less admired by young urban teens—but simply set out to provide the best possible footwear to championship athletes. Period. Once the product platform was established, the company developed innovative ways to communicate with consumers. It demonstrated that it had a clear understanding of what was cool as defined by end users, not by a bunch of guys in Beaverton, Oregon. While Nike paid close attention to music, to style, to vernacular, and to contemporary cultural icons such as Spike Lee, it never took its eye off the product.

The same was true of Starbucks. Howard Schultz has stated that he did not set out to create a great brand; it just happened over time. He focused, rather, on creating a great product, building great cafés, hiring great people, and delivering shareholder value. Those became the four cornerstones of the brand.

Grassroots Marketing

In 1984, Nike decided not to invest the tens of millions of dollars demanded by the International Olympic Committee to become an official sponsor of the Summer Olympic Games in Los Angeles. Instead, the company decided to engage in a more seat-of-the-pants method, "grassroots marketing," in which massive murals of Nike-sponsored athletes were painted on downtown L.A. buildings. Though Nike never invoked the word "Olympic" anywhere in this marketing effort, it gained the company recognition as one of the most visible sponsors of the 1984 Olympic Games, a feat that must have driven the guys in Switzerland a little crazy.

A more recent grassroots marketing effort was undertaken by Fresh Samantha, a young juice company based in Maine, which hired three young employees to drive up and down the East Coast in a Winnebago, towing a huge brightly colored bottle-shaped balloon of its nonpasteurized, natural fruit juice concoctions. The campaign became such a popular roadside attraction that it was featured on NBC's *Today* show. In February 2000, Fresh Samantha juices, a specialty product dreamed up by a family who had gone back to the "grass roots" in rural Maine, was acquired for a considerable sum by Odwalla, the largest purveyor of fresh fruit juices on the West Coast. Which means that before not so very long, the combined companies are likely to find themselves facing the classic "big company" quandary of "teaching the elephant to dance."

Like its ostensibly noncommercial cousin, grassroots politics, grassroots marketing represents an attempt to galvanize support by doing an end-run around mainstream and conventional marketing practices, primarily, paid advertising in the mass media. Conducted properly, and by the right company, this approach can be quite effective. It draws on the communications theorist Marshall McLuhan's seminal concept that "the medium is the message." In other words, it's not just what you say, but how and where you say it that's important. Avoiding the mass media can communicate a kind of authenticity to consumers.

If you want to observe grassroots marketing in action, pay attention to what the beverage companies are up to in your area. Coca-Cola recently hired New York–based Cornerstone Promotions, which specializes in hiring "street teams" to hand out free samples and flyers about products at unexpected places like movie lines, parking lots, and street corners. (Cornerstone was founded in the late nineties by two music industry executives, Jon Cohen and Rob Stone, who put together a group of DJ's around the country to help promote products. Clients included Nike's Quick Six shoes and a doomed Web start-up called Boo.com.)

When PepsiCo brought out a new line of juice-based noncarbonated soft drinks called Fruitworks, to go up against Snapple and Coca-Cola's Fruitopia, it asked its ad agency, DDB Digital in New York, to go the grassroots route. DDB Digital created an entertainment-oriented Web site, gave out lots of free samples at rock concerts, and kicked off a national promotion on MTV's *Total Request Live*. At the time, Steven Marrs of DDB Digital commented to the *New York Times*, "These kids are not . . . ones to be marketed to. They have a deep desire to go out and create their own space in the world. So we work with them to build the brand, and give expression to who they are." Marrs maintained that young people were "almost hard-wired to *reject* direct pitches that dictate what is cool or not cool."

"In talking to this market," said Steve Hicks, DDB Digital's creative director, "it's important to be cool, but you can't just say, 'Hey we're cool.'"

Unfortunately, many big and truly unhip companies are bumping into one another in the grassroots area of the marketplace, trying to say all the right things while wearing just the right corporate clothing. The lines between grassroots marketing and mass marketing continue to blur. At the height of the dot-com boom, a few digital start-ups preached the value of a digital variant of grassroots marketing known as "viral" marketing, in which the consumer is exposed to the brand on a one-to-one basis, often in the form of e-mail, usually unsolicited. The rationale here is partly to save costs and partly to "seed" the brand with key influencers, who, as the marketing-lingo term implies, presumably have lots of friends to influence. Microsoft's free Hotmail e-mail service is the textbook example of this strategy. Anyone receiving a message from a Hotmail user in effect also receives an ad for the service. The approach is undoubtedly effective, though it's difficult to gauge how well many of those companies would have done without the incessant press coverage that they received for free in lieu of paid advertising. Early IPO moves like Netscape and

Amazon.com must have accumulated the equivalent of several hundred million dollars' worth of advertising—in mass media vehicles like newspapers, radio, and television—while proclaiming in their press releases that they were building their brands without resorting to advertising in the mass media. It was amusing to watch while it lasted, or at least while the media had an interest in freshly minted technology company IPOs. And if the presence of extensive "Hotmail" brand identification on every outbound e-mail from a Hotmail user is not advertising, then I don't know what is.

When Cool Becomes
Too Hot to Handle

The underlying problem with strategies to market a company as "cool," particularly to the notoriously fickle demographic subsection known as "rebellious youth," is that cool can suddenly become "too cool for school," which can be a dangerous position for any brand, even the strongest, to be in. At the peak of Nike's "street chic" period, in the mid-eighties, a number of tough urban kids started attacking one another to steal their rivals' high-priced Nike shoes, along with their Starter jackets and jewelry. Though not widespread, this social phenomenon generated a serious challenge for the brand. A certain *New York Post* writer (who shall here remain nameless) saw in this tragic situation the opportunity to make a name for himself by attacking Nike, something he did every chance he could get.

About the same time as this controversy was brewing, I clicked on the TV one night to see the Reverend Jesse Jackson—founder of the Chicago-based civil rights group called Operation PUSH (People United to Save Humanity)—announcing that his organization was "looking into" the issue of Nike. In particular, he and his group were interested in dissecting the relationship that Nike had to its customers and employees in the black community. A few years earlier, he had put similar pressure on Coca-Cola with the slogan "Don't choke on Coke." Obviously, Jesse Jackson likes well-known brands.

Dick Donahue, Nike's recently appointed president; Liz Dolan, Nike's head of PR; and I flew to Chicago to speak with Jackson's appointed representatives at PUSH. They demanded to see a list of figures outlining Nike's employment policies regarding minorities and a precise accounting of where Nike's revenues went in terms of minority suppliers like advertising agencies and media companies. As Nike's head of corporate advertising, I personally knew that we had never advertised directly to any minorities. We focused on athletes of every age, color, and gender. We did not have an "ethnic marketing budget," as some companies do. By that time we were becoming a mass brand that had strength across nearly every consumer segment, probably precisely because we did not segment or fractionalize our efforts. We bought time on network and cable sports programming, and prime-time and late-night network TV. We also spent 20 percent of the budget in national print magazines like *Sports Illustrated, People,* and *Rolling Stone.* The problem was, we were not spending much money in minority-owned media that were represented by PUSH.

The meeting was a disaster. The twenty-some representatives from PUSH did not want to listen to anything we had to say. Worse, on the way out of what was supposed to be a private meeting, we were ambushed by a phalanx of special interest media, with reporters waving microphones and cameras in our faces. A few weeks later, we sifted through all of the demands that had been issued to Nike by PUSH; the core demand was for Nike to create an African American marketing program and to spend millions of dollars on companies sympathetic to if not direct members of PUSH.

Nike refused, for the reasons explained above, and the net result of the ensuing furor was a nationwide boycott of Nike products by PUSH. In the years that followed we did retain the services of a multiethnic advertising agency, Muse, Codero and Chen, in Los Angeles, to work with our core agency, Wieden & Kennedy. Their mandate was to help us extend our corporate advertising messages in ways that were more relevant to Asian, Hispanic, and African American consumers. Some exceptional "Just Do It" print work came from this relationship. Nike partnered with MCC because it had evolved to a point where it needed to more completely understand all minorities, not just the needs of one special interest group.

Using Your Superhuman Powers for Good

One of the best things that happened to Nike as a direct result of the pressure from PUSH was the realization that though we were doing great things for lots of people in need, as a *brand* Nike was getting little to no credit for any of it. In this respect, we were completely off the public radar. In 1992 Nike wrote more than a thousand checks to different charities around North America. This effort resulted in many millions of dollars being contributed to causes that included drug abuse, domestic violence, high school dropout programs, literacy, cancer research, AIDS, and public television, to name just a few. Certainly all of these causes were worthy and important, but few bore even a remote connection to Nike's core business. More important, Nike's assets—athletes, players, coaches, its connection with the games we play, particularly as kids—could not be easily leveraged through most of those programs.

Nike Supports Kids' Sports

Studying this problem, I became convinced that there must be some way to use our brand values to build up a reservoir of goodwill that would at the same time leverage our brand equity. It certainly seemed that Nike could become a major player at doing good, as well as doing well. A golden opportunity presented itself during a lunch meeting with Deion Sanders. Deion was an NFL football player and major league baseball player—another two-sport athlete like Bo Jackson. Throughout the lunch, Deion sat there with his sunglasses on, playing it cool, clearly engaging with the group just enough to participate, but just as clearly wishing that he were elsewhere.

Then we somehow alighted on the subject of Boys and Girls Clubs, and Sanders lit up. He took off his shades and began to tell his story. He grew up a poor kid on the wrong side of the highway in Fort Myers, Florida. As a teen I had spent a summer in Fort Myers myself, so I was curious and urged him to continue. Deion went on to explain that if it had not been for the Boys and Girls Club in Fort Myers, he probably would not have become a professional player of even one major league sport, let alone two. Instead, he said, he was pretty certain that he would have ended up in jail or dead, like some of his friends. He also told us that he had developed his speed when he would run home from the club late at night near a cemetery that was a shortcut to his house. "My feet barely touched the ground," he said.

Sanders then shared with us a long-cherished dream of building the world's greatest Boys and Girls Club in Atlanta, where he then lived. He wanted to name it the Deion Sanders Prime Time Center for Youth. He would buy big black buses that would scoop up children from surrounding neighborhoods and shuttle them safely to and from the center.

Before the meeting was over Sanders had drilled us on what Nike was going to do for kids and sports. We told him that we were already the largest corporate contributor to the Boys and Girls Clubs of America, but that we knew we could do more. I shook Sanders's hand and told him that I would personally look into the matter.

A few days later, I had a casual conversation with Steve Miller, head of Nike sports marketing, and Mark Thomashow, head of business affairs for Nike advertising. At the time, Portland, Oregon, was failing to pass school funding levies, and a number of sports, music, and arts programs had been cut. As a result, many Portland-area families had to "pay to play," some having to contribute more than two hundred dollars for a child to play one sport. A number of cities around the country were finding themselves in the same situation.

All three of us knew intuitively how good sports were for kids. We decided to throw out a net and see what kind of data we could come up with that would buttress a big proposal to Phil Knight and Tom Clarke to fund a program to increase kids' access to sports.

I asked Liz Dolan, head of corporate communications at Nike, for anything she might have on the positive effects of sports in kids' lives. One three-year study she located found that Los Angeles school district girls who competed in at least one team sport were 85 percent less likely to experience teen pregnancy or drug abuse or to drop out. Other studies showed that sports provided the first break in the color barrier between kids, serving as the means by which friendships were forged between elementary school children of different races and socioeconomic backgrounds.

Shortly thereafter, we proposed that Nike focus all of its nonprofit giving on creating sports opportunities for kids. We agreed to participate only if a proposal came to us that in some way helped provide outlets for children to play sports—even if it was simply to enable them to play safely in the inner cities of North America. Otherwise, we gracefully declined. Saying no was hard at first, but we soon appreciated the power of what we had set out to do. Every employee was proud of the program, and soon Nike provided matching contributions to any employee who gave to a local sports league or spent money on its equipment or uniforms.

As part of its effort, Nike also began to recruit adult mentors who could supervise children after school at playgrounds around the country. Programs like "Midnight Basketball" in Chicago, which essentially keeps the lights on in city parks and provides adult supervision and had been supported by Nike in the past, now became models for similar programs in other cities. We sponsored massive donations of products and the remodeling of playgrounds and basketball courts with Nike "regrind" materials—a cushioned surface made from recycled Nike shoes. We worked even more closely with the Boys and Girls Clubs, and spent Nike advertising dollars to air public service announcements for the organization with Denzel Washington as a proud alumnus. In the months that followed we learned that the majority of Nike's sponsor-athletes had played at a Boys and Girls Club at some point while they were growing up. No athlete turned us down when we asked them to stop by a local club while they were in town or to help with a public service announcement. Like Deion Sanders, they all appreciated the value of the games they played as kids—and the club where they played them.

Microsoft's Missed Opportunity

Given the success of this model, imagine what a company like Microsoft could have done in its relevant realm of education. Bill and Melinda Gates have recently contributed billions of dollars toward improving the quality of life in developing countries and toward supporting libraries, among other charities. But Microsoft, the company, has missed an enormous opportunity to become the protagonist for learning through personal computing—a role uniquely within the scope of its business. Apple was well ahead of its rival when it distributed Macs free or at low cost to schools and universities around the country. That campaign was still paying dividends to the company nearly twenty years later, when its "Think Different" campaign for the new iMacs sought to forge a link between revolutions in design and revolutions in thought—a distinctly "Apple" take on the educational process.

In this context, it's hard not to cite Microsoft as a superb case in point of playing the game of "hiding the elephant" badly—or or not playing the game at all. For years Microsoft prided itself on being a "pure product" company, whose merchandise could stand on its own merits and required no boost from PR or advertising. The Goliath of Redmond had become something of a joke in the marketing world for running unmemorable television advertising, and for failing to transmit any sort of vision. At the time of the decision by Judge Thomas Penfield Jackson to break apart the company (later reversed by a higher U.S. court of appeal), Rich Silverstein, co-chairman of Omnicom Group's Goodby, Silverstein & Partners (which has done great work for Starbucks and Nike) offered a comment on Microsoft's marketing efforts: "I have no idea what Microsoft feels. They touch so many people in the reality of the product, yet they have so little understanding of how to give back."

Ironically, Microsoft once worked with Nike's advertising agency, Wieden & Kennedy, and after spending two painful years trying to help workaholic Microsoft engineers disconnected from reality see the world and technology as consumers saw them, the agency resigned from the account. The emotional drain on the agency had become acute. As a client, Microsoft did not have the capacity, the respect, or the courage to trust the people who had created magic time and time again for Nike. The day the agency resigned the account, one member of the creative team sent an e-mail to everyone in the agency proclaiming simply, "Ding, dong. The evil witch is dead."

The Soul of Starbucks

The Starbucks Foundation has become another example of a brand using its superhuman powers for good. I once took a trip with Howard Schultz to his summer home in East Hampton on Long Island. On the way there, he confided in me that he had undergone a profound experience a few days earlier that had moved him deeply. He explained that it was the single most rewarding thing he had done with his newfound wealth from Starbucks. He had traveled back to his high school in one of the poorest sections of Brooklyn to visit his old football coach. Schultz had been a high school quarterback and had been awarded a college scholarship for his skill on the field. Now, he found that the school's sports facilities were in far worse shape than he ever imagined.

Schultz proceeded to write a rather large check and asked that it be directed toward upgrading the school's sports and fitness facilities so that they would be state-of-the-art for decades to come. He did so anonymously, without issuing any Starbucks press releases proclaiming the deed. In fact, I am certain that Schultz won't like my mentioning this. (Sorry, Howard.)

After relating this story, he said that it was time for Starbucks as a company to give back in a more meaningful way. This was 1996 and for the first time in the history of the business, it looked like Starbucks might have some breathing room. It was grossing somewhere near $750 million in revenues, and the future looked bright. Individual stores had long been supporters of their own communities, but Schultz was thinking about undertaking something on a national level. "I want to do something about literacy," he explained. He wanted to use all the proceeds from his then upcoming book, *Pour Your Heart into It,* to start the program. The advance alone would total more than a half million dollars.

Literacy may not have been an immediately obvious cause for Starbucks to support, but in fact, it was ideal. Literacy and enlightenment have always been at the heart of the coffeehouse tradition, and the café has been a "penny university" for centuries, a place where people could gather to learn, to work, to study, or simply to read.

"Once we have established a beachhead around literacy," I suggested, "we should move into cultural literacy and do whatever we can to expose our customers to the arts and to cultures that they are not familiar with." This was another genetic link to the classic image of the coffeehouse, which I felt could also inspire the 24,000 baristas that we had working at the time, most of whom were young, college-age students. Four months later Schultz appeared on the *Oprah Winfrey Show* with his book in hand. On the show Oprah announced the Starbucks "All Books for Children" book drive, which would be taking place at every Starbucks in America.

In 1999 Schultz found a way to make the program even more relevant to him personally. A lifetime baseball fan, he befriended major league baseball home run hitter Mark McGwire and struck a deal with him for the 1999 season. For every home run McGwire hit, Starbucks would donate $5,000 to local literacy organizations in the community in which Mark had knocked it out of the park.

Pfizer: A Good News Drug Story

In early 2000, in an unexpected move, the global pharmaceutical giant Pfizer announced that it would donate a crucial AIDS drug called fluconazole to South Africa. Fluconazole is the treatment of choice for a painful and lethal AIDS-related brain disease known as cryptococcal meningitis. The offer to provide the drug free of charge, as opposed to cutting its price sharply, came as something of a surprise to AIDS activists, who had been calling upon the company to lower its cost to a level commensurate with a generic version of the drug available in Thailand.

But Pfizer decided to do something better, and gain something from it: goodwill, also known as brand equity. To the nearly four million people in South Africa with AIDS, and to the millions of others around the world concerned by the ravages of the disease, Pfizer would no longer be a focus of resentment, but of respect and even gratitude.

Warming Up the Web at eBay

On the shores of Lake Atitlan, in a tiny Mayan village about a hundred miles west of Guatemala City, Karina Stahl arrives by boat carrying bags filled with a few days' change of clothing, and four gleaming new Compaq Presario laptop computers, complete with a DVD drive. The kit also included a server, a monitor, and Spanish/English translation software, all courtesy of eBay, the on-line auction house, where Karina Stahl works.

Since 1998, eBay has donated fifteen computers and two printers to a private school in San Pedro, Guatemala, whose 350 students pay tuition of about five dollars a month. This may not sound like a lot to most readers, but their parents must struggle to meet their tuition payments.

This is not simply an act of charity by eBay. Karina Stahl's project bears a direct relationship to the evolution of the eBay brand. The San Pedro region is known worldwide among collectors for its unique handicrafts of woven and beaded place mats, napkins, hats, and scarves. Stahl, director of the eBay Foundation, is hoping to market these goods directly to consumers via eBay, cutting out the middlemen who sharply reduce the income available to the craftspeople.

"Karina is passionate about the school project," Meg Whitman, chief executive of eBay, revealed in an interview with the *New York Times* about the initiative. "All 1,200 of our employees know about the school; it's part of our culture now. We have a bulletin board in our office with the children's photographs on it."

Dancing Elephants Versus Bad News Bears

All brands, as stated in the first chapter and repeated several times since, are organic. Like all living things, they start small and weak and, if they prove adept at surviving their environments, grow large and strong, before—one day—they die. Of course, a very few great brands could be considered immortal, but even those exceptions to the rules of survival will experience their ups and downs.

An important thing to remember is that all great brands were once infants. And all of today's global giants—Coca-Cola, Sony, Nike, Disney, even GM and GE—were at one time, not all that long ago, little more than mom-and-pop shops. But in each case, the creators of the brands we have come to know and respect were endowed with a commitment to building a brand that was larger than any single product or service, greater than any single new technology. This core belief in these brands' values allowed them to prosper and grow with change, to overcome fierce competition and end up on top.

Just as the imperatives of growth cannot be ignored, neither can the responsibilities of power and size. To become a globe-spanning Goliath is every brand's dream, but also its worst nightmare, if the public begins to suspect that the brand they helped to grow has turned against them. The solution is in one way simple—to "teach the elephant to dance"—but in another way complex, because that dance must be carefully aligned with your deepest brand values. Taking refuge in cheap labels like "cool" and "hip" can yield short-term results, but over the long haul, "hip" and "cool" are just labels—so thin you can peel them away with a thumbnail. The Maslowian approach to the problem is to attach the brand to a higher principle, which connects to the core business yet provides emotional benefits that transcend the physical ones. At Nike, we realized that we weren't in the charity business, we were in the sports business, and we needed to find ways to "give back" that emphasized the many social benefits that participation in sports can confer. At Starbucks, our connection to the venerable coffeehouse tradition showed us the way to promoting literacy. At Amazon.com it was literature; at Pfizer, health; at eBay, using technology and the Internet to give local crafts businesses global stretch. In each case, the brand and the benefits provided a synergy that wasn't just about squeezing the last dollar and cent out of every last revenue stream, but about building goodwill.

Coping with negative problems engendered by growth and size is a problem that every brand should have at least once in its life. It's one of the rites of passage of success. But long before you get there, I suggest that you think deeply about how you can tap your unique, superhuman powers—those talents unlike no other that you and/or your company possess—to improve the quality of life in the world around you. If you are a small company, your efforts may not amount to all that much in the beginning, but over time you will build a deep reservoir of goodwill that will set you apart and prove invaluable should bad luck—or bad perceptions—befall you.

–8–

brand future

Brand Principle #8
*Relevance, simplicity, and humanity
—not technology—
will distinguish brands in the future.*

The principles covered thus far have been applied to the business environment we face today with an eye to the future, but I'm convinced that they will be relevant for decades to come. My conviction is fueled in part by the past. One of the greatest and most enduring brands of all time, Coca-Cola, pioneered some of the best practices contained in these pages. The soda bar of the early twentieth century, the retail platform from which Coca-Cola laid much of its brand foundation, also served to inspire the reinvention of the coffeehouse by Starbucks seventy years later. Brands like Nike simply gave notions like "emotional ties" a new spin.

Back to Basics

I've been fortunate to witness these concepts at work from a position within great companies. More recently, as a consultant, I have applied them to businesses both big and small, to old dogs and new dogs. I have shared them with the world's premier entertainment company, the fastest-growing financial firm in America, one of the oldest and most recognized brands on earth, the world's third largest architectural firm, and the most trusted brand of jeans ever made.

Much as I enjoyed the task of reinvigorating established brands, I found the challenge of helping newcomers in the technology sector—some of them from scratch—to be equally engaging. After leaving Starbucks in 1998, I took on a project with a company at the forefront of Web-based comparison shopping. The Santa Clara, California–based mySimon.com provided instantaneous price comparisons of branded merchandise across more than a thousand different vendors, something virtually impossible to do in the Old Brand World. What intrigued me about this new company was that its core proprietary technology—a virtual learning agent that could scan Web sites for millions of products at blinding speeds—appeared to be heading where most brands feared technology would go: to reducing everything to price. The concept was new at the time, but clearly had enormous potential to change the way people shop, as well as to create issues for brands that did not want to be reduced to price-only comparisons. Brands and merchants most feared from such a process that consumers would abandon traditional loyalties to their most trusted—or, before the Web, most geographically convenient—points of purchase in favor of sellers offering the best price that could be found. Or that they would quickly abandon one brand for another if it was cheaper.

A few of these fears were allayed, however, by one of the most intriguing discoveries that mySimon.com made about their e-commerce site's users: that less than 20 percent of shoppers bought from the merchant with the lowest listed price, preferring instead to shop at a merchant they trusted. Further, in most shopping occasions, "brand switching" as a result of multiple-brand price disclosure did not appear to be happening. To the surprise of some believers in technology's power to fundamentally alter the rules of the marketing game, brand dynamics were still operative in precisely the place where few thought branding would have any relevancy whatsoever. What surprised me most was the way branding mattered a great deal when it came to retailers.

Given this reality, mySimon CEO Josh Goldman began to move his business model so that mySimon could enable on-line merchants, for a small fee, to present themselves more completely by presenting information above and beyond merely price. Not unlike the Yellow Pages phone directory strategy, the company enabled merchants to present themselves more creatively, often bringing their own logo and other corporate imagery, as well as more complete information about shipping costs, restocking fees, and anything else that would set them apart from their competitors.

When I first met the team at mySimon it was being pursued by several large media companies that saw great value in the technology. The thirty-person company had a dilemma: sell now for tens of millions of dollars and walk away, or rebuff the offers and build a brand on the back of the technology that could be far more valuable down the road. I had been brought in to speak with the board about what challenges they might anticipate in building a brand. A few days later one of the board members called me to say that I had convinced them to take the more difficult path. They wanted to build a brand and they wanted my help.

One of the first challenges was the development of a logo. The first-generation logo for mySimon was an animated character that served as the guide for the Web site itself. Management was evenly split on whether to keep him or dump him. We decided to keep him as a means to inject some warmth and personality to the brand and to the shopping experience, something that was in short supply on the Web. We set out to create a dozen different variations of the character, each serving as a trusted shopping guide for different areas of the Web site. The character gave the company something few technology brands had: a human face, even if it was an animated one. The company began to grow with relatively little marketing spending and by that holiday period became the number one shopping site on the Internet, surpassing Yahoo! Shopping. In the spring of 2000 mySimon was sold to CNET for approximately $700 million.

"They recognized the value of the technology," my board member friend told me later about the acquisition. "But they were most impressed by how quickly we had built such a creative brand."

Another challenge that I eagerly took on was Tellme Networks of Mountain View, California. With only forty employees in a deep double garage in Palo Alto, California, Tellme seemed poised to become the world's first major "voice portal" to the Web and speech-recognition enterprise provider, giving access to the Web via one of the oldest forms of information technology—the telephone. Through a free 800 number, callers could tap Web-based information to place calls to restaurants, airlines, and hotels all on the same free call. They could also quickly check stock quotes, movie times, sports scores, weather, horoscopes, and late-breaking news or traffic reports. For fun (and brand character) you could even play blackjack against someone who sounded an awful lot like Sean Connery. Tellme made the Internet more human and personable, more relevant, and much simpler. The Web was no longer solely accessible through the display on an electronic device, be it a PC or a WAP (Wireless Application Protocol) device or PDA. It could be reached with your own voice from any phone, from anywhere in the United States, at any time of day, for free. All you needed was your voice. Tellme made money via brief ads (five to seven seconds) with the service, by speech-enabling corporate Web sites, and by helping other companies improve their phone-based customer service programs.

We worked to provide this budding brand with strategic guardrails broad enough not to confine the creativity that abounds in such an unpredictable, emerging industry, yet tight enough so that the stream of brilliant refugees from Microsoft, Netscape, and Excite could focus on refining specific applications of the underlying technology. We identified core brand values ("Fast, Fresh, Friendly, Trustworthy") and a brand mantra ("Simple Everyday Connections") that united the elements of the consumer service. In most technology companies this would have been viewed as mushy babble. But Tellme—and I—were blessed to have a CEO, Mike McCue, who cared a great deal about what kind of brand the company was building. He admired what other visionary brands had done. He would do whatever was necessary so that Tellme might have such a chance.

The shakeout of the technology sector in 2000 and 2001 left few tech brands unscathed. Even in this harsh environment, however, mySimon prevailed and Tellme closed a $120 million financing round in a period when very few technology companies could acquire any fresh cash. Tellme received industry recognition for its brand development work and, more important, was also receiving more than ten million calls a month less than six months after launching its service to the public.

Despite these efforts, over the long haul these brands may not last—at least not as strong brands recognizable to the general public. Tellme, for example, is shifting its business model away from the consumer side toward what appears to be a far more profitable enterprise side. But I believe both brands survived the initial storm to fight another day because they built their brands on more solid foundations, they offered simple services that people really wanted, and they were exciting new businesses that meant much more to their employees and customers than just another new application of technology. Whether it is the fact that Tellme offers a human voice or that mySimon offers a human face, both companies have gone to great lengths to present their brands in a more organic, personal form than the average pure-play tech concern. Yes, they both had great technology. But unlike 99 percent of the industry, those brands also had heart.

Despite the much-needed reality check for the bulk of the sector, technology won't stop its forward path because of a downturn in the economy, or the stock market. It is only a matter of time and product improvement before our economy realizes the as yet largely unfulfilled promise of more friction-free commerce made possible by more pervasive technology with greater transmission speeds. The advent of the "networked society" will not be marked by a particular event; instead it will simply evolve. If it were a book, we would be midway through the third chapter of an interesting piece of literature for which there are no Cliffs Notes and no summary. We're all going to have to read the complete text as the story is written.

Fortunately, we have now completed a crash—and I do mean *crash*—course in how technology may or may not deliver on its platinum promise. We've learned a great deal from the initial dot-com boom, as well as the subsequent doom and gloom. It was an epic experiment that tested both conventional and unconventional wisdom in a few short years. Most industrial revolutions take decades to fully materialize; this one took about thirty-four months. The experience served as a free MBA for anyone who wanted to participate and it has given every business school on the planet much to ponder for a decade or two. It has also provided a new appreciation for keeping part of the family nest egg in established, well-run, solidly boring Old Economy brands.

Some of the greatest mistakes were committed in the assumption that technology or the Web itself would provide a stand-alone solution or the exclusive means by which to position or promote a brand. By now it has become clear that the Web is emerging as just one more means to an end, one more arrow in the quiver, one more tool for building and maintaining a business. It is an amazing new tool, with capabilities like those of few others before it. But most of those capabilities are so complex that they far outstripped the average person's ability to understand, much less trust and use them. Given its early developmental stage, the Web remains unpredictable and unreliable and will remain so for years. In that sense, the future will be a lot like Microsoft software.

The Importance of the Seven Core Values

In times of uncertainty, it pays to study societal values. What we collectively desire and what we most abhor are sentiments that can swing like a pendulum, making or breaking the fortunes of companies and whole industries along the way. As powerful as any emerging technology may be, it must ultimately conform to our values, not the reverse. So which way is society moving? What will customers desire most from brands in the future? How will they relate to them? What brand values will be most important, most universal, and most capable of enduring the inevitable shifts in economic prosperity or the intensifying global issues of energy management, human rights, and environmental protection? What must brands do to attract and retain great employees, their only real sustainable competitive advantage? And how will the mass media, which have provided the foundation for marketing and communications programs for much of the past century, evolve?

The best anyone can do when faced with such questions and confronted with change is to focus on the timeless values that have propelled brands forward across the ages. As technology unfolds, find ways to leverage so as to unleash a core brand value that you already deliver. It is unlikely that new technology will change the values of your brand. It can, however, make those values more deliverable, more accessible, and, quite possibly, more relevant.

In addition to the brand development principles already covered, I've developed a list of core values that all brands should pay attention to in the journey ahead. Some of these have already benefited from new technology. Some have been undermined by it. All apply to any company in any industry, regardless of size.

1. Simplicity
2. Patience
3. Relevance
4. Accessibility
5. Humanity
6. Omnipresence
7. Innovation

1. Simplicity

Six blistering years after Netscape's IPO ushered in the dot-com hysteria in 1995, a number of things had become crystal clear to the world's venture capitalists, investors, dot-com employees, the business press, analysts, and the consuming public. The following incredible discoveries might actually have remained buried in obscurity forever, were it not for the timely contributions of the storied geniuses of Silicon Valley and Red-mond, Washington.

- It's hard to make a profit giving things away.
- The last mile to a customer's home is the most expensive one.
- Most of us have a life away from our computer screens.
- The world is not going to beat a path to very many Web sites.
- Technology has to be *simple* in order to survive.

That last discovery, *simplicity,* was the most difficult for the hard-core technologists and former-technologists-turned-venture-capitalists to grasp. After all, they had *created* the stuff. They *knew* how it worked. How could anyone *not* know how it worked? Who did not know what a meta-tag was? Who could not *care*—deeply—what a meta-tag was?

In the March 5, 2001, issue of *Time* magazine, the cultural critic Wal-ter Kirn presented a refreshing analysis of why our technology-dependent economy—presumably both its new and old segments—had headed so deeply into the Dumpster, so fast.

> There's a recession because nothing works. I'm talking about the New Economy here. Cell phones. Satellite TV. PDAs. Computers. The stuff that was supposed to make us rich but won't make us rich be-cause it doesn't work.
>
> Remember the Old Economy? Things worked then. Steel didn't break. Refrigerators cooled food. A pound of wheat was a pound of wheat, and people could grind it into flour and eat it. A hamburger consisted of two buns and a patty of ground meat, and a cheeseburger was a hamburger plus cheese.
>
> Now suppose we applied the reliability standards and pricing schemes of New Economy products to the items above. One-inch-thick steel would only be one inch thick on weekend nights and holi-days. During weekday business hours, it would be one-third of an inch thick; and if one carried the steel outside one's "area," it would cost six times as much. Refrigerators would chill eggs and butter for only three or four hours before they "crashed," entailing a call to an 800 number. A pound of wheat would be a pound of wheat*—meaning that it would neither weigh a pound nor be composed of grain without the purchase of a 12-month contract. A hamburger would be defined as two buns around a paper coupon promising the delivery of a meat patty as soon as meat-patty technology was rolled out nationally.

The complexity that Kirn skewers refers not only to technology, of course. Creative pricing schemes and unreliable service are not limited to cell phone providers. Too many marketing programs tie customers into knots trying to save money or simply to acquire a product. And, for our purposes in this book, too many brands try to be everything to everyone, and seek to compete in every available market segment, whether they understand it or not. In the process, they do nothing well. No wonder consumers have developed a basic distrust of business, which all too often makes promises on which it can't deliver.

During my time at Starbucks, we had plenty of opportunities to run gimmicky promotions similar to those of other restaurant chains. We could have offered "$1.99 Grande Mocha Mondays" and "Two Fer Tuesdays," bonus packs or happy-hour pricing for coffee after lunch, a period when you could hear a pin drop in most Starbucks stores. We took heat for not providing punch cards (volume discounts) for some of our customers. But we didn't want to play games. We wanted to keep it simple. We wanted to reward our customers with consistently better service, not a sometimes cheaper cup of coffee.

2. Patience

A second common brand development mistake—and another utopian bubble punctured by the dot comets—was the prevailing assumption that brands could be built on Internet time. Many of the most lavishly funded start-ups persuaded themselves that they could become premier brands in a matter of months. A closely related, equally insidious belief was that *marketing*—whether it be viral Web-based viral e-mail and banners or Super Bowl commercials—equaled *brand building*.

Companies like Amazon.com, Netscape, eToys, Pets.com, Webvan, and Drugstore.com (to name but a few) received record levels of private- and public-sector financing. They gained widespread notoriety for their early best-in-category positions, their multibillion-dollar valuations, and their flagrant disregard for near-term profitability. A number of smaller companies, as well as analysts and investors, interpreted the apparent success of this behavior as a sign that traditional business logic didn't matter anymore and invoked the "Amazon Amendment" wherever possible. It was all about grabbing real estate (share-of-mind, share-of-clicks, share-of-whatever) while the real estate was cheap.

Oddly, Amazon.com's Jeff Bezos possessed an amazing amount of patience himself. But while he was content to sit back and let profitability manifest itself much later, he was not content to let someone else become the world's biggest on-line retailer. It's hard to fault Jeff for hitting the gas pedal by adding first music, then appliances, then hardware, and then just about everything under the sun, to his original business model of bookselling. He had the first-mover advantage, plenty of cash, and trusting investors. He also knew that no matter what steps he took to grow it, his brand would go only as far as it could be trusted. But in his race to define a new industry he may have added more breadth to his brand platform than it could handle at such a young age.

One of the more patient New Economy companies has been AOL. It never possessed bleeding-edge technology and was in fact scoffed at by anyone with a "real" Internet service, rather than the closed system within which AOL prefers to keep its many millions of users. AOL plodded forward and gave very little away for free. It was simple, it was sensible, it was patient. And it is no surprise that AOL has prevailed where few other technology concerns have, so much so that it grew rich and powerful enough to take over Time Warner, one of the few blue-chip media companies that historically pursued a solid technology base on its own.

Many factors will influence how fast a brand can move forward without tearing apart at the seams or running out of money. Companies make mistakes, they miss opportunities, and they lose momentum every now and then to someone better than them. It's the natural ebb and flow of organizations that are ultimately human. So what *is* the right pace for developing a brand? How long should it take?

The answer depends on what kind of brand you want to create. If you want to create a great one, know this: great endeavors take time and some things simply cannot be sped up. The average pregnancy is nine months, after all, and it takes the better part of two decades to raise a child. It took NASA decades to put a man on the moon. Even Cheez Whiz required countless years of research and development before it was perfected. Brands are no different. Push them too hard, too fast, and they will eventually fail. The explosion of the Internet in the last half of the nineties created a handful of exceptions to this rule. But even there, look at AOL. Compared to most Internet companies it resembles Father Time.

3. Relevance

It's human nature to seek out like-minded people. To visit places that inspire you, to listen to music that tickles your ears like no other. It's also quite fundamental to long for something unique, a rare find, an oddity that brings you joy for reasons that you may not even be able to articulate. Think for a moment about people who have spent $250 on a single Beanie Baby, or the neurosurgeon who trades Matchbox cars by night. Thanks to the Internet it is no longer difficult to find someone or something consistent with your own values. Somewhere out there are sites for Triumph Motorcycle enthusiasts and sites for collectors of tacky seventies home furnishings, or eighteenth-century undergarments. And there is a single site that can meet most if not all of these longings, yearnings, and urges. It is called eBay.

The question of relevance becomes particularly acute when individual needs come up against the capacities of the traditional large business. The old "one-to-many" model of traditional marketing has been forever transformed by the Web. If you can articulate what you want, chances are good that you will find it. But since the rise of the new universe of the Web, new expectations from consumers have arisen that require *mass customization*. With the ease of access to companies that the Web has provided, the challenge of meeting a vast variety of individual needs has become a great opportunity for those businesses willing to take it on.

Mass customization combines the benefits of mass production and mass distribution with the ability to make multiple cost-effective adjustments to the core product or service in order to meet the more exacting needs of a particular customer or market segment. If you're looking for a good working example of mass customization in action, look no farther than your local Starbucks. The company could never have achieved what it did simply by selling one or two different varieties of coffee, no matter how good those cups were. Starbucks was built to accommodate the most idiosyncratic requests for coffee drinks imaginable. I recently overheard a customer nonchalantly order a double-tall, nonfat, half-caff, not-too-hot caramel machiatto with two Equals. The unfazed barista served it up flawlessly.

The only way Burger King was able to make its early run at McDonald's was with its "Have It Your Way" campaign. Where McDonald's was built to achieve incredible efficiencies through mass production and the prepreparation of a strictly defined selection of products in advance of ordering, some of its competitors saw an opportunity in giving customers exactly what they wanted, even if it took a minute or two longer.

Dell Computers is a textbook example of mass customization. The company builds and ships the products that have been specifically requested. Many national magazines today produce "split runs" whereby different versions of the cover may be shot and printed to suit the taste of particular distribution outlets and markets. I suspect we have seen only the beginning of such select printing, a tactic that Time Warner pioneered in the early nineties.

Nike didn't reach its market position by designing a handful of shoes and then building millions of them. Today it sells more than 50,000 different SKUs (Stock Keeping Units) across its apparel, footwear, and accessory lines. The average life span for those products is between three and six months. Nike has developed the ability to produce on a massive level and achieve economies of scale, but has done so by creating a broad array of unique offerings that make the brand relevant to people whether they walk, run, or waddle. More recently, Nike has led the mass-customization pack in the sports and fitness field by letting visitors to its Web site customize their own pair of shoes, right down to such essential details as color, a personal name, and some styling features.

How can you extend your core product or service in ways that make it unique and more relevant to current and future customers? It may not be as hard as you think. You may find that customers are willing to pay a premium for a product tailored to their own tastes and preferences. Just a few years ago people scoffed at the idea of a $2.50 cup of coffee. Starbucks proved that if you deliver value as perceived by the customer, you could be very profitable and generate serious volume. Too many companies engineer themselves to cut costs rather than add to the value or relevance of their products. Start with your customers and allow them to define "value" in their terms. Build and manage your profitability from there.

4. Accessibility

One of the greatest frustrations for any company is the affliction that Catherine Viscardi Johnson, formerly the head of sales and marketing for Condé Nast, one of the world's premier magazine publishing companies, had dubbed *marketing interruptus*. She described the syndrome to me in the course of a discussion about integrating mySimon.com's Web-based comparison-shopping technology with the content of such magazines as *Vogue* and *Glamour*.

"The problem with most brands and the magazine publishing industry," she explained, "is the way we create desire with great advertising and editorial but don't consummate the union; we don't complete the sale. Readers want the products but are left searching the back of the magazine for an 800 number that isn't usually much help, and most of the brands we advertise can't afford to build great Web sites, much less a direct commerce business. It's *marketing interruptus!*"

In the future, the gaps between desire, shopping, and purchase will

get a lot narrower. Brands like Williams-Sonoma, Eddie Bauer, and Crate
& Barrel are already vertically integrated: they combine retail store platforms (limited primarily to major markets) with strong direct-mail catalogs and Web platforms. Find an item in one of their catalogs and you
will be able to buy it quickly, with either a phone call or a visit to their
Web site. Request an item in their stores that is not in stock and you will
be connected directly to the Web-based or phone fulfillment system.

Consumer brands that lack such a well-executed retail presence or a
robust catalog need to give potential customers the ability to easily purchase an advertised item over the phone or the Web while the ad is in their
lap or on the television or computer screen. As information technology
matures and becomes more widespread, it will be foolhardy for any company to advertise a product or service and not then be able to provide the
consumer with a simple means to fulfill his or her desire—immediately.

A poorly staffed outsourced 800 number is not an acceptable solution
anymore. Consumers want to connect directly with the brands, and to
speak to someone who is well informed about the products. If you are
spending a significant amount of money to attract a potential customer's
attention, be certain you have the proper mechanisms in place to close
the deal. Or at the very least, point them to an authorized retailer that
has the item they are looking for. Brands will need to keep careful track
of all their products at every point in the supply chain.

Obviously, consumers won't always be able to get what they want,
today or in the future. But they will try. And thanks to emerging technologies their demands will be more direct than ever before, and if you
don't listen to them someone else probably will. But before you completely change your business and become accessible 24/7 in every corner
of the world in order to win the prize for consumer centricity, I should
tell you that I'm not so sure that the consumer is always right. Consumers should always be respected, for sure, but I'm not convinced they
are always right. Give them everything they want and you will most
likely go broke. A lot of consumers thought they should have free home
delivery of groceries. Look what that did to Webvan, Home Grocer.com,
and a million stock market investors. I haven't yet met a consumer that
doesn't want both better services and lower taxes from their government.

But the fact is, much of what stands between a brand and a demanding customer will change in the years to come, especially if the existing
intermediary, the middleman, fails to add real value to either the brand or
the customer. In some cases there will be a direct disintermediation of

some layer, some go-between. I suspect, for example, that we will see fewer wholesalers and distributors in the future, and in their place a new kind of company may step in. An intelligent Web-based shopping agent like mySimon is one example of re-intermediation that may occur.

Traditional brands that utilize resellers will eventually establish more direct sales to customers. This is inevitable, and for good reason. Not every retailer can stock every product a brand makes, particularly in the case of the larger brands. And some of the most important products for a brand should not be made in large quantities. Statement or niche products that probe the edges of the brand and the emerging interests of consumers are important to companies, particularly those that are trying to shake a Goliath image and keep their edge. Occasionally, a brand may decide to apply mass-marketing pressure to a limited, niche product to create unrequited demand and some fire around the larger brand. Volkswagen's introduction of limited-production Bugs in exclusive colors is a great example of this strategy. Initially, the cars could only be purchased over the Web—a brilliant use of a new medium to exploit an old idea without spending a ton of money. In the years ahead, brands and consumers will forge more direct and personal relationships that reinforce the power and role that brand values play. Most consumers aren't asking for the world from the brands they desire. They simply want an open relationship that is respected.

5. Humanity

One thing that struck me early in my career as an aspiring copywriter in journalism school was how some brands like Coke, Levi Strauss, and Kodak felt human to me, while most others felt lifeless and cold, incapable of creating an emotional response. In any supermarket or shopping mall there are several hundred brands that fall into this category. I puzzled over why I would describe brands in terms I normally reserved for describing people—attributes like "reliable," "fun," "creative," "hip," "driven," "solid," "smart," "responsive," "entertaining," "compassionate," "respectful," and "knowing." Looking for the answer, I read everything I could about brands, about human behavior, about marketing and the culture of business. Were my responses simply the result of effective advertising, or were they the product of something deeper and more enduring than whatever the ad agency or copywriter had managed to bring to the account? Though I didn't find the definitive answers then, I realized one thing: eliciting such feelings could not be an accident.

In the years that followed, as I cut my teeth in product management and advertising, I learned that the ability to build a brand that evokes positive human qualities was quite valuable. Today, in this age of widespread distrust of large organizations, that ability is invaluable. People trust people they know; getting to know someone means getting to know his behaviors, attitudes, and values. The same is true of becoming acquainted with a brand. Convey your human values wherever you can. If all companies are made up of people, why do so many of them feel so lifeless? Here's a quick prescription for adding some humanity to your brand.

LAUGH AT YOURSELF.

Don't be afraid to poke fun at yourself and your product. Look at the lighter side. People like to laugh; it's good for them and it's good for you. If you do this well and do it honestly you will gain enormous respect. You will also set yourself apart from 99 percent of all other companies. Remember that it's just a job. You're not curing cancer. And if you are, see the next paragraph.

SHOW GENUINE COMPASSION.

Have a heart, and by that I mean don't just settle for writing a check to a charity. Show that you care about your customers, the community they live in, and, as important, your own employees. No one wants to work for or patronize an evil empire, and bad karma is one enormous boomerang that knows where you live and shows up when you least need the visit. Give a damn. And give back.

STAND FOR SOMETHING.

Anything. If you don't stand for something you stand for nothing. But don't be all things to all people; you'll never please everyone. Just make sure your friends far outnumber your enemies. Connect your brand with something much larger, more timeless, and more interesting than just your company, no matter how great you think it is. Even IBM and AOL Time Warner are specks in the greater view. When IBM attached itself to the simple slogan "Think," it represented a strong effort at becoming a protagonist for something larger than itself. And when Apple, many years later, came up with the clever slogan "Think Different," the ungrammatical nature of the exhortation and its meaning said two very important things: (1) Apple was different from IBM, and (2) that difference was embodied in a capacity and a willingness to break rules in the spirit of Albert Einstein, John Lennon, and James Dean.

LISTEN AND WATCH.

Some humans are just unable to listen. It's been my experience that most of these people don't have very many friends. Brands that listen and observe the world around them show respect and are a lot smarter than brands that are intentionally deaf and blind. Remember, you learn more with your mouth shut. Get out and see the world your customers and your employees live in. Do it often. Observe and absorb.

ADMIT YOUR MISTAKES.

No one's perfect—not even you. When you screw up, own up to it quickly. Thanks to the Information Age and rising consumer interest in corporate behavior, the future will become ever more transparent. Wear clean underwear that fits.

FIND YOUR SOUL.

Every company has a heart, a brain, and a soul. The brain is usually in finance or operations, the heart is somewhere between the CEO and marketing, but the soul should be present in every department and in everyone in the company. Your soul is in your culture, for better or worse. Start there to rediscover it if you have lost it. Once you have it, protect it, honor it, and *never, never* lose it in a merger. Think Chrysler.

BECOME A MORE HUMAN EMPLOYER.

Many of the dot coms gave us shiny new textbook examples of how not to treat employees. Let's look at the case of InfoSpace and its founder, Naveen Jain. In January 2001, InfoSpace experienced an exodus of its executive leadership and a tumbling stock price. It was not an unusual circumstance for that time period, when lots of technology companies were coming apart at the seams and execs were heading for the exits. But an article in the *Seattle Post-Intelligencer* (January 23, 2001) provided an interesting insight into what it must have been like to be in such a place at such a time.

Chief Executive Arun Sarin stepped down after just nine months, reportedly to spend more time with his family. Given the pace at companies like InfoSpace, an Internet infrastructure company, I don't question his motivations, and I am personally happy for Arun and his family. What was strange, though, was that President Russell Horowitz and CFO Rand Rosenberg immediately followed him out the door. InfoSpace's founder, Jain, had to return to the company's day-to-day operations as CEO and do damage control. When the news of the musical chairs broke, the stock dropped 21 percent. Jain blamed the departures on the inability of Sarin and Rosenberg to commit the amount of time needed for the business.

"What this company needs is people who will be living here, working 16-hour days, seven days a week," insisted Jain. Obviously, he had learned some valuable management skills at Microsoft, where he had worked for seven years. A few weeks later, *The Industry Standard* carried a story on InfoSpace that included information about six lawsuits brought against Jain by former employees who claimed that he had reneged on stock-option agreements. Four lawsuits had been settled at a cost of millions of dollars, and two were still pending. One former InfoSpace VP, Mark Kaleem, settled a similar suit for $4.5 million. Another, Kent Plunkett, filed a suit after being fired, he says, for not voluntarily reducing his own stock-option grant. That suit was settled for $10.5 million.

Jain remained upbeat:

> "Internal morale is extremely, extremely, extremely positive," he insists. "I can forward you e-mails where people say, 'We will give up our lives for this company. We will work 24 hours a day [up from 16 the month before], now that you are back. Now we have a cause. We have a reason to live.'" (*The Industry Standard*, February 5, 2001)

I wonder if this sort of workplace ethic, which is all too typical of the entire technology sector, can't be traced back to industry leaders like Bill Gates in their early years, who in published accounts so often strike us as men without lives beyond their jobs. To me, the sector has long been inhuman, and its inhumanity is painfully reflected in the thin, hollow brands of so many of those companies. How is it that most technology advertising seems thin, bland, and lifeless? Why is it that their products are devoid of human feelings? (Think of Microsoft PowerPoint Clip Art.) Look no further than their conduct on the job. *The New Yorker* writer Ken Auletta recently observed at a high-tech industry conference in New York that Bill Gates was the kind of guy who if you happened to be visiting him in his office would go and get himself a Coke without asking you if you cared for one.

How is it that a lot of kids in places like Redmond, Washington, who live in large expensive houses, have been effectively orphaned to school systems, nannies, and day-care centers? Mom and Dad live at the office, working "16-hour days, seven days a week," to quote InfoSpace CEO Jain. And for what? Are *they* curing cancer? Knowing the pace and stress of such a life, I truly question how much productivity and creativity are possible. When Nike was at the top of its game, the average employee worked eight or nine hours, tops. And that included a daily one-hour workout.

Another once-prominent start-up in Bellevue, Washington, assembled its employees for a pep talk at just about the time the wheels appeared to be falling off the home-delivered grocery and drug shopping carts. Its CEO was not a particularly warm or charismatic leader, but he had been a roaring success at Microsoft. During his presentation he spoke about the values that would set their brand apart, values that would enable them to change the world, and then he cited a list of brand attributes that the advertising agency had helped him drum up. As the audience sat listening passively, he concluded his presentation with one final, critically important brand attribute:

"And last but not least, we're going to have *fun*!"

A friend of mine, an employee of the company who was in the audience that day, recalled this remark by his boss as one of the weirdest things he had ever heard anyone say. There was nothing *fun* about that company; fun was hardly the reason that anyone—including its founder—had come to work there. They were there to make pots of money and retire young—and *then* maybe have some fun. The business model was already strained as it was and the stock was heading toward a dollar. Fun could not be slapped onto this scenario like cheese onto a sandwich. As my friend commented, "If our survival now depended on our ability to be 'fun,' then I figured we were all in deep trouble."

He quit a few weeks later.

6. Omnipresence

A number of New Economy pundits have suggested that, thanks to the Internet, there is no longer any need for traditional, "interruptive" media tools such as television, radio, and print advertising. I am always amused by people who view the world in black and white, in terms of either/or. Great brands need both. Humans are curious creatures; we love to graze and check out the world around us. Many consumers enjoy reading ads as much as they do the editorial content in magazines. It is no secret that during some destination viewing events like the Academy Awards or the Super Bowl, the commercials often wind up being more entertaining and memorable than the programming itself. This is not intended as a blanket defense of traditional advertising. Much of it is really quite bad and doesn't belong anywhere we can see or hear it, be it on a computer screen or on television. In the future, advertising will have to be more intelligent, more entertaining, and more rewarding than it is today. I suggest that all major advertisers contemplate this: Imagine that in the future television viewers can get free TV but have to allow advertising from fifty brands. If they could pick from thousands of brands' advertising, would your brand be on the short list? How welcome are you?

As we transition from analog to digital technology, there will be countless new ways beyond traditional media for a company to present itself to potential customers. But it may be reckless to assume that the unfettered access of traditional mass media will survive unscathed. I suspect that the mass media will remain a part of business and of our daily lives for the simple reason that large companies will be around for quite some time. Big companies can provide the financial means by which to support mass media since they can justify, if not leverage, the mass reach. On the other end of the scale, the Internet has made possible cheaper one-to-one relationships between brands and consumers. In truth, on-line or direct-mail advertising is all that many companies can afford. But for those who can afford to establish a more dynamic media presence, I highly recommend investigating all forms of media, on-line and off-line, paid and unpaid, and work toward a strategy of omnipresence to your core target audience. And remember to make everything tie together.

Building a brand entirely on the Web is difficult, to say the least. Making a transition from traditional marketing to include a stronger Web presence, as Charles Schwab has done, is perhaps a better model to follow. Some consumer brands have opened their own retail stores as one more method of establishing a stronger, more complete market presence. Some, such as Warner Brothers and Disney, may have overdone it a bit and have scaled back expansion efforts. Nike's approach to Nike Town may prove to be the wisest approach. There are only a handful of the stores around the world, but as a showpiece for the brand and all of its products, Nike Town was never intended to replace traditional retail or its marketing efforts. It is one more way in which the brand has become "present" within its key markets.

One thing "omnipresence" does *not* mean is running irritating Web banners across a thousand different Web sites or airing the same commercial four times in one thirty-minute television program. If anything, this behavior drives brands in reverse. I don't think I am alone when I become irritated at brands that think I didn't see them the forty-ninth time around. Not only is it creating an unfavorable experience for customers, it is an absolute waste of money for the company. At Nike, we retired commercials and print ads while they were still fresh. We respected consumers' time when we had their attention. We also respected their intelligence.

Ultimately, brand omnipresence rests on the principle that there are many potential positive influences on brand image other than network television or unsolicited e-mail campaigns. When pay-per-view, commercial-free TV first appeared in North America, smart brands hedged their bets and began to explore ways to integrate their product into entertainment content, should the commercial break cease to exist. Some companies managed to do this well and their products and services were a seamless element of a larger story. Other companies garishly buy their way into Hollywood films, but such forced attempts at product placement are all too obvious to today's sophisticated audiences.

The better brands select only those programs or venues that are genuinely relevant to them, and then build a relationship with the content developer. Nike never paid a dime for product placement in the time I was there, but it did establish direct relationships with hundreds of directors, set designers, and art directors as well as musicians, actors, and other icons in the public eye. Nike allowed celebrities to shop at a discreet, off-the-radar Nike Town of sorts in Los Angeles. When an actor wanted to take his kids shopping, he or she could do so in peace at Nike rather than get mobbed at a shopping mall. Nike was repaid the favor with the opportunity to design boots for *Batman* or the shoes for Michael J. Fox when he hovered on his skateboard in *Back to the Future*. Nike also made props and crew jackets for Spike Lee's 40 Acres and a Mule production company. As a company, Nike thoroughly enjoys helping the creative community. In return, its products show up in all the right places.

Starbucks eventually built a working café on the David E. Kelley production lot for *Ally McBeal;* earlier, the show had made a habit of shooting in real Starbucks stores, which was flattering, but also created considerable havoc for Starbucks regulars, not to mention location costs for the show. Starbucks didn't write its product into the script; Kelley did. We just made it a lot easier for him. Starbucks also has a long waiting list of baristas in Los Angeles who are eager and willing to work as extras when Ally needs her morning latte.

Brand omnipresence is also about placing your brand where it *needs* to be, where it does the most good for the community. When a local grade school goes looking for help with a literacy program it should seek it from local businesses. Through the Starbucks Foundation, Starbucks supports literacy efforts in every community it operates in. Smart brands initially underwrite such programs where they do business and support programs that are consistent with their own unique brand values. Besides helping the community, these efforts add another dimension to the brand presence in the marketplace that traditional advertising cannot provide.

7. Innovation

We continue to move toward an "idea economy," where we place a higher value on the ability to continually innovate and to develop new products, services, and revenue streams than on simply executing an existing concept or business model. We also hear all too often about the need to "reinvent" our businesses, and have been instructed, ad nauseam, about the value of *transformational* rather than *incremental* thinking, about *transforming* rather than simply *renewing* businesses.

So how does one accomplish this? The best way is with people— people whom you respect, and for whom you do whatever you can to help them unleash their potential. Innovation happens when great people—and not necessarily creative people—are brought together in an inspiring environment where they are valued and rewarded for taking risks and challenging the status quo. It happens where rebels and mavericks feel comfortable. If a company is genuinely outstanding, it develops a culture where innovation is not an isolated event nor an exception, but instead is the ongoing process or rule. Corporate cultures that achieve this level of innovative continuity are rare and exceptional, 3M being one of the notable examples. But such cultures can also be fragile, especially when they are forced into relationships with partners that do not bring out the best in both parties. Take the case of the Daimler-Chrysler merger, which was supposed to be a union made in heaven.

As was reported in *Newsweek* (December 11, 2000),

Chrysler was the world's most profitable and cost-efficient carmaker, while Daimler was renowned as the planet's premier luxury-car maker.

This mass-to-class marriage became a new model for a global auto-motive powerhouse. But in remarkably short order DaimlerChrysler has become a disaster, dogged by transatlantic culture clashes and questions about Daimler's union not only with Chrysler but also with Japanese and Korean mass automakers as well. At the moment the company's most notable American export is talent. Virtually the en-tire "dream team" that built hot models and big profits in the 1990s has left Chrysler, leaving behind chaotic operations and costs spin-ning out of control.

In an earlier chapter we examined the story of Chrysler's innovations in the nineties, specifically how the Dodge Viper came to be. It was, you'll remember, Bob Lutz who was credited with much of the creativity and hard-nosed attention to cost controls in that era. As the merger began to take shape in 1998, Lutz was given no role in the new company by Chrysler's chairman, Bob Eaton, who, according to the *Newsweek* ar-ticle, resented the attention Lutz had been receiving. So shortly after the merger Lutz left, and the nucleus of the design team eventually followed him, including the design chief, Tom Gale, and the head of production, Dennis Pawley. "The guys who were the soul of Chrysler walked out the door," observed the auto analyst Maryann Keller. And Lutz, as I men-tioned, was later picked up by GM.

The fallout from this merger is not unique. Even small companies, brought together with the best of intentions, can form a disastrous union. Although some of the most gifted and creative people can be high main-tenance and difficult to keep happy, in a world where product life cycles will most likely continue to shorten, no one can rest on laurels for very long. For that reason alone, it pays to develop a culture that attracts, in-spires, and retains innovative people, bright lights that thrive on trans-formational rather than incremental change, and to reward those who originate innovative solutions wherever they are found. The cost of re-placing critical intellectual capital has always been great. In the future it will only become greater.

The View from the Continental Divide

Just before leaving Nike, I found myself standing in the northern Rocky Mountains at the Continental Divide, the place where east meets west. As I stood on this remarkable site, I found myself pondering an acute brand dilemma the company was facing. For the last six years, since the onset of the "Just Do It" campaign, we had been on a roll. No matter how far we continued to stretch the swoosh, it still seemed primed for more. But I knew such growth could not last forever—not at that torrid pace.

Before "Just Do It" became inscribed in the global lexicon, early swooshers had taken inspiration from a slogan written for Nike in the seventies by a small local agency. "There is no finish line" was one hell of a brand-positioning statement, and it was regrettable that Nike didn't have much of an advertising budget back then to put behind it. Standing there on the ridge, I began to realize the profound wisdom—and the obligation—inherent in such a statement when applied to business. *We would move fast and we would never stop. Never.*

As I mulled over concepts like perpetual motion, annual compound growth rates, and brand mortality, I noted dark clouds from the west bumping up against a ridge to the north. Watching the gray haze of rain descend from the clouds as they ascended the ridge on which I was standing, I was struck by a brand-development analogy that is as fresh and relevant today as it was a decade ago. At the crest of the ridge, the rain would fall to earth and run in one of two directions. Very little would stay right on top, as it was steep and rocky down both sides, with little soil to absorb the water.

To the east of the Continental Divide, toward the Great Plains, hundreds of small rivers, streams, and creeks poke along, slowly but surely, to the Missouri, which then drains into the Mississippi, which takes in the Ohio River before heading straight south to the Gulf of Mexico. This forms an incredibly large albeit slow-moving body of water, save for the occasional hundred-year flood. From an elevation of just a little more than a mile above sea level, at the start, there's still enough downward slope for gravity to pull that water along a winding route of roughly 2,500 miles before it reaches the sea. There's not a lot of whitewater on this journey across the gentle, sometimes imperceptible valleys of the Plains.

This gradual flow reminded me of the process whereby most brands were formed in the early and mid-twentieth century: a slow, steady, predictable, workmanlike journey that ultimately led to brands that were a little broad around the waist. Now, hold that thought for a moment while we look west.

From where I was standing, rainfall draining to the west of the continent would join a handful of small streams, such as Idaho's famous Henry's Fork, before dropping into the Snake River, a ride that in certain stretches is too wild for all but the most daring river runners. Unlike the rivers of the flatlands of Nebraska and Kansas, the Snake cuts through a canyon thousands of feet deep that separates Idaho and Washington before joining the mighty Columbia. After coursing through a series of some twenty dams, the water spills into the Pacific Ocean at Astoria, Oregon, a fraction of the water's eastward journey.

The west slope reminded me of brand development in these early years of the new century—a sometimes dizzying ride broken up by dams of indecision that provide inflection points where energy and resources are gathered and then unleashed so the process can start all over again. Mergers, acquisitions, and quantum leaps in technology build up behind a series of dams and give everyone reason to strap on a life jacket and paddle like hell if they're caught downstream. The canyon walls that loom overhead in the Snake and Columbia River gorge also form deep ruts that are hard to see beyond. Spend much time there and you mistake the ruts for the horizon. Many New Economy jobs are like that.

Today, most brands find themselves living in the wilder West; few can enjoy the idyllic if not lazy pace of the Mississippi. Most of the dot-com brands experience the equivalent of running the upper Yangtze River in class six rapids in an expensive but irrelevant canoe with a broken paddle. Nearly all of them get wet; most don't make it to the end.

In the future, brands will have to be a lot wiser about navigating the inevitable rapids ahead of them. They will need to understand that speed is not as important as arriving safely. They will learn to portage their businesses around the really frothy sections or have the wherewithal— and patience—to seek out someone who has been there before and has that wisdom. Ten years ago most successful companies scoffed at the idea of hiring a consultant for anything, particularly in the area of brand development. Given the accelerating pace of change in markets, consumer behaviors, and technologies, it may not be wise to be so closed-minded about looking for help outside the company. No one has all the answers—I get stumped often enough, too—but everyone must reach informed decisions by whatever means necessary.

There is nothing quite as exciting or as terrifying as not knowing what awaits you around the bend of a river that you are rafting for the first time. As a young man, I found such a white-knuckle pursuit to be pure exhilaration, just another rodeo ride, even one time when I nearly died. Now, as a middle-aged father of two, the roar of unseen crashing water makes my heart pound between my ears and my palms sweat around the oars. As it should. I have learned all too well what can happen when things go wrong, and I have acquired a deep respect for moving water that lies beneath an idyllic surface. I never fully understood the concepts of mass and inertia until I was pinned underwater against a submerged tree, tangled in ropes connected to a raft caught in the current above me.

Developing a brand can be a lot like that. Perhaps it's not as life-threatening, but it's just about as surprising. On the surface, most businesses look pretty straightforward and it's easy to lull ourselves into thinking that a present course is the best possible one, even the only one, worth pursuing. We want to believe that our brand will succeed if we do one or two things well. This is especially true if we have had any modicum of success. But brands are complicated concepts and, like a river, they cannot be entirely controlled. Brands derive their power from people—customers, employees, intermediaries, stakeholders, the press—and the relationships and experiences they have with your company. How well these people understand and respect your brand and its values will determine its strength. In the New Brand World, it is not about controlling what these people think. It is about inspiring them to believe in what you do, and what kind of company you are trying to be. It is also about meeting or exceeding their expectations 365 days a year.

A great brand foundation is built with many different bricks by many different people and over many years. For that reason I can think of no better organizing concept for a company than the brand itself. A brand gives employees a common understanding not just of what they do for a living but of *how* they must do it. They also make someone or something accountable. They provide companies with a conscience. They give it heart. And over time, a brand that is universally understood, inside and outside the company, will create a spirit and a soul whose value to the company cannot by overestimated. And if all goes well, the brand becomes an enduring and rewarding part of everyday life for many, and Wall Street will place a value on your brand that is many times greater than your annual revenue because they believe it will survive for years to come.

This book is meant to speak to a broad cross-section of companies big and small, but I'd like to take this opportunity to send a message to the truly large company, the global juggernaut, the multinational hairball that drives anarchists crazy.

Large corporations have an enormous influence on our personal and collective quality of life. They are more influential than the governments of some nations. This gives cause to stop and wonder. In the United

States we have many checks and balances on our national government, the world's single most powerful institution. Thank Thomas Jefferson and a bunch of other visionaries who came together during one hot Philadelphia summer for that. But we lack a constitution for powerful companies. I doubt that we will arrive at a global mechanism for regulating companies anytime soon. As a goal, it's right up there with world peace.

So in the meantime, I propose this: Let's all become better, more respected, more meaningful, and more trusted brands. Not just bigger but better. If we take the principles of this book to heart—if we create emotional connections that transcend our products and services, if we respect our employees, our customers, and the environment around us—then I think we have a chance at changing the world for the better. But it's really important that the big guys step up to the plate.

Big corporations are not abstract concepts. They are made up of living, breathing people like you and me. Improving these companies will happen when employees, customers, and stakeholders—not just special interest groups—demand change. Companies cannot exist without employees, stockholders, and customers. These people fuel the enterprise. They keep it alive. If you work for or invest in a company that you think should do better, speak up or shut up. Do not complain. Be part of what changes the company for the better.

My goal in writing this book has been to touch enough people to serve as a catalyst for improving the way businesses interact with the world around them. Even if just one massive company takes a different and better path forward, and leads by example for others to follow, then this will have been a huge success for me. But I know how hard it is for a large company to change. The aircraft carrier analogy—that it takes miles for an aircraft carrier to change course—isn't big enough to fit most global corporations today. So I am hopeful that if enough small companies lead the way to the New Brand World, the bigger companies will be inspired to change their ways, too. And if I am right about what consumers want, all businesses big and small will eventually have to change in order to survive.

It has become clear in the wake of the tragedy of September 11, and the events since, that globalization is not an option, subject to debate. It is not an "either/or," but a "how." Contrary to what some may believe, globalization is not limited to or defined by large multinational corporations. Likewise, it is not a recent phenomenon, but one that began when prehistoric man first left one cave for another, one valley for the next. It grew in significance as religious ideologies spread across continents, quite often with violence, and it accelerated further when explorers set sail across uncharted oceans for the unknown. Notable twentieth-century events—two World Wars, the development of weapons of mass destruction, the introduction of mass media, the rise of "superpowers," and the creation of the Internet—are just milestones along the path of an unending journey, in the course of which many human traits have remained largely unchanged. As it always has been, the world is beset by religious conflicts, ignorance, poverty, intolerance, and hate. And for these ancient ills, globalization must become part of the solution, not a perpetuator of the problem.

In the last decade the world has grown smaller, and as it continues to do so we face the danger of becoming even more conflicted if we can't figure out a better way to evolve, a better way to live in some form of harmony. We share one environment, and it doesn't take the warnings of scientists to make us see that we live in a closed system. We are bound to the planet earth. You know the saying—with apologies to Thomas Wolfe—"You can't go home again"? Well, I think it's healthier to recognize that you can't really leave home, either.

The imbalance of wealth, timeless ideological conflicts, and a growing resentment toward powerful institutions (private and public) have intersected in a way that must be met with action, not rhetoric. We are at what is perhaps one of the most important crossroads in the history of civilization, a profound time in which corporations and other NGOs (Non-Governmental Organizations)—as opposed to governments—can and should become a part of a more creative and collective solution to these problems. We are living in a time when everyone, not just the military or our elected officials, should take a leadership role.

One opportunity to do so will be for all companies, large and small, regional and global, to step up and use their superhuman powers to help improve the quality of life where it is needed most, and with actions rather than words. This is no longer about just writing a check to a local charity in a wealthy community. All companies must move beyond the idea of providing only pure financial support. Who better than the world's largest beverage companies to make sure that children in developing countries have clean water to drink? Who better than the world's biggest footwear and apparel companies to help clothe the poorest in the grip of winter? Who better than the world's smartest logistics consulting companies to help figure out how to orchestrate and deliver aid to hard-to-reach areas? Who better than the world's best advertising agencies to help develop messages about the value of a free and open society? Who better than the world's most successful computer, telecommunications, and software companies to bridge the gap between the connected and the unconnected in isolated parts of the world? As valuable as an organization like the Red Cross is, it steps in only when everything else fails. It's time to stop treating the symptoms and force changes to the underlying conditions. It won't be easy. It won't be quick. But it will be worth the effort.

Our society has not rewarded companies that divert a significant portion of their assets to help the less fortunate. We lack any recognized system for accounting for goodwill. There is but one bottom line and it is entirely driven by transactions, earnings-per-share, market caps, and market share. No component of the bottom line that Wall Street follows reflects heart, goodwill, or conscience. At a minimum, that has to change.

The world needs an acceptable accounting method for how companies treat their employees, how they treat the communities in which they operate, and how lightly they walk on the land and develop sustainable businesses. Companies need to be measured against one another, and not against the standards set subjectively by a special-interest group. We have no broadly shared context for informed decisions in this matter. This was, at least in part, what Phil Knight had in mind in July 2000 when he addressed the United Nations on the need for greater corporate responsibility and the means by which to monitor and measure it.

> Finally, [global businesses need] an internationally recognized set of generally accepted social accounting principles and monitoring organizations certified to measure performance [that] would bring greater clarity to the impact of globalization and the performance of any one company. The F.L.A. [Fair Labor Association] is one such attempt. The Ethical Trading Initiative has a set of standards and has experimented with monitoring. The International Confederation of Free Trade Unions has another set of standards, as do its member secretariats. . . .
>
> One of the greatest potentials lies in the nature of the UN itself, and its organizations. The UN Environmental Program, the International Labor Organization, the resident directors and staffs in countries around the world have vast and untapped competencies that we can all learn from and share. All the key parties here at the table have extraordinary things to offer. Real solutions that improve people's lives will result if we can make this partnership work.

I fully expect companies with an established social conscience like Nike and Starbucks to rise to the challenge and lead others toward the goal of improving people's lives around the world as they go about their business. I know both of those companies well. They *are* good companies. Perhaps no other brand has taken more cheap shots—too many of them ill-informed and malicious—on the issue of globalization than Nike. But Nike has never been one to shy away from a challenge. That has and will always be the trait of a leader. Nike has become one of the most transparent companies on earth. Few other brands can withstand such scrutiny.

And to all those companies standing in the shadows, watching brands like Nike take the lightning bolts, know this: the future is going to be increasingly transparent, and you should start planning for it. Better yet, go beyond planning and begin making positive changes in how you do your business and how you can share your success.

To me, the best possible change would be for all businesses, large and small, to use their unique talents, their resources, and their passion to build brands that are respected far beyond Wall Street, and not just because they have become effective cash cows. Perhaps there will be a way for many of them to improve social conditions, collectively. As Phil Knight argued above, the United Nations has been a critically valuable institution in the last half century for governments big and small. We need an analog for business.

In his November 2001 keynote address to a global gathering of representatives for Business for Social Responsibility, Starbucks CEO Howard Schultz highlighted one of the greatest challenges that we face in the New Brand World, the imbalance between profits and benevolence, and the need for business leaders to step up.

> The opportunity to do the right thing has never been as important as it is right now. Building a sustainable enterprise is about having a conscience and having heart. . . . As a business you care about doing the right thing because it is who you are, not because it is good press. Those with the backbone to do the right thing will sustain greatness in their business.

For the sake of humanity, I hope that society will reward companies that make their brands better, not simply bigger. Achieving this will require that we stop measuring our success merely in terms of the strength of financial numbers, and that we begin to account for goodwill, business ethics, and corporate contributions to creating a world better than the one we know today.

In this book I make the case that clearly defined and broadly shared brand values provide a much better organizing principle for an enterprise than an EPS target, market share goal, or stock price. The latter are merely financial performance measures. They don't tell us anything about *how* to get there. If we take it one step further and envision a future in which brands will be more closely scrutinized and held more accountable for their global impact, then it is inevitable that they will also become a conscience for companies. And if enough companies adopt this thinking and commit to building better, more compassionate brands, brands that are measured more completely, we just may succeed in establishing a powerful collective conscience for some of the most significant forces in the free world.

Personally, I can't think of a better thing for any business to do.

index